the medieval outlook + romanticism - 102.

great classical oratory in 5

SELECTED
SHELBURNE ESSAYS

By PAUL ELMER MORE

NEW YORK

OXFORD UNIVERSITY PRESS

PRINTED IN THE UNITED STATES OF AMERICA

CONTENTS

PREFACE

THE material here reprinted is selected from the eleven volumes of Shelburne Essays published between 1904 and 1921, and the reader may be curious to know how they came to be written and why they were so named,—the answer to which questions involves a bit of autobiography.

My earlier years were divided between the private desire to be a poet and the open necessity of making a living. As for the poetical ambition it is sufficient to say that it resulted in the composition of tragedies in verse and a huge epic, which in due season were given to the flames. These, however, were preceded by a volume of lyrics which I imprudently published, and which the world, including the author, has willingly let die, and followed by a translation of one hundred epigrams translated from the Sanskrit of Bhartrihari which, for the intrinsic merit of the originals, has, I think, some permanent value. As for the public occupation, I first, after college graduation, taught for a while in an academy, then went to the Harvard Graduate School for three years, and at their conclusion obtained a position at Bryn Mawr, where I held out for two years. At the last named place my duties embraced instruction in Sanskrit, lecturing on Greek and Latin literature, besides courses in Horace, Lucretius, Homer, and Aristotle. How I came to be chosen for such a post has always been something of a puzzle to me. For I had refused to stand for the doctoral degree at Harvard, to the consternation of my master in oriental studies, and when President M. Cary Thomas, in one of her prowling excursions for instructors, asked Professor Goodwin whether I was competent to carry the proposed burden, he replied, as he afterwards informed me, that I was not, nor was any one else in the country. For the first of which statements I can vouch the accuracy; at any rate the experience at Bryn Mawr made clear to me that my proper life work was not in teaching.

So it happened that rather recklessly I threw up my job, and at a nominal price rented a dilapidated little farm-house near the village of Shelburne, N. H., that lies along the peaceful valley of the Androscoggin. There for three summers and two winters, with no human habitation in view, and with only a dog, named Râj after the canine hero of the last book of the *Mahâbhârata,* and a cat for constant companions, I took upon myself to live as a hermit after a mild Epicurean fashion of my own.

This was the experiment described in the first of the Shelburne Essays. Three maiden aunts, as may there be read, wagged their heads ominously; my nearest friend inquired cautiously whether there was any taint of insanity in the family; an old grey-haired lady, a veritable saint who had not been soured by her many deeds of charity, admonished me on the utter selfishness and godlessness of such a proceeding. But I clung heroically to my resolution. Summer tourists in that pleasant valley may still see the little red house among the pines, empty now I believe (this was in 1904); and I dare say gaudy coaches still draw up at the door as they used to do, when the gaudier bonnets and hats exchanged wondering remarks on the cabalistic inscription over the lintel, or spoke condescendingly to the great dog lying on the steps. As for the hermit within, having found it impossible to educe any meaning from the tangled habits of mankind while he himself was whirled about in the imbroglio, he had determined to try the efficacy of undisturbed meditation at a distance. So deficient had been his education that he was actually better acquainted with the aspirations and emotions of the old dwellers on the Ganges than with those of the modern toilers by the Hudson or the Potomac. He had been deafened by the "indistinguishable roar" of the streets, and could make no sense of the noisy jargon of the market place. But—shall it be confessed?—although he discovered many things during his contemplative sojourn in the wilderness, and learned that the attempt to criticise and not to create literature was to be his labour in this world, nevertheless he returned to civilization as ignorant of its meaning as when he left it.

Hence the long series of essays, critical and philosophical, and hence the non-committal name attached to them.

To be exact, the retirement at Shelburne was broken by a brief visit to my home in St. Louis, and the summers were enlivened by association with a group of Harvard men who had cottages about Philbrook's farm house some three quarters of a mile down the valley. And for two of his vacations my brother, Louis T. More, then instructor in physics at the University of Nebraska, came east to join me. His first visit was in answer to an invitation, which, as the last gasp of poetic ambition, I may be excused for copying out from the same initial essay of the series:

> Brother, awhile your impious engines leave;
>   Nor always seek with flame-compelling wires
> Out of the palsied hand of Zeus to reave
>   His dear celestial fires.
>
> What though he drowse upon a tottering bench,
>   Forgetful how his random bolts are hurled!
> Are you to blame? or is it yours to quench
>   The thunders of the world?

Come learn with me through folly to be wise:
　　Think you by cunning laws of optic lore
To lend the enamelled fields or burning skies
　　One splendour lacked before?

A wizard footrule to the waves of sound
　　You lay,—hath measure in the song of bird
Or ever in the voice of waters found
　　One melody erst unheard?

Ah, for a season close your magic books,
　　Your rods and crystals in the closet hide;
I know in covert ways a hundred nooks,
　　High on the mountain side,

Where through the golden hours that follow noon,
　　Under the greenwood shadows you and I
May talk of happy lives, until too soon
　　Night's shadows fold the sky.

And while like incense blown among the leaves
　　Our fragrant smoke ascends from carven bowl,
We'll con the lesser wisdom that deceives
　　The Questioner in the soul,

And laugh to hoodwink where we cannot rout:—
　　Did Bruno of the stubborn heart outbrave,
Or could the mind of Galileo flout,
　　The folly of the Grave?

It was all a very amateurish business, a sort of mixed imitation of Thoreau and the Hindu eremites; but for most of the time I was alone and thrown back upon myself. And if I returned to the world with the riddle of existence still unsolved—who can say that he has solved that mystery finally?—yet the direction so to speak of my thinking was fixed by those years of solitary reflection, and the essays that followed, at least the more serious of them, were successive attempts to discover the meaning of life. It was the sense of this direction and this purpose, however ill carried out, that led Mr. Walter Lippmann to write as he did in the *Saturday Review of Literature,* 15 March 1930:

"Mr. More, besides being a scholar of extraordinary attainments, is by way of being an adept in the mysteries of faith and in his own right something of a spiritual genius. The Shelburne Essays and the five volumes of the Greek Tradition are more than the monumental work of a literary critic. They are a record of continuous religious discovery within a nature that combines in exquisite proportions a delicate sensibility with a hard-headed instinct for reality. It makes no particular difference whether one agrees with all his particular judgments; to read him is to enter an austere and elevated realm of ideas and to know a man who, in the guise of a critic, is authentically concerned with the first and last things of human experience."

Laudatum a laudato. The little vanity of quoting such a eulogy from so eminent a publicist will be pardoned, I trust, to one whose pathway through literature has been plentifully sprinkled with abuse. And apart from vanity, Mr. Lippmann's language, however it may overshoot the mark in generous appreciation, does express, better than I could do, the intention, if not the actual achievement, of all my writing since those Shelburne days. There has been a "continuous religious discovery"; and there has been an attempt to deal with "the first and last things of human experience," though this interest may have been obscured by the fact that the most of the essays were written hastily in the intervals of time snatched from the busy life of a journalist and editor.

And there is another reason why I would call the attention of the reader of this volume to the inner intention, or purport, of my work as a whole. In looking over the present selection I find that, with one or two exceptions, I have omitted those essays which deal more systematically with my philosophic and religious development. This was done because the search for truth came into the open, so to speak, and reached its conclusion, so far as any such quest can be concluded, in the treatises published together under the name of the Greek Tradition and written in the main after the series of Shelburne Essays from which I have drawn was closed. To have included the earlier essays bearing immediately on the problems of philosophy and religion and sociology would have given but a scattered and even misleading notion of the evolution of my ideas. The essays actually chosen are thus for the most part of a biographical and critical type. They represent what was one of the dominant influences of my literary career, that of Sainte-Beuve, though in saying this I should add that our courses intellectually were in opposite directions, —his away from faith towards complete scepticism and a sort of naturalism controlled by classical taste, whereas mine was towards a slow submission to the dogmas of religion.

As it is, what strikes me most forcibly is the fact that the essays here selected will appear very old-fashioned to those caught by the present trend of ideas. For the one thing characteristic of modern criticism, as exemplified eminently by so influential a writer as I. A. Richards, is the complete absence of any search for the meaning of life, and in place of that an absorbing interest in what might be called the problem of aesthetic psychology,—which is indeed no more than a late-born offspring of the romantic heresy of art for art's sake. For this old-fashioned note I offer no apology; I am utterly convinced that literature divorced from life is an empty pursuit, and that an honest search for the meaning of life must lead to the simple faith of theism.

With the exception of the study of Criticism the essays follow the chronological order of publication, and, save for a few minor corrections, the original text is reproduced exactly. The last four of the essays are from volumes the copyright of which is held by Houghton Mifflin Company, and I have to thank those publishers for their liberal permission to reprint.

P. E. M.

CRITICISM

OF all Matthew Arnold's books I sometimes think that not the least precious is the slender posthumous volume published by his daughter in 1902. It was long his habit to carry in his pocket a narrow diary in which he jotted down engagements for the day, mingled with short quotations from the books he was reading to serve as amulets, so to speak, against the importunities of business. The quotations for a selection of years printed by Mrs. Wodehouse from these *Notebooks* form what might be called the critic's breviary. Here, if anywhere, we seem to feel the very beating of the critic's heart, and to catch the inner voice of recollection and duty, corresponding to the poet's "gleam," which he followed so devoutly in his life. I do not know to what work in English to liken it unless it be the notebooks containing quotations from Marcus Aurelius and Epictetus written down by the author of the *Characteristics* with his comments, which Dr. Rand edited in 1900 as the *Philosophical Regimen of Anthony, Earl of Shaftesbury.*

Nor is it mere chance that Matthew Arnold and Shaftesbury should have left for posthumous publication these private memoranda, which with all their differences of form and substance are in their final impression upon the mind so curiously alike; for the two men themselves, in their outlook on life and in their relation to their respective ages, had much in common, and there is perhaps no better way to reach a dispassionate understanding of the virtue and limitations of criticism than by comparing Arnold with his great forerunner of the early eighteenth century. Both men were essentially critical in their mental habit, and both magnified the critic's office. "I take upon me," said Shaftesbury, "absolutely to condemn the fashionable and prevailing custom of inveighing against critics as the common enemies, the pests and incendiaries of the commonwealth of Wit and Letters. I assert, on the contrary, that they are the props and pillars of this building; and that without the encouragement and propagation of such a race, we should remain as Gothic architects as ever." And the purpose of Shaftesbury in upholding the function of criticism was much the same as Arnold's; he too was offended by the Gothic and barbarous self-complacency of his contemporaries—the Philistines, as he might have called them. As Arnold protested that the work of the English romantic revival was doomed "to prove hardly more lasting than the productions of far less splendid epochs"; that Byron was "empty of matter," Shelley "incoherent," and Wordsworth "wanting in completeness and variety," just because they lacked critical background; so his predecessor censured the literature of his day. "An English author would be all genius," says Shaftesbury. "He would reap the fruits of art, but without study, pains, or application. He thinks it necessary, indeed (lest his learning should be called in question), to show the world that he errs knowingly against the rules of art."

Against this presumption of genius on the one hand and the self-complacency of Philistinism on the other, both critics took up the same weapons—the barbs of ridicule and irony. With Shaftesbury this method was an avowed creed. His essays are no more than sermons on two texts: that of Horace, *"Ridiculum acri Fortius et melius magnas plerumque secat res—* a jest often decides weighty matters better and more forcibly than can asperity"; and the saying of Gorgias

Leontinus,[1] which he misinterprets and expands for his own purpose, "That humour was the only test of gravity; and gravity of humour. For a subject which would not bear raillery was suspicious; and a jest which would not bear a serious examination was certainly false wit." With this touchstone of truth he proceeds to test the one-sided enthusiasm of his day, the smirking conceits, the pedantic pretensions, and the narrow dogmatisms whether of science or religion. "There is a great difference," he says, "between seeking how to raise a laugh from everything, and seeking in everything what justly may be laughed at. For nothing is ridiculous except what is deformed; nor is anything proof against raillery except what is handsome and just." The comic spirit is thus a kind of purgation of taste, and a way of return to nature. How deliberately Matthew Arnold used this weapon of ridicule in the service of sweet reasonableness, which is only his modern phrase, a little sentimentalised, for eighteenth-century nature; how magisterially he raised the laugh against his enemies, the bishops and the great austere toilers of the press and the mighty men of political Philistia, no one needs be told who has enjoyed the elaborate irony of *Culture and Anarchy* or of *Friendship's Garland.*

Sweet reasonableness, or "sweetness and light," to use the phrase as Arnold took it from Swift's *Battle of the Books,* is, I have suggested, little more than the modern turn for the deist's nature and reason; how nearly the two ideals approach each other you may see by comparing the "good-breeding," which is the aim of Shaftesbury's philosophy, with the "culture" which is the end of Arnold's criticism. "To philoso-

---

[1] Quoted by Aristotle; τὴν μὲν σπουδὴν διαφθείρειν γέλωτι τὸν δὲ γέλωτα σπουδῇ.

phise," said the former, "in a just signification, is but to carry good-breeding a step higher. For the accomplishment of breeding is, to learn whatever is decent in company or beautiful in arts, and the sum of philosophy is, to learn what is just in society and beautiful in Nature and the order of the world." I have wondered sometimes whether Matthew Arnold had these words in mind when he formulated his definition of culture; whether his famous command is really but another echo from the ancient quarrel of the deists. The whole scope of the essay on *Sweetness and Light* is, he avows, "to recommend culture as the great help out of our present difficulties; culture being a pursuit of our total perfection by means of getting to know, on all the matters which most concern us, the best which has been thought and said in the world [Shaftesbury, too, like Arnold, is insistent on the *exemplaria Græca*]; and through this knowledge, turning a stream of fresh and free thought upon our stock notions and habits."

There is, I trust, something more than a pedantic curiosity in such a parallel, which might yet be much prolonged, between the author of *Culture and Anarchy* and the author of the *Characteristics*. It proves, if proof be necessary, more clearly than would any amount of direct exposition, that Matthew Arnold's method of criticism was not an isolated product of the nineteenth century, but that he belongs to one of the great families of human intelligence, which begins with Cicero, the father of them all, and passes through Erasmus and Boileau and Shaftesbury and Sainte-Beuve. These are the exemplars—not complete individually, I need not say—of what may be called the critical spirit: discriminators between the false and the true, the deformed and the normal; preachers of harmony and proportion and order, prophets of the religion of taste. If they deal much with the criticism of literature, this is because in literature more manifestly than anywhere else life displays its infinitely varied motives and results; and their practice is always to render literature itself more consciously a criticism of life. The past is the field out of which they draw their examples of what is in conformity with nature and of what departs from that norm. In that field they balance and weigh and measure; they are by intellect hesitators, but at heart very much in earnest.

These critics are sometimes contrasted to their detriment with the so-called creative writers, yet they themselves stood each among the first writers of his day, and it is not plain that, for instance, Tennyson, in any true estimation, added more to the intellectual life of the world than Matthew Arnold, or Lucretius than Cicero, though their method and aim may have been different. The more significant comparison at least is not with the so-called creative writers, but with the great fulminators of new creeds—between Matthew Arnold and the Carlyles and Ruskins and Huxleys of his day; between Shaftesbury and, let us say, Rousseau; Boileau and Descartes; Erasmus and Luther; Cicero and St. Paul. Such a contrast might seem at first to lie as much in efficiency as in quality. In the very nature of things the man who seizes on one deep-reaching idea, whether newly found or rediscovered, and with single-hearted fervour forces it upon the world, might appear to have the advantage in power over the man of critical temper, who weighs and refines; who is for ever checking the enthusiasm of the living by the authority of the dead; and whose doctrine, even though in the end he may assert it with sovereign contempt of doubters, is still the command to follow the well-tried path of common-sense. Better the half-truth that makes for action and jostles the world out of its ruts, men cry, than such a timid search for the whole truth as paralyses the will, and may after all prove only an exchange of depth for breadth. That might appear to be the plain lesson of history; yet I am not so sure. Is there not a possibility that in our estimate of these powers we are a little betrayed by the tumult of the times, just as we are prone in other things to mistake bustle for movement? The critical spirit, as it has been exercised, may have its limitations and may justly be open to censure, but I doubt if its true reproach will turn out in the end to be a lack of efficiency in comparison with the more assertive force of the reformers. I am inclined to believe, for instance, that the balancing spirit of Erasmus is really more at work among us to-day than that of the dogmatic and reforming Luther; that Cicero's philosophy, though they would gape to hear it said, is really more in the hearts of the men you will meet in the street than is the theology of St. Paul. This may be in part because the representatives of the critical spirit, by their very lack of warping originality and by their endeavour to separate the true from the false, the complete from the one-sided, stand with the great conservative forces of human nature, having their fame certified by the things that endure amid all the betrayals of time and fashion.

I know the deductions that must be made from that kind of fame. Cicero, it will be said, when in his *De Finibus* he brought together the various experiences of antiquity in regard to the meaning and values of life, weighing the claims of Stoic and Epicurean and the others, may have stood for something more comprehensive and balanced than did St. Paul with his new dogma of justification by faith. Yet St. Paul's theory of justification by faith, though it may be losing for us its cogent veracity, was the immediate driving force of history and a power that remade the world, while Cicero's nice discussions remained a luxury of the learned few. In one sense that is indisputably true; and yet, imprudent as it may sound, I question whether it is the whole truth. When I consider the part played by Stoic and Epicurean philosophies in the Renaissance and the transcendent influence of Cicero's dissertations upon the men of that day; when I consider that the impulse of Deism in the eighteenth century, as seen in Shaftesbury and his successors, was at bottom little more than a revival of this same Stoicism, as it had been subdued to the emotions by Cicero and mixed with Epicureanism; that Shaftesbury was, in fact, despite his worship of Epictetus, almost a pure Ciceronian; and when I consider that out of Deism sprang the dominant religion and social philosophy of our present world—when I consider these and many other facts, I question whether Cicero, while he certainly represents what is more enduring, has not been also, actually and personally, as dynamic an influence in civilisation as St. Paul, though the noise, no doubt, and the tumult have been around the latter.

We are still too near Matthew Arnold's day to determine the resultant of all the forces then at work, yet it would not be very rash even now to assert that his critical essays will be found in the end a broader and more lasting, as they are a saner, influence than the exaggerated æstheticism of Ruskin or the shrill prophesying of Carlyle or the scientific dogmatism of Huxley. No, if there is any deduction to be made to the value of criticism, it is not on the side of efficiency. It is well to remember Matthew Arnold's own words. "Violent indignation with the past," he says, "abstract systems of renovation applied wholesale, a new doctrine drawn up in black and white for elaborating down to the very smallest details a rational society for

the future—these are the ways of Jacobinism. . .
Culture [it is his word here for criticism] is always
assigning to system-makers and systems a smaller share
in the bent of human destiny than their friends like."

Perhaps it is a secret inkling of this vanity of the
critic in its widest bearing, besides a natural antagonism of temper, that leads so many to carp against
him and his trade. The inveterate hostility of "creative" writers to criticism is well known, and has been
neatly summed up by E. S. Dallas in *The Gay
Science* :

Ben Jonson spoke of critics as tinkers, who make more
faults than they mend; Samuel Butler, as the fierce inquisitors
of wit, and as butchers who have no right to sit on a jury;
Sir Richard Steele, as of all mortals the silliest; Swift, as dogs,
rats, wasps, or, at best, drones of the learned world; Shen-
stone, as asses, which by gnawing vines first taught the advantage of pruning them; Burns, as cut-throat bandits in the path
of fame; Walter Scott, humorously reflecting the general sentiment, as caterpillars.

The droll thing about it is that every one of these
critics of criticism was so ready to act himself as
butcher or ass or caterpillar. It is a common trick of
the guild. For a modern instance, turn to Mr. Horace
Traubel, the shirt-sleeved Boswell of Walt Whitman,
and you will find pages of conversation recorded in
which the seer of Camden belabours the professors of
criticism and in almost the same breath exercises the
art upon his brother poets with delightful frankness
and at times rare penetration. But this ancient feud
of the gentlemen of the pen is a special form, due in
part to special causes, of the hostility that so often
manifests itself against the critical spirit in general.
The man of system and the man of unhesitating
action are likely to feel something like contempt for
the mind that balances and waits. The imperial

Mommsen felt this contempt, and showed it, in his treatment of Cicero; it is rife even yet in the current tone of condescension towards Erasmus as compared with Luther, to which Matthew Arnold replied by calling Luther "a Philistine of genius"; Warburton showed it in his sneers at Shaftesbury as the man of taste, and Cardinal Newman has, with splendid politeness, echoed them; Matthew Arnold was equally feared and despised in his own lifetime, and it is an odd fact that you will to-day scarcely pick up a piece of third-rate criticism (in which there is likely to be anything at work rather than the critical spirit), but you will come upon some gratuitous fling against him. Most bitter of all was Henry Sidgwick's arraignment of "The Prophet of Culture" in *Macmillan's Magazine* for August, 1867. There if anywhere the critical spirit was stabbed with its own weapon. You will recall the image of the pouncet-box:

Mr. Arnold may say that he does not discourage action, but only asks for delay, in order that we may act with sufficient knowledge. This is the eternal excuse of indolence—insufficient knowledge. . . One cannot think on this subject without recalling the great man who recommended to philosophy a position very similar to that now claimed for culture. I wish to give Mr. Arnold the full benefit of his resemblance to Plato. But when we look closer at the two positions, the dissimilarity comes out: they have a very different effect on our feelings and imagination; and I confess I feel more sympathy with the melancholy philosopher looking out with hopeless placidity "from beneath the shelter of some wall" than with a cheerful modern liberal, tempered by renouncement, shuddering aloof from the rank exhalations of vulgar enthusiasm, and holding up the pouncet-box of culture betwixt the wind and his nobility.

Such an onslaught on our prophet of culture as a languid and shrinking dilettante was fair enough in the heat of controversy and was at least justified by its own art, if not by certain affectations of its victim's style; but I protest against accepting it as essentially true. Any one might perceive that Matthew Arnold had beneath the irony and suavity of his manner a temper of determined seriousness; that, like the bride of Giacopone di Todi in his sonnet, his Muse might be young, gay, and radiant outside, but had

> a hidden ground
> Of thought and of austerity within.

It would be interesting in this respect to continue the comparison of Arnold and Shaftesbury, and to show how near together they stood in their attitude towards nature and society and in their religion, and how profound was their own enthusiasm beneath their hostility to the sham or undisciplined enthusiasms of the day. Lord Shaftesbury might say that we have "in the main a witty and good-humoured religion," as Matthew Arnold might ridicule the sourness of the Nonconformists and the bleakness of the reformers in whose assemblies any child of nature, if he shall stray thither, is smitten with lamentation and mourning and woe; but there was solemnity enough, however we may rate their insight, in their own search for the God that sits concealed at the centre. Shaftesbury's creed became the formula of the deists. "Still ardent in its pursuit," the soul, he says, "rests not here, nor satisfies itself with the beauty of a part, but, extending further its communicative bounty, seeks the good of all, and affects the interest and prosperity of the whole. True to its native world and higher country, 'tis here it seeks order and perfection; wishing the best, and hoping still to find a just and wise administration. And since all hope of this were vain and idle if no universal mind presided; since without such a supreme intelligence and providential care the distracted universe must be condemned to suffer infinite calamities; 'tis here the generous mind labours to discover that healing cause by which the interest of the whole is securely established, the beauty of things and the universal order happily sustained." Matthew Arnold condensed that rhetoric into a pharse: "The stream of tendency, not ourselves, which makes for righteousness."

But the strongest evidence of their austerity of purpose is seen in those private notebooks which led me to couple their names together in this study of the spirit of criticism. This is not the time to deal at length with that sober and anxious self-examination of the noble Lord, as Shaftesbury's enemies in the Church were so fond of calling him. It is one of the important documents to show how completely Deism was a revival of pagan morality. It is, in brief, no more than a translation of the great maxims of antiquity into modern purposes: the inner record of a man seeking character in the two elements of attention (προσοχή) and the harmony of life (*veræ numerosque modosque vitæ*), and of a man who thought that this pursuit must be maintained unrelentingly. Of the two books it may seem strange that Matthew Arnold's, which consists merely of brief quotations without comment, should really open to us more intimately the author's heart than does the direct self-questioning of Shaftesbury's. Yet a book more filled with sad sincerity, a more perfect confession of a life's purpose, will scarcely be found than these memoranda. "I am glad to find," he wrote once in a letter to his sister, "that in the past year I have at least accomplished more than usual in the way of reading the books which at the beginning of the year I had put down to be read. . . The importance of reading, not slight stuff to get through the time, but the best that has been written, forces itself upon me more and more every

year I live." Now the *Notebooks* not only preserve
some of these annual lists of books to be read, but
show, in quintessential phrase, just what the books
actually read meant to him. Some of the quotations
are repeated a number of times, and if frequency of
repetition can be taken as a criterion the maxim closest
to Arnold's heart was the sentence, from what source
I do not know: *"Semper aliquid certi proponendum
est*—always some certain end must be kept in view."
It is but an expansion of the same idea that he
expresses in the words set down more than once from
some French author: "A working life, a succession
of labours which fill and moralise the days!" and in
the beloved command of the *Imitation:* *"Cum multa
legeris et cognoveris, ad unum semper oportet redire
principium*—when you have read and learned many
things, it is necessary always to return to one principle." That principle he sets down in aphorisms and
exhortations from a hundred diverse sources—nowhere, perhaps, more succinctly than in the broken
phrases of the stoic Lucan:

> servare modum, finemque tenere
> Naturamque sequi—
> Nec sibi, sed toti genitum se credere mundo—
> In commune bonus.

(To preserve measure, to hold fast to the end, and follow
nature—To believe oneself born not for oneself alone but for
all the world—good for the community of mankind.)

He might well have applied to his own pursuit of
culture the eulogy he quotes concerning another:
"Study, which for most men is only a frivolous amuse-
ment and often dangerous, was for Dom Rivet a
serious occupation consecrated by religion."

It was not a mere dilettante of sweetness and light
who day by day laid such maxims as these upon his

breast; it was not one who held up the pouncet-box of culture betwixt the wind and his nobility. Matthew Arnold, if any man in his generation, was by temperament a stoic for whom duty and submission and reverence made up the large part of life; and there is something of what we call the irony of fate in the thought that he who made σπουδαιότης, *high seriousness,* the test of great literature, should have suffered the reproach of levity. Yet, after all, fate is never quite blind in these things, and if criticism has thus drawn upon itself the censure of men like Sidgwick we may feel assured that in some way it has failed of the deeper truth. Those reproaches may in part be due to prejudice and revenge and the inevitable contrast of temperaments; they may err in ascribing to the critic a want of efficiency, as they may be wantonly perverse in denouncing him for frivolity; but they have a meaning and they cannot be overlooked. Now the future is often a strange revealer of secret things, and there is no surer way to detect the weak side of a leader than by studying the career of his disciples, or even of his successors.

You are familiar with the story of the concluding chapter of Pater's *Renaissance*—how it was withdrawn from the second edition of that book because the author "conceived it might possibly mislead some of those young men into whose hands it might fall"; and how it was restored, with some slight changes, to the later editions where it now stands. And you know the moral of that essay: that life is but an uncertain interval before the universal judgment of death, a brief illusion of stability in the eternal flux, and that "our one chance lies in expanding that interval, in getting as many pulsations as possible into the given time." And "of this wisdom," he concludes, "the poetic passion, the desire of beauty, the love of art for art's sake, has most; for art comes to you professing frankly to give nothing but the highest quality to your moments as they pass, and simply for those moments' sake." That philosophy of the Oxonian Epicurus and its scandal in a very un-Epicurean land are familiar enough; but perhaps we do not always stop to think how plausibly this doctrine of crowning our moments with the highest sensations of art flows from Matthew Arnold's definition of criticism as the disinterested endeavour "to know the best that is known and thought in the world, irrespectively of practice, politics, and everything of the kind."

The next step from Pater's Epicureanism, and so by a further remove from Arnold's criticism, brings us to one whose name, unfortunately, must always be mentioned with regret, but who is more significant in the development of English letters than is sometimes allowed. At the time when Paterism, as a recent writer has said, was "tripping indelicately along the Oxford High and by the banks of the Cherwell," a young votary of the Muses from Dublin came upon the scene, and began to push the doctrine of Pater as far beyond what the master intended as Pater had gone beyond Matthew Arnold. This is the young man who "would occasionally be seen walking the streets carrying a lily or a sunflower in his hand, at which he would gaze intently and admiringly." He had fashioned himself deliberately to pose as the head of a new sect of "æsthetes," as they styled themselves, who expanded Arnold's excluded tribe of Philistines to embrace all the sober citizens of the world. The fate of Oscar Wilde is still like a fresh wound in the public memory. What I wish to call to your mind is the direct connection (strengthened no doubt by influences from across the Channel) between Pater's philosophy of the sensation-crowded moment and such a poem as that in which Wilde attempted to concentrate all the passionate moments of the past in his gloating revery upon *The Sphinx*. He was himself not unaware of the treachery of the path he had chosen; the sonnet which he prefixed to his book of poems is sincere with the pathos of conscious insincerity, and is a memorable comment on one of the tragic ambitions of a century:

> To drift with every passion till my soul
> Is a stringed lute on which all winds can play, ·
> Is it for this that I have given away
> Mine ancient wisdom, and austere control?
>
> .   .   .   .   .   .
>
> Surely there was a time I might have trod
> The sunlit heights, and from life's dissonance
> Struck one clear chord to reach the ears of God:
> Is that time dead? lo! with a little rod
> I did but touch the honey of romance—
> And must I lose a soul's inheritance?

The answer to the poet's query he was himself to write in *The Ballad of Reading Gaol*:

> Silently we went round and round,
>   And through each hollow mind
> The Memory of dreadful things
>   Rushed like a dreadful wind,
> And Horror stalked before each man,
>   And Terror crept behind.

This Memory of dreadful things is the too logical end, step by step, of the philosophy of the sensation-crowded moment; the concealed suspicion of it in Matthew Arnold's definition of criticism was the justification, if any there be, of the contempt hurled upon him by some of his contemporaries.

It is necessary to repeat that such a derivation from Matthew Arnold is essentially unfair because it leaves out of view the real purpose and heart of the man.

If we could not read his great moral energy in his *Essays,* as I trust we all of us can, and if we did not know the profound influence of his critical philosophy upon the better life of our age, we could still dispel our doubts by looking into the *Notebooks,* in which memory is not turned to dreadful things for the soul's disgrace, but is the guide and impulse to strong resolution and beautiful forbearance. Yet withal it remains true that the Epicureanism of Pater and the hedonism of Oscar Wilde were able to connect themselves in a disquieting way with one side of Matthew Arnold's gospel of culture; and it behooves us who come upon the heels of this movement and who believe that the critical spirit is still to be one of the powers making in the world for right enjoyment, it behooves us to examine the first definition of culture or criticism— the words had about the same meaning as Arnold used them—and see whether something was not there forgotten. The fault lay not in any intrinsic want of efficiency in the critical spirit, nor in any want of moral earnestness in Matthew Arnold or Shaftesbury: that we have seen. But these men were lacking in another direction: they missed a philosophy which could bind together their moral and their æsthetic sense, a positive principle besides the negative force of ridicule and irony; and, missing this, they left criticism more easily subject to a one-sided and dangerous development.

To the nature of that omission, to the *porro unum necessarium,* we may be directed, I think, by the critical theory of the one who carried the practice, in other respects, to its lowest degradation. In Oscar Wilde's dialogue on *The Critic as Artist,* one of the most extraordinary mixtures ever compounded of truth flaunting in the robes of error and error assuming the gravity of truth, you will remember that the advocate of criticism at the height of his argument proclaims the true man of culture to be him who has learned "the best that is known and thought in the world" (he uses Matthew Arnold's words), and who thus, as Matthew Arnold neglected to add, "bears within himself the dreams, and ideas, and feelings of myriad generations." The addition is important, how important, or at least how large, may be seen in the really splendid, if somewhat morbid, passage in which the idea is developed. Let me quote at some length:

To know anything about oneself, one must know all about others. There must be no mood with which one cannot sympathise, no dead mode of life that one cannot make alive. Is this impossible? I think not. By revealing to us the absolute mechanism of all action, and so freeing us from the self-imposed and trammelling burden of moral responsibility, the scientific principle of Heredity has become, as it were, the warrant for the contemplative life. It has shown us that we are never less free than when we try to act. It has hemmed us round with the nets of the hunter, and written upon the wall the prophecy of our doom. We may not watch it, for it is within us. We may not see it, save in a mirror that mirrors the soul. It is Nemesis without her mask. It is the last of the Fates, and the most terrible. It is the only one of the Gods whose real name we know.

And yet, while in the sphere of practical and external life it has robbed energy of its freedom and activity of its choice, in the subjective sphere, where the soul is at work, it comes to us, this terrible shadow, with many gifts in its hands, gifts of strange temperaments and subtle susceptibilities, gifts of wild ardours and chill moods of indifference, complex multiform gifts of thoughts that are at variance with each other, and passions that war against themselves. And so, it is not our own life that we live, but the lives of the dead, and the soul that dwells within us is no single spiritual entity, making us personal and individual, created for our service, and entering into us for our joy. . . It can help us to leave the age in which we were born, and to pass into other ages, and find ourselves not exiled from their air. It can teach us how to escape from our experience, and to realise the experiences of those who are greater than we are. The pain of Leopardi crying out against life becomes our pain. Theocritus blows on his pipe, and we laugh with the lips of nymph and shepherd. In the wolfskin of Pierre Vidal we flee before the hounds, and in the armour of Lancelot we ride from the bower of the Queen. We have whispered the secret of our love beneath the cowl of Abelard, and in the stained raiment of Villon have put our shame into song. We can see the dawn through Shelley's eyes, and when we wander with Endymion the Moon grows amorous of our youth. Ours is the anguish of Atys, and ours the weak rage and noble sorrows of the Dane. Do you think that it is the imagination that enables us to live these countless lives? Yes: it is the imagination; and the imagination is the result of heredity. It is simply concentrated race-experience.

Now, this theory of race-experience, as Oscar Wilde formulated it, lends itself, no doubt, to an easy fallacy. I am aware of the rebuke administered to one who was by the range of his knowledge and by his historic sense much more justified in such a presumption than was Oscar Wilde. "Is it not the strangest illusion," exclaimed the biographer of Renan, "to believe that the mere reading of the Acts of the martyrs is sufficient to give us their soul, to transfer to us in its real intensity the ardour which ravished them amidst their tortures? . . . Those who have lost all the energy of living and acting may, if they choose, shut themselves up in this kingdom of shadows; that is their affair. But that they should proclaim theirs as the true life, is not to be conceded to them." Séailles was right. These men, whether it be a paradox-monger like Oscar Wilde or a great scholar like Renan, should have laid to heart the favourite maxim of Matthew Arnold, *semper aliquid certi proponendum est:* true culture has always before its eyes a definite end and is for self-discipline, not for revery. Nor am I unaware that the theory as expressed by Oscar Wilde, is mixed up with his own personal taint of decadence. One thing at least is certain: that the way of the true critical spirit is not to free us, as he boasts, from "the self-imposed and trammelling burden of moral responsibility." His avowal in the same dialogue that the sole aim of art is to produce the "beautiful sterile emotions" so hateful to the world, his shameless vaunt that "there is nothing sane about the worship of beauty," his whole philosophy of the ego as above the laws of society, cannot be severed from the memory of dreadful things in which his own song ended: such a philosophy is in fact a denial of the validity of that very race-experience out of which he attempts to derive it. In this respect again he should have remembered the maxim of Matthew Arnold: "A working life, a succession of labours that fill and moralise the days." The aim of culture is not to merge the present in a sterile dream of the past, but to hold the past as a living force in the present. In omitting these aspects of criticism Pater and, to a greater extent, Oscar Wilde fell into extravagance far more deleterious to culture than was any omission or incompleteness on the part of Matthew Arnold.

Nevertheless, with all its false emphasis and its admixture of personal error, that positive and emotional reassumption of the past, that association of the contemplative life (the βίος θεωρητικός) with the rapture of memory, contains the hint of a great truth which must be grasped and properly exercised if criticism is to confirm itself against such hostility as has hitherto kept it on the defensive. I would not say even that the mysticism, out of which Oscar Wilde's critical theory really springs, though expressed in the modish language of scientific evolution, is essentially

perverse. For in a very true sense the past of mankind, by the larger race-memory and particularly by
that form of it which we call literature, abides as a
living reality in our present. We suffer not our individual destiny alone but the fates of humanity also.
We are born into an inheritance of great emotions—
into the unconquerable hopes and defeated fears of an
immeasurable past, the tragedies and the comedies of
love, the ardent aspirations of faith, the baffled questionings of evil, the huge laughter at facts, the deep-
welling passion of peace. Without that common
inheritance how inconceivably poor and shallow would
be this life of the world and our life in it! These
recorded emotions are, indeed, not for us what they
were in actuality, nor by sitting at our own ease with
memory can we enter into the exact emotions of the
martyr at the stake and the hero in his triumph.
These things are now transmuted into something the
same and different, something less and greater. The
intensity of the actual moment they cannot possess, but
on the other hand with this loss of separate reality
they are associated with life as a whole, and in that
unity of experience obtain, what they lacked before, a
significance and design. They bear in a way the same
relation to practical life as that life bore to the ideal
world out of which it arose and into which it is continually passing. And thus this larger memory, in its
transmuting and unifying power, may not unmean-
ingly be regarded as the purpose of activity, and literature may not too presumptuously be cherished as the
final end of existence. Some such mystery as this was
hinted in the Greek and Gnostic doctrine of the *logos,*
the Word, and in the Hindu name for the creator as
vâcas pati, Lord of the Word. And if such a theory
sounds too absurdly metaphysical for the ears of prudent common-sense, consider that Homer, no philoso-

pher of empty phrases surely, meant nothing very
different when he judged of actions by their fame in
future story. To him the warring of armies for ten
long years and the desolation of Troy were for no
other purpose than that the inner life of the race might
be enriched by memory:

> Thus the gods fated, and such ruin wove
> That song might flourish for posterity.

And in this theory of memory criticism has an
important office. We are beginning to hear a good
deal these days about the French metaphysician, M.
Henri Bergson, of whom Prof. William James has
avowed himself a willing disciple, and whose disquisi-
tions on *Matière et mémoire* and *L'Évolution créatrice*
are perhaps more talked of than any other recent books
of philosophy. I do not pretend to pronounce on
the full scope of his theories, but his conception of the
function of memory is rich with applications to the
matter we have in hand. Our consciousness, that is
to say our very self, is not, he says, a thing born new
with each moment, not a *mens momentanea,* but an
uninterrupted stream of activity, and what we now
feel is directly bound up with what we have felt before.
Nor is this consciousness, on the other hand, a mere
heaping together indiscriminately of perceptions and
emotions, but it is an active faculty, or, I should prefer
to say, the servant of some active faculty, that depresses
this particular experience into the background and
centres attention upon that other experience, thus by a
process of criticism secreting the present, so to speak,
out of the past. Such a philosophy finds a new and
profound truth in the saying of Pascal: *"La mémoire
est nécessaire à toutes les opérations de l'esprit—*
memory is necessary to all the operations of the mind."
This notion of the active memory is, I am told by

those who should know, mixed up in Bergson with a questionable metaphysic, yet in itself alone it should seem to be nothing more than the laborious expression of a very simple fact. We have all of us met now and then in our daily intercourse a man whose conversation impressed us immediately as possessing a certain ripeness of wisdom, a certain pertinency and depth of meaning. If we wished to characterise such a man in a single word, we should perhaps say that he was essentially educated. We feel that he has within him some central force which enables him to choose consistently amidst the innumerable conflicting impulses and attractions and dissipations of life, that he moves forward, not at haphazard, but by the direction of some principle of conduct, and that he can be depended upon for counsel and comfort. Well, if you stop to analyse this quality of mind, which we will call education, you will discover in every case, I believe, that the determining trait is just the force of a critical memory. I do not mean by this the mere facility of recalling the emotions and events and spectacles which have come to a man with the years; for such undisciplined reminiscence may be but a shabby wisdom to the man himself, as it may be the very contrary of joy to his hearer. I mean rather the faculty of selection as well as of retention, the weighing of cause and effect, the constant and active assumption of the past in the present, by which the events of life are no longer regarded as isolated and fortuitous moments, but are merged into a unity of experience. Those in whom this faculty rules are commonly the possessors of practical wisdom, but there are others, a few, who by its virtue are raised into another kind of wisdom. With these men the selective, reconciling memory is associated, more or less consciously, with the Platonic reminiscence in such a manner that not only are the past and present of passing time made one but our ephemeral life is fitted into that great ring of eternity which Henry Vaughan saw as in a dream. So it is that to them the things which others behold as sudden unrelated facts are made shadows and types of the everlasting ideas; and with the accumulation of knowledge they grow ripe in vision,

> Till old experience do attain
> To something like prophetic strain.

And as our private memory is not a merely passive retention of sensations, so in literature the critical spirit is at work as a conscious energy of selection. The function of criticism, as thus understood, is far removed from the surrender to luxurious revery which the impressionists believed it to be; nor is the good critic, as Anatole France said, he who recounts the adventures of his soul amid masterpieces; he is rather one who has before him always the *aliquid certi,* the definite aim of a Matthew Arnold. He does not, like Oscar Wilde, seek by losing the present in the past to throw off "the self-imposed and trammelling burden of moral responsibility"; he is rather one whose life is "a succession of labours that fill and moralise the days"—not in the narrow didactic sense, it need scarcely be said, but in so far as his task is a continual weighing of values. But the critical spirit is also something deeper than Matthew Arnold perceived, or, at least, clearly expressed. The error of criticism in his hands, as in the hands of his predecessors, was that in the exercise of judgment it used the past too much as a dead storehouse of precepts for schoolmastering the present; it was not sufficiently aware of the relation of this faculty of judgment to the indwelling and ever-acting memory of things. Here is the one touch of insight needed, I think, to raise criticism, while not

forgetting its special duty of discrimination and judgment, to a more independent and self-respecting *genre*.
In its conscious creation of the field of the present out
of the past it takes an honoured, if not equal, place
by the side of those impulses, more commonly recognised as creative, which are continually adding new
material for its selective energy. "Valuing is creating," said Nietzsche; "to value is the treasure and
jewel among all things valued." The critical spirit is
thus akin to that force of design or final cause in the
Aristotelian sense, which we are beginning once more
to divine as the guiding principle, itself unchanged,
at work within the evolutionary changes of nature;
and in so far as it becomes aware of this high office it
introduces into our intellectual life an element outside
of alteration and growth and decay, a principle to
which time is the minister and not the master.

Literary criticism is, indeed, in this sense only the
specific exercise of a faculty which works in many
directions. All scholars, whether they deal with
history or sociology or philosophy or language or, in
the narrower use of the word, literature, are servants
of the critical spirit, in so far as they transmit and
interpret and mould the sum of experience from man
to man and from generation to generation. Might not
one even say that at a certain point criticism becomes
almost identical with education, and that by this
standard we may judge the value of any study as an
instrument of education, and may estimate the merit
of any special presentation of that study? It is at
least, in the existing chaos of pedagogical theories, a
question worthy of consideration.

LAFCADIO HEARN

THERE was something almost as romantic in Mr. Hearn's life as in his books. He was, I believe, the child of an Irish father and a woman of the Greek islands; his early manhood he passed in this country, and then converted himself into a subject of the Mikado, taking a Japanese wife and adopting the customs and religion of the land. On his death this winter (1904) he was buried with full Buddhist rites, being the first foreigner so distinguished in Japan; and almost his last act was to pass by cablegram on the final proofs of his most serious attempt to transfer the illusive mystery of the Orient into Western speech. His *Japan, an Interpretation* thus rounded out what must be deemed one of the most extraordinary artistic achievements of modern days. For it is as an art of strange subtlety that we should regard his literary work, an art that, like some sympathetic menstruum, has fused into one compound three elements never before brought together.

In the mere outward manner of this art there is, to be sure, nothing mysterious. One recognises immediately throughout his writing that sense of restraint joined with a power of after-suggestion, which he has described as appertaining to Japanese poetry, but which is no less his own by native right. There is a term, *ittakkiri*, it seems, meaning "all gone," or "entirely vanished," which is applied contemptuously by the Japanese to verse that tells all and trusts nothing to the reader's imagination. Their praise they reserve for compositions that leave in the mind the thrilling of a something unsaid. "Like the single stroke of a bell, the perfect poem should set murmuring and undulating, in the mind of the hearer, many a ghostly aftertone of long duration." Now these ghostly reverberations are precisely the effect of the simplest of Mr. Hearn's pictures. Let him describe, for instance, the impression produced by walking down the deep cañon of Broadway, between those vast structures, beautiful but sinister, where one feels depressed by the mere sensation of enormous creative life without sympathy and of unresting power without pity,—let him describe this terror of Broadway, and in a few words he shall set ringing within you long pulsations of emotion which reach down to the depths of experience. Or, let him relate by mere allusion the story of hearing a girl say "Good-night" to some one parting from her in a London park, and there shall be awakened in your mind ghostly aftertones that bring back memories of the saddest separations and regrets of life. He employs the power of suggestion through perfect restraint.

But this self-restrained and suggestive style is merely the instrument, the manner, so to speak, of his art. If we examine the actual substance of his writings, we shall discover that it is borrowed from three entirely distinct, in fact almost mutually destructive, philosophies, any one of which alone would afford material for the genius of an ordinary writer. He stands and proclaims his mysteries at the meeting of three ways. To the religious instinct of India,—Buddhism in particular,—which history has engrafted on the æsthetic sense of Japan, Mr. Hearn brings the interpreting spirit of Occidental science; and these three traditions (Hindu, Japanese, and European) are fused by the peculiar sympathies of his mind into one rich and novel compound,—a compound so rare as to have introduced into literature a psychological sensation unknown before. More than any other recent author, he has added a new thrill to our intellectual experience.

Of Japan, which gives the most obvious substratum to Mr. Hearn's work, it has been said that her people, since the days of ancient Greece, are the only genuine artists of the world; and in a manner, if we do not forget their Chinese teachers, this is true. There was a depth and pregnancy in the Greek imagination which made of Greek art something far more universally significant than the frail loveliness of Japanese creation, but not the Greeks themselves surpassed, or even equalled, the Japanese in their all-embracing love of decorative beauty. To read the story of the daily life of these people, as recorded by Mr. Mortimer Menpes and other travellers, is to be brought into contact with a national temperament so far removed from Western comprehension as to seem to most of us a tale from fairyland. When, for instance, Mr. Menpes, with a Japanese friend, visited Danjuro, he found a single exquisite *kakemono,* or painting, displayed in the great actor's chamber. On admiring its beauty, he was told by the friend that Danjuro had taken pains to learn the precise character of his visitor's taste, and only then had exhibited this particular picture. To the Japanese the hanging of a kakemono or the arranging of a bough of blossoms is a serious function of life. The placing of flowers is indeed an exact science, to the study of which a man may devote seven years, even fourteen years, before he will be acknowledged a master. Nature herself is subjected to this elaborate system of training, and often what in a Japanese landscape seems to a foreigner the exuberance of natural growth is really the work of patient human artifice.

There is no accident [writes Mr. Menpes] in the beautiful curves of the trees that the globe-trotter so justly admires: these trees have been trained and shaped and forced to form a certain decorative pattern, and the result is—perfection. We in the West labour under the delusion that if Nature were to be allowed to have her sweet way, she would always be beautiful. But the Japanese have gone much farther than this: they realise that Nature does not always do the right thing; they know that occasionally trees will grow up to form ugly lines; and they know exactly how to adapt and help her. She is to them like some beautiful musical instrument, finer than any ever made by human hands, but still an instrument, with harmonies to be coaxed out.

And the same æsthetic delicacy, touched with artificiality if you will, pervades the literature of this people. We are accustomed, and rightly, to regard the Japanese as a nation of imitators. But their poetry, we are assured by Mr. Hearn, is the one original art which they have not borrowed from China, or from any other country; and nowhere better than in their poetry can we observe the swiftness and dexterity of their imagination and that exquisite reserve with its haunting echo in the memory. To reproduce in English the peculiar daintiness of these poems is, we are told and can well believe, quite an impossibility; but from the seemingly careless translations scattered through Mr. Hearn's pages we do at least form some notion of their art in the original. Many of these stanzas are mere bits of folk-lore or the work of unknown singers, like this tiny picture of the cicada:

> Lo! on the topmost pine, a solitary cicada
> Vainly attempts to clasp one last red beam of sun.

That is light enough in English, but even one entirely ignorant of the Japanese language can see that, in comparison with the rhythm of the original,[1] it is like the

---

[1] Sémi hitotsu
Matsu no yū-hi wo
Kakaé-keri.

step of a quadruped compared with the fluttering of a moth. It contains only sixteen syllables in the original; and indeed all these poems are wrought into the brief compass of a stanza, like certain fragile little vases painted inside and out which are so highly prized by connoisseurs. Yet these tiny word-paintings, by virtue of their cunning restraint, are capable at times of gathering into their loveliness echoes of emotion as wide-reaching as love and as deep as the grave:

Perhaps a freak of the wind—yet perhaps a sign of remembrance,—
This fall of a single leaf on the water I pour for the dead.

. . . .

I whispered a prayer at the grave: a butterfly rose and fluttered—
Thy spirit, perhaps, dear friend!

To have been able to convey through the coarser medium of English prose something of this æsthetic grace, this deftness of touch, and this suggestiveness of restraint, would in itself deserve no slight praise. But beneath all this artistic delicacy lies some reminiscence of India's austere religious thought, a sense of the nothingness of life strangely exiled among this people of graceful artists, yet still more strangely assimilated by them; and this, too, Mr. Hearn has been able to reproduce. We feel this shadow of India's faith lurking in the sunshine of many of the lightest of the stanzas,—a touch of swift exotic poignancy, if nothing more. We feel it still more strongly in such poems as these, which are inspired by the consciousness of endless change and of unceasing birth and death and again birth:

All things change, we are told, in this world of change and sorrow;

But love's way never changes of promising never to change.

. . . . . .

Even the knot of the rope tying our boats together
Knotted was long ago by some love in a former birth.

Endless change, a ceaseless coming and going, and
the past throwing its shadow on into the future,—
that is the very essence of Hindu philosophy; but how
the tone of this philosophy has itself become altered
in passing from the valley of the Ganges to the
decorated island of the Mikado! Over and over again
Buddha repeats the essential law of being, that all
things are made up of constituent parts and are subject
to flux and change, that all things are impermanent.
It is the *All things pass and nothing abides* of the
Greek philosopher, deepened with the intensity of
emotion that makes of philosophy a religion. In this
ever-revolving wheel of existence one fact only is certain, *karma,* the law of cause and effect which declares
that every present state is the effect of some previous
act and that every present act must inevitably bear its
fruit in some future state. As a man soweth so shall
he reap. We are indeed the creatures of a fate which
we ourselves have builded by the deeds of a former
life. We are bound in chains which we ourselves
have riveted, yet still our desires are free, and as our
desires shape themselves, so we act and build up our
coming fate, our karma; and as our desires abnegate
themselves, so we cease to act and become liberated
from the world. Endless change subject to the law
of cause and effect—not even our personality remains
constant in this meaningless flux, for it too is made
up of constituent parts and is dissolved at death as
the body is dissolved, leaving only its karma to build
up the new personality with the new body. From the
perception of this universal impermanence springs the

so-called "Truth" of Buddhism, that sorrow is the attribute of all existence. Birth is sorrow, old age is sorrow, death is sorrow, every desire of the heart is sorrow; and the mission of Buddha was to deliver men out of the bondage of this sorrow as from the peril of a burning house. The song of victory uttered by Gotama when the great enlightenment shone upon him, and he became the Buddha, was the cry of a man who has escaped a great evil.

But because the Buddhist so dwells on the impermanence and sorrow of existence, he is not therefore properly called a pessimist. On the contrary, the one predominant note of Buddhism is joy, for it too is a gospel of glad tidings. The builders who rear these prison houses of life are nothing other than the desires of our own hearts, and these we may control though all else is beyond our power. To the worldly this teaching of Buddha may seem wrapped in pessimistic gloom, for deliverance to them must be only another name for annihilation; but to the spiritually minded it brought ineffable joy, for they knew that deliverance meant the passing out of the bondage of personality into a freedom of whose nature no tongue could speak. It is an austere faith, hardly suited, in its purer form, for the sentimental and vacillating,—austere in its recognition of sorrow, austere in its teaching of spiritual joy.

Yet the wonderful adaptability of Buddhism is shown by its acceptance among the Japanese, certainly of all peoples the most dissimilar in temperament to the ancient Hindus. Here the brooding of the Hindu over the law of impermanence melts into the peculiar sensitiveness to fleeting impressions so characteristic of the Japanese, and the delicacy of their æsthetic taste is enhanced by this half-understood spiritual insight. And it deepens their temperament: I think that the feeling awakened by all these dainty stanzas of something not said but only hinted, that the avoidance of ittakkiri to which Mr. Hearn alludes, the echoing reverberations that haunt us after the single stroke of the bell, are due to the residuum of Hindu philosophy left in these vases of Japanese art. "Buddhism," writes Mr. Hearn, "taught that nature was a dream, an illusion, a phantasmagoria; but it also taught men [men of Japan, he should say] how to seize the fleeting impressions of that dream, and how to interpret them in relation to the highest truth."

Buddhism when it passed over to Japan came into contact with the national religion of Shinto, a kind of ancestor-worship, which proclaimed that the world of the living was directly governed by the world of the dead. On this popular belief the doctrine of karma was readily engrafted, and the two flourished henceforth side by side. Faith in the protecting presence of ancestors and faith in the present efficacy of our own multitudinous preëxistence were inextricably confused. To the Japanese Buddhist the past does not die, but lives on without end, involving the present in an infinite web of invisible influences not easily comprehensible to the Western mind.

And the Indian horror of impermanence and the rapture of deliverance have suffered like transformation with their causes. First of all, the sharp contrast between the horror and the joy is lightened. The sorrow fades to a fanciful feeling of regret for the beauty of the passing moment,—the same regret that speaks through a thousand Western songs such as Herrick's "Gather ye rosebuds while ye may," and Malherbe's "Et rose elle a vécu ce que vivent les roses," but touched here in Japanese poetry with a little mystery and made more insistent by some echo of Hindu brooding. And the joy, severed from its spiritual sustenance, loses its high ecstasy and becomes almost indistinguishable from regret. Sorrow, too, and joy are impermanent, and the enlightened mind dwells lingeringly and fondly on each fair moment garnered from the waste of Time. Here is no longer the spiritual exaltation, the *dhyâna,* of the Indian monk, but the charmed impressions of the artist. The religion of the Ganges has assumed in Japan the mask of æsthetic emotionalism.

Now this refinement of emotionalism Mr. Hearn by his peculiar temperament has been able to reproduce almost miraculously in the coarser fibre of English. But more specially he has sought to interpret the deeper influence of India on Japan,—the thoughts and images in which we see the subtlety of the Japanese turned aside into a strange new psychology. One may suppose that some tendency to mingle grace and beauty with haunting suggestions was inherent in the Japanese temper from the beginning, but certainly the particular form of imagination that runs through most of the tales Mr. Hearn has translated is not the product of Japan alone. Nor is it purely Hindu: the literature of India includes much that is grotesque but hardly a touch of the weird or ghostly, for its religious tone is too austere and lacks the suggestive symbolism which that quality demands. Out of the blending of the stern sense of impermanence and moral responsibility with the flower-like beauty of Japan there arises this new feeling of the weird. How intimately the two tempers are blended and how rare their product is, may be seen in such sketches as that called *Ingwa-banashi: A Tale of Karma.*

Had it been that Mr. Hearn's art sufficed only to reproduce the delicacy and haunting strangeness of Japanese tales, he would have performed a notable but scarcely an extraordinary service to letters. But into the study of these byways of Oriental literature he has carried a third element, the dominant idea of Occidental science; and this element he has wedded with Hindu religion and Japanese æstheticism in a union as bewildering as it is voluptuous. In this triple combination lies his real claim to high originality.

Now the fact is well known to those who have studied Buddhism at its genuine sources that our modern conception of evolution fits into Buddhist psychology more readily and completely than into any dogmatic theology of the West. It is natural, therefore, that the Western authors quoted most freely by Mr. Hearn in support of his Oriental meditations should be Huxley and Herbert Spencer. For the most part these allusions to Western science are merely made in passing. But in one essay, that on *The Idea of Preëxistence,* he endeavours with something of philosophic system to develop the harmony between evolution and the Buddhist conception of previous existences, a conception which, as he shows, has little in common with the crude form of metempsychosis embodied by Wordsworth in such poems as *Fidelity* and *Intimations of Immortality.* To justify his theory he turns to Professor Huxley and quotes these words: "None but very hasty thinkers will reject it on the ground of inherent absurdity. Like the doctrine of evolution itself, that of transmigration has its roots in the world of reality; and it may claim such support as the great argument from analogy is capable of supplying." Again, in his essay on Nirvâna he compares the doctrine of impermanence, out of which the conception of Nirvâna springs as a natural corollary, with similar ideas in evolutionary science. "Every feeling and thought," so he quotes from Herbert Spencer, "being but transitory; nay, the objects amid which life is passed, though less transitory, being severally in the course of losing their individualities, whether quickly or slowly,—*we learn that the one thing permanent is the Unknowable Reality hidden under all these changing shapes.*"

The parallel is at once apt and misleading. In both Oriental faith and Occidental science we do indeed have the conception of all phenomena, including that ultimate phenomenon which we name our personality, —we do indeed have the conception of these as suffering endless flux and change behind which lies a permanent inexpressible Reality. The parallel so far is close and makes possible the peculiar blending of traditions which, as I have said, is the chief mark of originality in Mr. Hearn's essays. But in the next step the two diverge as far as the rising sun is from the setting. To Mr. Spencer and all the spokesmen of science it is the impermanent sphere of phenomena that is alone knowable, whereas the permanent Reality hidden from the eyes is the great Unknowable. To the Buddhist on the contrary, all impermanence is wrapt in illusion, as indeed the very meaning of the word would seem to imply, whereas the permanent Reality, though inexpressible, is alone knowable. The difference is of great importance when we come to consider the effect of interpreting Japanese ideas in Occidental terms. It even seems that Mr. Hearn himself is not aware of the gulf set between these two methods of viewing existence, and that consequently he has never measured the full originality of this realm of sensation which his art has opened by spanning a bridge between the two. In the fusion of Mr. Hearn's thought the world of impermanent phenomena is at once knowable and unknowable: it is the reality of Western cognition, and therefore is invested with an intensity of influence and fulness of meaning impossible to an Oriental writer; and at the same time it is the unreality of Eastern philosophy, and hence is involved in illusion and subtle shadows into which it threatens momentarily to melt away. It is a realm of half reality, this phenomenal world, a realm of mingled spirit and matter, seeming now to tantalise the eyes with colours of unimaginable beauty that fade away when we gaze on them too intently, and again to promise the Soul that one long-sought word which shall solve the riddle of her existence in this land of exile. It is a new symbolism that troubles while it illumines. It leads the artist to dwell on the weirder, more impalpable phases of Japanese literature, and to lend to these subconscious motives a force of realism which they could never possess in the original. The perception of impermanence is accompanied with a depth of yearning regret quite beyond the frailer beauty of the songs of the East which could see little gravity of meaning in phenomena dissevered from the spirit, and equally beyond the songs of the West composed before science had carried the law of material mutability into the notion of personality. From this union with science the Oriental belief in the indwelling of the past now receives a vividness of present actuality that dissolves the Soul into ghostly intimacy with the mystic unexplored background of life. As a consequence of this new sense of impermanence and of this new realism lent to the indwelling past, all the primitive emotions of the heart are translated into a strange language, which, when once it lays hold of the imagination, carries us into a region of dreams akin to that world which our psychologists dimly call the subliminal or subconscious. The far-reaching results of this psychology on literature it is not easy to foresee. Mr. Hearn has nowhere treated systematically this new interpretation of human emotions, but by bringing together scattered passages from his essays we may form some notion of its scope and efficacy.

Beauty itself, which forms the essence of Mr. Hearn's art as of all true art, receives a new content from this union of the East and the West. So standing before a picture of nude beauty we might, in our author's words, question its meaning. That nudity which is divine, which is the abstract of beauty absolute,—what power, we ask, resides within it or within the beholder that causes this shock of astonishment and delight, not unmixed with melancholy? The longer one looks, the more the wonder grows, since there appears no line, or part of a line, whose beauty does not surpass all memory of things seen. Plato explained the shock of beauty as being the Soul's sudden half-remembrance of the World of Divine Ideas: "They who see here any image or resemblance of the things which are there receive a shock like a thunderbolt, and are, after a manner, taken out of themselves." The positive psychology of Spencer declares in our own day that the most powerful of human passions, first love, when it makes its appearance, is absolutely antecedent to all individual experience. Thus do ancient thought and modern— metaphysics and science—accord in recognising that the first deep sensation of human beauty known to the individual is not individual at all. Must not the same truth hold of that shock which supreme art gives? The emotion of beauty, like all our emotions, is certainly the inherited product of unimaginably countless experiences in an immeasurable past. In every æsthetic sensation is the stirring of trillions of trillions of ghostly memories buried in the magical soil of the brain. And each man carries within him an ideal of beauty which is but an infinite composite of dead perceptions of form, colour, grace, once dear to look upon. It is dormant, this ideal,—potential in essence, —cannot be evoked at will before the imagination; but it may light up electrically at any perception by the living outer sense of some vague affinity. Then is felt that weird, sad, delicious thrill, which accompanies the sudden backward-flowing of the tides of life and time.

So, again, to follow Mr. Hearn, it is easy to infer how this perception of the indwelling of the past gives a wonderful significance to the thraldom of love,—to first love most of all, when the shock of emotion comes untroubled by worldly calculations of the present. What is the glamour, we ask with our author, that blinds the lover in its sweet bewildering light when first he meets the woman of his involuntary choice? Whose the witchcraft? Is it any power in the living idol? Rather it is the power of the dead within the idolater. The dead cast the spell. Theirs the shock in the lover's heart; theirs the electric shiver that tingled through his veins at the first touch of one girl's hand. We look into the eyes of love and it is as though, through some intense and sudden stimulation of vital being, we had obtained—for one supercelestial moment—the glimpse of a reality never before imagined, and never again to be revealed. There is, indeed, an illusion. We seem to view the divine; but this divine itself, whereby we are dazzled and duped, is a ghost. Our mortal sight pierces beyond the surface of the present into profundities of myriads of years,—pierces beyond the mask of life into the enormous night of death. For a moment we are made aware of a beauty and a mystery and a depth unutterable: then the Veil falls again forever. The splendour of the eyes that we worship belongs to them only as brightness to the morning star. It is a reflex from beyond the shadow of the Now,—a ghost-light of vanished suns. Unknowingly within that maiden-gaze we meet the gaze of eyes more countless than the hosts of heaven,—eyes otherwhere passed into darkness and dust.

And if we turn to another and purer form of love, it is the same force we behold. So long as we supposed the woman soul one in itself,—a something specially created to fit one particular physical being,—the beauty and the wonder of mother-love could never be fully revealed to us. But with deeper knowledge we must perceive that the inherited love of numberless millions of dead mothers has been treasured up in one life;—that only thus can be interpreted the infinite sweetness of the speech which the infant hears,—the infinite tenderness of the look of caress which meets its gaze.

So too when we listen to the harmonies of instrumental music or the melody of the human voice, there arises a strange emotion within us which seems to magnify us out of ourselves into some expanse of illimitable experiences, to lift us above the present cares of our petty life into some vast concern—so vast that the soul is lost between the wonderings of divine hope and divine fear. Great music is a psychical storm, agitating to fathomless depths the mystery of the past within us. Or we might say that it is a prodigious incantation. There are tones that call up all ghosts of youth and joy and tenderness;—there are tones that evoke all phantom pains of perished passion;—there are tones that revive all dead sensations of majesty and might and glory,—all expired exultations,—all forgotten magnanimities. Well may the influence of music seem inexplicable to the man who idly dreams that his life began less than a hundred years ago! He who has been initiated into the truth knows that to every ripple of melody, to every billow of harmony, there answers within him, out of the Sea of Death and Birth, some eddying immeasurable of ancient pleasure and pain.

Genius itself, the master of music and poetry and all art that enlarges mortal life, genius itself is nothing other than the reverberation of this enormous past on the sounding board of some human intelligence, so finely wrought as to send forth in purity the echoed tones which from a grosser soul come forth deadened and confused by the clashing of the man's individual impulses.

Is it not proper to say, after reading such passages as these, that Mr. Hearn has introduced a new element of psychology into literature? We are indeed living in the past, we who foolishly cry out that the past is dead. In one remarkable study of the emotions awakened by the baying of a gaunt white hound, Mr. Hearn shows how even the very beasts whom we despise as unreasoning and unremembering are filled with an inarticulate sense of this dark backward and abysm of time, whose shadow falls on their sensitive souls with the chill of a vague dread,—dread, I say, for it must begin to be evident that this new psychology is fraught with meanings that may well trouble and awe the student. In the ghostly residuum of these meditations we may perceive a vision dimly foreshadowing itself which mankind for centuries, nay for thousands of years, has striven half unwittingly to keep veiled. I do not know, but it seems to me that the foreboding of this dreaded disclosure may account for many things in the obscure history of the race. By reason of this terror the savage trembled before the magician who seemed to have penetrated the mysteries of nature about him. Among the free-hearted Greeks it showed itself in many ways, even in persecutions and deaths, as later among the Christians. It expressed itself mythologically in the haunting legend of Prometheus, who, by stealing the celestial fire (a symbol of forbidden prying into natural laws), brought on himself torment and chains and on mankind a life of brutal labour.

But more particularly in the Christian world this formless terror has taken to itself a body and a name; it is the heart of the inquisition, which has always followed with excommunications and tortures the unveiling of the recondite powers of nature. It has thus made of itself a potent factor of civilisation—some would say against civilisation, yet he is a very bold man or a very ignorant man who would brush away this long protest of religion against scientific discoveries as the mere vapourings of superstition. If we examine this bitter warfare between science and revelation, we shall find the Church actuated throughout by one ever-present, obscure dread, and when the source of this dread is made clear to us we shall be slow to condemn her conduct. We shall at least have sympathy with her in the struggle, for if she has been a persecutor, she has also been the champion of a losing cause.

At the first, indeed, she was victorious. In the conflict with what remained of Greek philosophy and science the prophets of the new revelation were easily victors. "Ignorance is the mother of devotion," was the motto of Gregory, and ignorance won the day. We love to think of the bright naturalism of antiquity as suffering martyrdom with Hypatia, philosopher and mathematician,—

> Hypatia, fair embodiment
> Of learning's great delight.

And the picture of her naked body torn to pieces by oyster shells in the hands of a bigoted mob is an emblem of the dismemberment of the old nature-worship.

But the Church did not fare so well in the ceaseless conflict with learning, when, at the time of the Renaissance, she laid violent hands on the followers of Copernicus. It may seem to us now a futile crime that Giordano Bruno should have been burned at the stake for teaching the infinity of space and the revolution of the earth about the sun, and that Galileo should have been so harassed for the same cause.[1] But at bottom the question was one of vital importance to religion; and Bruno may have been right in saying that the sentence was pronounced against him with greater fear than he received it. Despite the narrow bigotry displayed, it was a sublime contest for the integrity of the human soul,—for who would believe that the divine drama of redemption was wrought out for a race of puny creatures inhabiting a mere atom in the illimitable expanse of space? Copernicus and his followers disabused us of the old belief that the universe revolved about the home of man. Henceforth the history of the earth was the insignificant story of one of the least of a countless multitude of worlds. The supremacy and lordship of man in creation were no longer conceivable, and in the triumph of science our personal pride received a fatal blow.

Custom and time, however, did in a way heal the wound, and things went well until the forces of science rallied once again under the banner of evolution. Volumes have been written to prove that the new belief only adds to the dignity of man, and Darwin himself professed never to understand the widespread opposition to his theory. But the new terror that aroused theological hostility was as firmly grounded as it was

---

[1] These statements I hold to be true, though the actual charges were in the name of theology.—Note added to this edition.

against the invasion of Copernicus centuries before.
There is no place for Providence or for the divine
prerogatives of the human soul in the law of evolution. We are made a brother to the brute and akin
to unclean things that crawl in the dust. Yet this
quarrel also was adjusted after a fashion, as the quarrels before it had been composed. What though ignorance is necessary to obscure our kinship with living
nature, as Pope Gregory declared; what though our
home is but a point in space; what though we are
inheritors of a past of brutal degradation;—still our
consciousness has no recking of these things, and
dwells serene in its assumption of divine supremacy
and isolation.

But now at the last we are shocked out of our security. We are made conscious of the shame of the hidden past, and the ancient haunting terror is revealed
in all its hideous nakedness. Have you ever by chance
strayed through a museum where the relics of old-
world life are gathered together,—filthy amphibians
armed with impenetrable scales, grotesque serpents
eight fathoms long that churned the seas, huge reptiles
that beat the air with wings of nightmare breadth?
The imagination recoils from picturing what the
world must have been when Nature exhausted herself to fashion these abhorrent monstrosities. We have
burrowed the soil and brought into the light of day
these reluctant hidden records of bestial growths.
Consider for a moment what it would mean if some
new geology should lay bare the covered strata of
memory in our own brain corresponding to these records of the earth; for there is nothing lost, and in
some mysterious way the memories of all that obscure
past are stored up within us. If evolution be true, we
are the inheritors in our soul of the experience and
life of those innumerable generations whose material

forms lie moulded in the bed-rock of earth. Consider the horror of beholding in our own consciousness the remembrance of such fears and frenzies, such cruel passions and wallowing desires as would correspond to those gigantic and abortive relics of antiquity. Would not the world in its shame cry out for some Lethean draught of sleep, though it were as profound as the oblivion of Nirvâna? This is the terror, then, that from the beginning has beset the upholders of religion, and has caused them to attack the revelations of natural science; for what faith or beauty of holiness can abide after such an uncovering? None, unless to obtain spiritual grace the whole memory and personality of a man be blotted out, and the spirit be severed from the experiences of the body by an impassable gulf. And I think the shadow of this dread is typified in the curse which Noah laid upon his son Ham.

The final outcome of this dread in all its nakedness we see foreshadowed in these fantasies and essays of an author, who, as I have attempted to show, has brought together into indissoluble union our Western theory of Darwin and that strange doctrine of metempsychosis which was carried to Japan with Buddhism and is so curiously engrafted on the laughing fancies of the people of the Mikado. To understand the tremendous realism of horror and gloom connected with this doctrine of everlasting birth and death, and rebirth, one must go to the burning valley of the Ganges, where the conception first laid hold of the human mind. But overpowering as this notion of endless unrest may be, a new shadow would seem to be added to it by contact with the scientific hypothesis of evolution which has been developed in the Occident. Evolution is a theory, drawn from the observation of outer phenomena, that man is the last product of myriads of generations of life reaching back into the past; but evolution has forborne to make any appeal to the inner consciousness of the human soul. Metempsychosis, on the contrary, is a half mystical theory evolved out of the consciousness of the soul, which in a dim way seems to carry remembrance of illimitable existence before its present birth. But this symbolic faith of the Orient has never sought confirmation in scientific study of the outer world. Now comes the blending of these two theories, and the result is a laying bare of those hideous realities (pray heaven they prove pseudo-realities in the end) that mankind has instinctively shunned and denounced.

It is because I see in Mr. Hearn's sketches and translations a suggestion of the incalculable influences that may spring from this union of the East and the West, that I have treated them with a seriousness that will seem to many readers greater than they deserve. The skeptical I would refer, in conclusion, to that little essay on the *Nightmare-Touch,* which attempts to account for the shuddering fear of seizure that so often troubles our dreams, and to associate that fear with the widespread superstitious dread of being *touched* by a ghost. The closing words of the essay have the sinister beauty and acrid odour of the flowers in some Rappaccini's garden:

Furthermore, through all the course of evolution, heredity would have been accumulating the experience of such feeling. Under those forms of imaginative pain evolved through reaction of religious beliefs, there would persist some dim survival of savage primitive fears, and again, under this, a dimmer, but incomparably deeper, substratum of ancient animal-terrors. In the dreams of the modern child all these latencies might quicken—one below another—unfathomably—with the coming and the growing of nightmare.

It may be doubted whether the phantasms of any particular

nightmare have a history older than the brain in which they move. But the shock of the touch would seem to indicate *some point of dream-contact with the total race-experience of shadowy seizure.* It may be that profundities of Self—abysses never reached by any ray from the life of sun—are strangely stirred in slumber, and that out of their blackness immediately responds a shuddering of memory, measureless even by millions of years.

CHRISTINA ROSSETTI

PROBABLY the first impression one gets from reading the *Complete Poetical Works* of Christina Rossetti, now collected and edited by her brother, Mr. W. M. Rossetti,[1] is that she wrote altogether too much, and that it was a doubtful service to her memory to preserve so many poems purely private in their nature. The editor, one thinks, might well have shown himself more "reverent of her strange simplicity." For page after page we are in the society of a spirit always refined and exquisite in sentiment, but without any guiding and restraining artistic impulse; she never drew to the shutters of her soul, but lay open to every wandering breath of heaven. In comparison with the works of the more creative poets her song is like the continuous lisping of an æolian harp beside the music elicited by cunning fingers. And then, suddenly, out of this sweet monotony, moved by some stronger, clearer breeze of inspiration, there sounds a strain of wonderful beauty and flawless perfection, unmatched in its own kind in English letters. An anonymous purveyor of anecdotes has recently told how one of these more exquisite songs called forth the enthusiasm of Swinburne. It was just after the publication of *Goblin Market and Other Poems,* and in a little company of friends that erratic poet and critic started to read aloud from the volume. Turning first to the devotional paraphrase which begins with "Passing away, saith the World, passing away," he chanted the lines in his own emphatic manner, then laid the book

---

[1] *The Poetical Works of Christina Georgina Rossetti*. With Memoir and Notes, etc. By William Michael Rossetti. New York: The Macmillan Co., 1904.

down with a vehement gesture. Presently he took it up again, and a second time read the poem through, even more impressively. "By God" he exclaimed at the end, "that's one of the finest things ever written!"

Passing away, saith the World, passing away:
Chances, beauty, and youth, sapped day by day,
Thy life never continueth in one stay.
Is the eye waxen dim, is the dark hair changing to grey,
That hath won neither laurel nor bay?
I shall clothe myself in Spring and bud in May:
Thou, root-stricken, shalt not rebuild thy decay
On my bosom for aye.
Then I answered: Yea.

Passing away, saith my Soul, passing away:
With its burden of fear and hope, of labour and play,
Hearken what the past doth witness and say:
Rust in thy gold, a moth is in thine array,
A canker is in thy bud, thy leaf must decay.
At midnight, at cockcrow, at morning, one certain day
Lo the Bridegroom shall come and shall not delay;
Watch thou and pray.
Then I answered: Yea.

Passing away, saith my God, passing away:
Winter passeth after the long delay:
New grapes on the vine, new figs on the tender spray,
Turtle calleth turtle in Heaven's May.
Though I tarry, wait for Me, trust Me, watch and pray:
Arise, come away, night is past and lo it is day:
My love, My sister, My spouse, thou shalt hear Me say.
Then I answered: Yea.

And Swinburne, somewhat contrary to his wont, was right. Purer inspiration, less troubled by worldly motives, than these verses cannot be found. Nor would it be difficult to discover in their brief compass most of the qualities that lend distinction to Christina Rossetti's work. Even her monotone, which after long continuation becomes monotony, affects one here

as a subtle device heightening the note of subdued
fervour and religious resignation; the repetition of the
rhyming vowel creates the feeling of a secret expectancy cherished through the weariness of a frustrate
life. If there is any excuse for publishing the many
poems that express the mere unlifted, unvaried prayer
of her heart, it is because their monotony may prepare
the mind for the strange artifice of this solemn chant.
But such a preparation demands more patience than
a poet may justly claim from the ordinary reader.
Better would be a volume of selections from her
works, including a number of poems of this character. It would stand, in its own way, supreme
in English literature,—as pure and fine an expression
of the feminine genius as the world has yet heard.

It is, indeed, as the flower of strictly feminine
genius that Christina Rossetti should be read and
judged. She is one of a group of women who
brought this new note into Victorian poetry,—
Louisa Shore, Jean Ingelow, rarely Mrs. Browning,
and, I may add, Mrs. Meynell. She is like them, but
of a higher, finer strain than they (καλαὶ δέ τε
πᾶσαι), and I always think of her as of her brother's
Blessed Damozel, circled with a company of singers,
yet holding herself aloof in chosen loneliness of
passion. She, too, has not quite ceased to yearn
towards earth:

> And still she bowed herself and stooped
>   Out of the circling charm;
> Until her bosom must have made
>   The bar she leaned on warm,
> And the lilies lay as if asleep
>   Along her bended arm.

I have likened the artlessness of much of her
writing to the sweet monotony of an æolian harp;
the comparison returns as expressing also the purely

feminine spirit of her inspiration. There is in her a
passive surrender to the powers of life, a religious
acquiescence, which wavers between a plaintive pathos
and a sublime exultation of faith. The great world,
with its harsh indifference for the weak, passes over
her as a ruinous gale rushes over a sequestered wood-
flower; she bows her head, humbled but not broken,
nor ever forgetful of her gentle mission,—

> And strong in patient weakness till the end.

She bends to the storm, yet no one, not the great
mystics nor the greater poets who cry out upon the
sound and fury of life, is more constantly impressed
by the vanity and fleeting insignificance of the bluster-
ing power, or more persistently looks for consolation
and joy from another source. But there is a difference. Read the masculine poets who have heard this
mystic call of the spirit, and you feel yourself in the
presence of a strong will that has grasped the world,
and, finding it insufficient, deliberately casts it away;
and there is no room for pathetic regret in
their ruthless determination to renounce. But this
womanly poet does not properly renounce at all, she
passively allows the world to glide away from her.
The strength of her genius is endurance:

> She stands there like a beacon through the night,
>   A pale clear beacon where the storm-drift is—
> She stands alone, a wonder deathly-white:
> She stands there patient, nerved with inner might,
>   Indomitable in her feebleness,
> Her face and will athirst against the light.

It is characteristic of her feminine disposition that
the loss of the world should have come to her first
of all in the personal relation of love. And here we
must signalise the chief service of the editor to his
sister. It was generally known in a vague way,

indeed it was easy to surmise as much from her published work, that Christina Rossetti bore with her always the sadness of unfulfilled affection. In the introductory Memoir her brother has now given a sufficiently detailed account of this matter to remove all ambiguity. I am not one to wish that the reserves and secret emotions of an author should be displayed for the mere gratification of the inquisitive; but in this case the revelation would seem to be justified as a needed explanation of poems which she herself was willing to publish. Twice, it appears, she gave her love, and both times drew back in a kind of tremulous awe from the last step. The first affair began in 1848, before she was eighteen, and ran its course in about two years. The man was one James Collinson, an artist of mediocre talent who had connected himself with the Preraphaelite Brotherhood. He was originally a Protestant, but had become a Roman Catholic. Then, as Christina refused to ally herself to one of that faith, he compliantly abandoned Rome for the Church of England. His conscience, however, which seems from all accounts to have been of a flabby consistency, troubled him in the new faith, and he soon reverted to Catholicism. Christina then drew back from him finally.

It is for a somewhat different reason that she refused the second suitor, with whom she became intimately acquainted about 1862, and whom she loved in her own retiring fashion until the day of her death. This was Charles Bagot Cayley, a brother of the famous Cambridge mathematician, himself a scholar and in a small way a poet. Some idea of the man may be obtained from a notice of him written by Mr. W. M. Rossetti for the *Athenæum* after his death. "A more complete specimen than Mr. Charles Cayley," says Mr. Rossetti, "of the abstracted scholar in appearance and manner—the scholar who constantly lives an inward and unmaterial life, faintly perceptive of external facts and appearances—could hardly be conceived. He united great sweetness to great simplicity of character, and was not less polite than unworldly." One might suppose that such a temperament was peculiarly fitted to join with that of the secluded poetess, and so, to judge from her many love poems, it actually was. Of her own heart or of his there seems to have been no doubt in her mind. Even in her most rapturous visions of heaven, like the yearning cry of the Blessed Damozel, the memory of that stilled passion often breaks out:

> How should I rest in Paradise,
> Or sit on steps of heaven alone?
> If Saints and Angels spoke of love,
> Should I not answer from my throne,
> Have pity upon me, ye my friends,
> For I have heard the sound thereof?

She seems even not to have been unfamiliar with the hope of joy, and I would persuade myself that her best-known lyric of gladness, "My heart is like a singing-bird," was inspired by the early dawning of this passion. But the hope and the joy soon passed away and left her only the solemn refrain of acquiescence: "Then I answered: Yea." Her brother can give no sufficient explanation of this refusal on her part to accept the happiness almost within her hand, though he hints at lack of religious sympathy between the two owing to a vein of infidelity in Cayley. Some inner necessity of sorrow and resignation, one almost thinks, drew her back in both cases, some perception that the real treasure of her heart lay not in this world:

> A voice said, "Follow, follow": and I rose
> And followed far into the dreamy night,

Turning my back upon the pleasant light.
It led me where the bluest water flows,
And would not let me drink: where the corn grows
    I dared not pause, but went uncheered by sight
    Or touch: until at length in evil plight
It left me, wearied out with many woes.
Some time I sat as one bereft of sense:
    But soon another voice from very far
        Called, "Follow, follow": and I rose again.
Now on my night has dawned a blessed star:
    Kind steady hands my sinking steps sustain,
And will not leave me till I go from hence.

It might seem that here was a spirit of renunciation akin to that of the more masculine mystics; indeed, a great many of her poems are, unconsciously I presume, almost a paraphrase of that recurring theme of the Imitation: "Nolle consolari ab aliqua creatura," and again: "Amore igitur Creatoris, amorem hominis superavit; et pro humano solatio, divinum beneplacitum magis elegit." She, too, was unwilling to find consolation in any creature, and turned from the love of man to the love of the Creator; yet a little reading of her exquisite hymns will show that this renunciation has more the nature of surrender than of deliberate choice:

> He broke my will from day to day;
> He read my yearnings unexprest,
>   And said them nay.

The world is withheld from her by a power above her will, and always this power stands before her in that peculiarly personal form which it is wont to assume in the feminine mind. Her faith is a mere transference to heaven of a love that terrifies her in its ruthless earthly manifestation; and the passion of her life is henceforth a yearning expectation of the hour when the Bridegroom shall come and she shall answer, Yea. Nor is the earthly source of this love forgotten; it abides with her as a dream which often is not easily distinguished from its celestial transmutation:

> O dream how sweet, too sweet, too bitter sweet,
>   Whose wakening should have been in Paradise,
> Where souls brimful of love abide and meet;
>   Where thirsting longing eyes
>   Watch the slow door
> That opening, letting in, lets out no more.
>
> Yet come to me in dreams, that I may live
>   My very life again though cold in death:
> Come back to me in dreams, that I may give
>   Pulse for pulse, breath for breath:
>   Speak low, lean low,
> As long ago, my love, how long ago.

It is this perfectly passive attitude towards the powers that command her heart and her soul—a passivity which by its completeness assumes the misguiding semblance of a deliberate determination of life—that makes her to me the purest expression in English of the feminine genius. I know that many would think this pre-eminence belongs to Mrs. Browning. They would point out the narrowness of Christina Rossetti's range, and the larger aspects of woman's nature, neglected by her, which inspire some of her rival's best-known poems. To me, on the contrary, it is the very scope attempted by Mrs. Browning that prevents her from holding the place I would give to Christina Rossetti. So much of Mrs. Browning—her political ideas, her passion for reform, her scholarship—simply carries her into the sphere of the masculine poets, where she suffers by an unfair comparison. She would be a better and less irritating writer without these excursions into a field for which she was not entirely fitted. The uncouthness that so often mars her language is partly due to an unreconciled feud between her intellect and her heart. She had neither a woman's wise passivity nor a man's controlling will. Even within the range of strictly feminine powers her genius is not simple and typical. And here I must take refuge in a paradox which is like enough to carry but little conviction. Nevertheless, it is the truth. I mean to say that probably most women will regard Mrs. Browning as the better type of their sex, whereas to men the honour will seem to belong to Miss Rossetti; and that the judgment of a man in this matter is more conclusive than a woman's. This is a paradox, I admit, yet its solution is simple. Women will judge a poetess by her inclusion of the larger human nature, and will resent the limiting of her range to the qualities that we look upon as peculiarly feminine. The passion of Mrs. Browning, her attempt to control her inspiration to the demands of a shaping intellect, her questioning and answering, her larger aims, in a word her effort to create,—all these will be set down to her credit by women who are as appreciative of such qualities as men, and who will not be annoyed by the false tone running through them. Men, on the contrary, are apt, in accepting a woman's work or in creating a female character, to be interested more in the traits and limitations which distinguish her from her masculine complement. They care more for the *idea* of woman, and less for woman as merely a human being. Thus, for example, I should not hesitate to say that in this ideal aspect Thackeray's heroines are more womanly than George Eliot's,—though I am aware of the ridicule to which such an opinion lays me open; and for the same reason I hold that Christina Rossetti is a more complete exemplar of feminine genius, and, as being more perfect in her own sphere, a better poet than Mrs. Browning. That disconcerting sneer of Edward FitzGerald's, which so enraged Robert Browning, would never have occurred to him, I think, in the case of Miss Rossetti.

There is a curious comment on this contrast in the introduction to Christina Rossetti's *Monna Innominata,* a sonnet-sequence in which she tells her own story in the supposed person of an early Italian lady. "Had the great poetess of our own day and nation," she says, "only been unhappy instead of happy, her circumstances would have invited her to bequeath to us, in lieu of the *Portuguese Sonnets,* an inimitable 'donna innominata' drawn not from fancy, but from feeling, and worthy to occupy a niche beside Beatrice and Laura." Now this sonnet-sequence of Miss Rossetti's is far from her best work, and holds a lower rank in every way than that passionate self-revelation of Mrs. Browning's; yet to read these confessions of the two poets together is a good way to get at the division between their spirits. In Miss Rossetti's sonnets all those feminine traits I have dwelt on are present to a marked, almost an exaggerated, degree. They are harmonious within themselves, and filled with a quiet ease; only the higher inspiration is lacking to them in comparison with her *Passing Away,* and other great lyrics. In Mrs. Browning, on the contrary, one cannot but feel a disturbing element. The very tortuousness of her language, the straining to render her emotion in terms of the intellect, introduces a quality which is out of harmony with the ground theme of feminine surrender. More than that, this submission to love, if looked at more closely, is itself in large part such as might proceed from a man as well as from a woman, so that there results an annoying confusion of masculine and feminine passion. Take, for instance, the twenty-second of the

Portuguese Sonnets, one of the most perfect in the series:

> When our two souls stand up erect and strong,
> Face to face, drawing nigher and nigher,
> Until the lengthening wings break into fire
> At either curvèd point,—What bitter wrong
> Can earth do to us, that we should not long
> Be here contented? Think. In mounting higher,
> The angels would press on us, and aspire
> To drop some golden orb of perfect song
> Into our deep, dear silence. Let us stay
> Rather on earth, Beloved,—where the unfit
> Contrarious moods of men recoil away
> And isolate pure spirits, and permit
> A place to stand and love in for a day,
> With darkness and the death-hour rounding it.

That is noble verse, undoubtedly. The point is that it might just as well have been written by a man to a woman as the contrary; it would, for example, fit perfectly well into Dante Gabriel Rossetti's *House of Life.* There is here no passivity of soul; the passion is not that of acquiescence, but of determination to press to the quick of love. Only, perhaps, a certain falsetto in the tone (if the meaning of that word may be so extended) shows that, after all, it was written by a woman, who in adopting the masculine pitch loses something of fineness and exquisiteness.[1]

[1] Mrs. Browning once wrote to a friend: "Please to recollect that when I talk of women I do not speak of them as many men do, . . . according to a separate peculiar and womanly standard, but according to the common standard of human nature." Miss Rossetti wrote to Augusta Webster: "In one sense I feel as if I had gone deep, for my objection seems to myself a fundamental one underlying the whole structure of female claims. Does it not appear as if the Bible was based upon an understood unalterable distinction between men and women, their position, duties, privileges?"—Note added to present edition.

A single phrase of the sonnet, that "deep, dear silence," links it in my mind with one of Christina Rossetti's not found in the *Monna Innominata,* but expressing the same spirit of resignation. It is entitled simply *Rest:*

> O Earth, lie heavily upon her eyes;
>> Seal her sweet eyes weary of watching, Earth;
>> Lie close around her; leave no room for mirth
> With its harsh laughter, nor for sound of sighs.
> She hath no questions, she hath no replies,
>> Hushed in and curtained with a blessed dearth
>> Of all that irked her from the hour of birth;
> *With stillness that is almost Paradise.*
> *Darkness more clear than noonday holdeth her,*
>> *Silence more musical than any song;*
> Even her very heart has ceased to stir:
> Until the morning of Eternity
> Her rest shall not begin nor end, but be;
>> And when she wakes she will not think it long.

Am I misguided in thinking that in this stillness, this silence more musical than any song, the feminine heart speaks with a simplicity and consummate purity such as I quite fail to hear in the *Portuguese Sonnets,* admired as those sonnets are? Nor could one, perhaps, find in all Christina Rossetti's poems a single line that better expresses the character of her genius than these magical words: "With stillness that is almost Paradise." That is the mood which, with the passing away of love, never leaves her; that is her religion; her acquiescent Yea, to the world and the soul and to God. Into that region of rapt stillness it seems almost a sacrilege to penetrate with inquisitive, critical mind; it is like tearing away the veil of modesty. I will not attempt to bring out the beauty of her mood by comparing it with that of the more masculine quietists, who reach out and take the kingdom of Heaven by storm, and whose prayer is, in the words of Tennyson:

> Our wills are ours, we know not how;
> Our wills are ours, to make them Thine.

It will be better to quote one other poem, perhaps her most perfect work artistically, and to pass on:

UP-HILL

> Does the road wind up-hill all the way?
>   Yes, to the very end.
> Will the day's journey take the whole long day?
>   From morn to night, my friend.
>
> But is there for the night a resting-place?
>   A roof for when the slow dark hours begin.
> May not the darkness hide it from my face?
>   You cannot miss that inn.
>
> Shall I meet other wayfarers at night?
>   Those who have gone before.
> Then must I knock, or call when just in sight?
>   They will not keep you standing at that door.
>
> Shall I find comfort, travel-sore and weak?
>   Of labour you shall find the sum.
> Will there be beds for me and all who seek?
>   Yea, beds for all who come.

The culmination of her pathetic weariness is always this cry for rest, a cry for supreme acquiescence in the will of Heaven, troubled by no personal volition, no desire, no emotion, save only love that waits for blessed absorption. Her latter years became what St. Teresa called a long "prayer of quiet"; and her brother's record of her secluded life in the refuge of his home, and later in her own house on Torrington Square, reads like the saintly story of a cloistered nun.

It might be said of her, as of one of the fathers, that she needed not to pray, for her life was an unbroken communion with God. And yet that is not all. It is a sign of her utter womanliness that envy for the common affections of life was never quite crushed in her heart. Now and then through this monotony of resignation there wells up a sob of complaint, a note not easy, indeed, to distinguish from that *amari aliquid* of jealousy, which Thackeray, cynically, as some think, always left at the bottom of his gentlest feminine characters. The fullest expression of this feeling is in one of her longer poems, *The Lowest Room,* which contrasts the life of two sisters, one of whom chooses the ordinary lot of woman with home and husband and children, while the other learns, year after tedious year, the consolation of lonely patience. The spirit of the poem is not entirely pleasant. The resurgence of personal envy is a little disconcerting; and the only comfort to be derived from it is the proof that under different circumstances Christina Rossetti might have given expression to the more ordinary lot of contented womanhood as perfectly as she sings the pathos and hope of the cloistered life. Had that first voice, which led her "where the bluest water flows," suffered her also to quench the thirst of her heart, had not that second voice summoned her to follow, this might have been. But literature, I think, would have lost in her gain. As it is, we must recognise that the vision of fulfilled affection and of quiet home joys still troubled her, in her darker hours, with a feeling of embittered regret. Two or three of the stanzas of *The Lowest Room* even evoke a reminiscence of that scene in Thomson's *City of Dreadful Night,* where the "shrill and lamentable cry" breaks through the silence of the shadowy congregation:

In all eternity I had one chance,
    One few years' term of gracious human life,
The splendours of the intellect's advance,
    The sweetness of the home with babes and wife.

But if occasionally this residue of bitterness in
Christina Rossetti recalls the more acrid genius of
James Thomson, yet a comparison of the two poets
(and such a comparison is not fantastic, however
unexpected it may appear) would set the feminine
character of our subject in a peculiarly vivid light.
Both were profoundly moved by the evanescence of
life, by the deceitfulness of pleasure, while both at
times, Thomson almost continually, were troubled by
the apparent content of those who rested in these joys
of the world. Both looked forward longingly to the
consummation of peace. In his call to *Our Lady of
Oblivion* Thomson might seem to be speaking for
both, only in a more deliberately metaphorical style:

Take me, and lull me into perfect sleep;
    Down, down, far hidden in thy duskiest cave;
While all the clamorous years above me sweep
    Unheard, or, like the voice of seas that rave
On far-off coasts, but murmuring o'er my trance,
A dim vast monotone, that shall enhance
    The restful rapture of the inviolate grave.

But the roads by which the two would reach this
"silence more musical than any song" were utterly
different. With an intellect at once mathematical
and constructive, Thomson built out of his personal
bitterness and despair a universe corresponding to his
own mood, a philosophy of atheistic revolt. Like
Lucretius, "he denied divinely the divine." In that
tremendous conversation on the river-walk he represents one soul as protesting to another that not for all
his misery would he carry the guilt of creating such a

world; whereto the second replies, and it is the poet himself who speaks:

> The world rolls round forever as a mill;
> It grinds out death and life and good and ill;
> It has no purpose, heart or mind or will. . . .
>
> Man might know one thing were his sight less dim;
> That it whirls not to suit his petty whim,
> That it is quite indifferent to him.

There is the voluntary ecstasy of the saints, there is also this stern and self-willed rebellion, and, contrasted with them both, as woman is contrasted with man, there is the acquiescence of Christina Rossetti and of the little group of writers whom she leads in spirit:

> Passing away, saith the World, passing away. . . .
> Then I answered: Yea.

THE GREEK ANTHOLOGY

IT is true, as others have already pointed out, that
Dr. Mackail in reëditing his volume of *Select
Epigrams* [1] has failed to take advantage of the labours
of certain German scholars during the intervening
sixteen years, [2] and has thus missed the proper historical perspective in his Introduction. And this is
regrettable, since such omissions leave the reader with
a feeling of uneasiness even where the purpose of a
book makes the neglected points of slight significance.
As a matter of fact, Dr. Mackail's volume is one of
the few really excellent works of English (or, one
may add, Continental) scholarship dealing with the
classics as a human production. Here in brief compass, and with suitable aids to comprehension, one has
the substance of a whole fascinating literature. Just
to have rendered the epigrams so closely, yet with
such unfailing charm, was a notable achievement.
Still more signal is the accuracy with which he has
selected what was essential in the great bulk of traditional matter, so as to leave in the end the impression
of something closed and complete in itself. Exi-
gencies of modern taste compelled him to omit the
more characteristic epigrams of Strato's *Musa Puerilis,*
as well as the too passionate and luxuriant numbers
of Rufinus, which might seem to form an integral
part of the Anthology; but a little reflection will show

[1] *Select Epigrams from the Greek Anthology,* edited with
revised text, translation, introduction, and notes, by J. W.
Mackail, professor of poetry in the University of Oxford.
New York: Longmans, Green & Co., 1906. The first edition
appeared in 1890.
[2] The most important work has been done by R. Reitzen-
stein, whose *Epigramm und Skolion* (Giessen, 1893) I have
drawn upon in this essay.

63

that these ardours of the flesh are almost as foreign to the heart of that literature as would be the more classical elevation of mind. If he has erred, it has been in the pardonable direction of hospitality. It would be hard to blame the maker of any anthology for including the perfect epitaphs of Simonides, and one can understand the temptation which led him to increase the number of these in his new edition. Yet I am not sure whether the artistic harmony of the book is not a little marred by such lines as these *On the Defenders of Tegea:*

Through these men's valour the smoke of the burning of wide-floored Tegea went not up to heaven, who chose to leave the city glad and free to their children, and themselves to die in the forefront of battle;

whether, if anything were to be added to the section of *Epitaphs,* that town of Arcady could not have furnished a more fitting example in the verses by its poetess, Anyte:

No bridal chamber for thee, nor pride of marriage—but above this marble tomb thy mother has raised a virgin figure, having thy stature and form, O Thersis; so can she speak to thee, even dead.

For it cannot be stated too strongly that the real Anthology is something far removed from the heroic poetry of Greece, something in which the note of the fifth century sounds as a sharp intrusion. Echoes of the older poets there are, of course—Homeric epithets and clear reminiscences of Lesbos and Teos. And, strange as it may seem, Plato on one of his sides comes closer to the spirit of the Anthology than does any other of the great writers, so that the transition from the opening scenes of the *Phædrus* to some of the epigrams in Dr. Mackail's section of *Nature* demands but a slight readjustment of the mind. Thus,

when Socrates and his ardent young friend come to
the plane-tree overhanging the Ilissus, they sit down
to talk, and Socrates says:

> A fair and shady resting-place, full of summer sounds and
> scents. There is the lofty and spreading plane-tree, and the
> agnus castus high and clustering, in the fullest blossom and
> the greatest fragrance; and the stream which flows beneath
> the plane-tree is deliciously cold to the feet. Judging from
> the ornaments and images, this must be a spot sacred to
> Achelous and the Nymphs; moreover, there is a sweet breeze,
> and the grasshoppers chirrup; and the greatest charm of all
> is the grass like a pillow gently sloping to the head.

If anything could save the authenticity of the epigrams attributed to Plato, it would be the similarity
of tone here and in his quatrain of the Anthology
beginning: "Sit down by this high-foliaged voiceful
pine." Or compare the scene of the *Phædrus* with
this longer idyl of some unknown poet:

> Here fling thyself down on the grassy meadow, O traveller,
> and rest thy relaxed limbs from painful weariness; since here
> also, as thou listenest to the cicalas' tune, the stone-pine
> trembling in the wafts of the west wind will lull thee, and the
> shepherd on the mountains piping at noon nigh the spring
> under a copse of leafy plane; so escaping the ardours of the
> autumnal dogstar thou wilt cross the height to-morrow; trust
> this good counsel that Pan gives thee.

With the exception of that tell-tale word *weariness,*
Socrates might have uttered these words on that
memorable day when he and his companion walked
together by the stream of Attica.

The resemblance is but momentary, of course, and
the graceful dallying of Plato is the balancing of himself, so to speak, for a plunge into the depths. His
conception of love and beauty that follows in this
same dialogue is as widely remote from the human
indulgence of the pseudo-Plato of the Epigrams as, to

make another comparison, Eros, the subduer, of the true Anacreon is different from the mischievous boy-Eros of the Anacreontica. These superficial resemblances merely serve to emphasize the contrast between the gravity (the σπουδαιότης one might say, had not the word been vulgarised since Matthew Arnold's time) of the genuine Greek literature, and the lightness, often triviality, of what supplanted it. For this fresh flowering of wit is not so much a continuation of the old schools of poetry, as a new *genre* sprung from the coalescing of two modes of expression very characteristic of Hellenic life, but hitherto kept in a subordinate place.

From an early date it had been the custom to enliven the symposium, or drinking part of the dinner, with the rivalry of song. There were regular rules for the sport. A subject was proposed, perhaps the lines of some well-known poet quoted, and then each man in turn had to display his ingenuity. Another form of verse adapted to the more religious needs of the people was the epigram, or actual inscription, whether it were the brief commemoration on stone of the dead, or some prayer or word of thanksgiving to the gods set up with a gift or statue in a temple. Great poets did not disdain to exercise their art in this way, and a few of the genuine epigrams of Simonides and his rivals from the fifth century are as perfect as any work of human wit can be. Brevity, dignity, and a certain rounded completeness were the essential qualities of such writing; and the elegiac couplet soon proved itself the inevitable medium. At an early date collections of inscriptions were made, and the forger followed in the field. From publishing spurious verses under the name of Simonides or another, it was an easy step to turn the epigram into an avowed form of literary expression.

Meanwhile, this trick of composing imaginary inscriptions made its way to the banquet hall. It introduced a new kind of lure to name some one of the illustrious dead, and then call on each guest to compose a suitable epitaph; for death in those days, as always, had its poignant appeal for a reflective Epicureanism. "Drink, for once dead you never shall return," is a refrain as new as it is old; and love?—

When I am gone, Cleobulus—for what avails? cast among the fire of young loves, I lie a brand in the ashes—I pray thee make the burial-urn drunk with wine ere thou lay it under earth, and write on it, "Love's gift to Death."

From such an example it is easy to see how the epitaph could merge with the erotic elegies which had been sung at the table. The two subjects flowed together naturally; and even where this did not occur, the peculiar form of the inscription imposed itself upon the elegy. From this contact came the epigram as we have it in the Anthology—a brief poem in elegiac metre, written for the most part in the closet, but with something of the point and self-sufficiency of the actual engraving on stone, combined with the zest and flavour of the banquet. It might take the form of an epitaph; it might, as the supposed accompaniment of a temple-gift, sum up some experience of life; it might, as the inscription of a statue, invite to repose by the wayside; again, freeing itself from these restrictions, it might merely philosophise on the vanity of things or play with the passions. It was distinctly a new *genre,* having well-defined rules and suited to the spirit of the disenchanted centuries after the political fall of Greece.

The beginning of the epigram as a recognised literary kind has been traced back to two poets, the founders of the Doric, or Peloponnesian, and the Ionian schools. Of the first of these, Anyte of Tegea, little is known. She was, apparently, a contemporary of Theocritus (the fact is important, considering the character of their inspiration), and about 300 B.C. published a book of epigrams which were much imitated in later ages. Meleager opens his garland of poets with the "many lilies of Anyte," and to another epigrammatist she was the "female Homer." There had existed for some time in Arcadia a school of bucolic poetry, largely, it may be supposed, of a popular sort ("soli cantare periti Arcades," says Virgil), in which the rustic gods, Pan and Hermes, and the nymphs played an important rôle. So far as is known, Anyte was the first to express this spirit of homely pastoral life in elegiac couplets for social usage. Only a handful of her poems have been preserved, but they are sufficient to show the exquisite transparency and delicate finish of her work. Some of them are on the humblest themes, such as this supposed inscription for a shepherd's crook, or pipe, or ivy cup:

> To bristly Pan and the Nymphs of the farm-yard, Theodotus, the shepherd, lays this gift under the crag, because they stayed him when very weary under the parching summer, holding out to him honey-sweet water in their hands.

Others are mottoes, actual or imaginary, for fountains and statues:

> I, Hermes, stand here by the windy orchard in the crossways nigh the grey sea-shore, giving rest on the way to wearied men; and the fountain wells forth cold stainless water;

or this, perhaps the most radiant of all the pictures in the Anthology:

> This is the Cyprian's ground, since it was her pleasure ever to look from land on the shining sea, that she may give fulfilment of their voyage to sailors; and around the deep trembles, gazing on her bright image.

(Was ever the beauty of the sea-born Aphrodite more magically conveyed?) These three epigrams Dr. Mackail gives in his selection. One wishes he could have made room for Anyte's pretty lines on the dead locust and cicada, or for one at least of her pathetic epitaphs on young girls dying in their first loveliness —so much might have been granted to the poetess for her position.

The gods of the fields and the sea in these epigrams prevail over those of the cup. For the wanton muse of *Wein und Weib* we must turn to the Ionian Asclepiades of Samos, whose singing, according to Theocritus, was as high above his own as the locust surpasses a frog in sweetness. Others before him, we may believe, had reduced the love-elegy to the brevity and turn of an epigram, but he first, it appears, was conscious of the full powers of this banquet Muse. His themes were those that are so familiar to us in the erotic poets of Rome who copied the Alexandrine school. There is the lover at the closed door of his beloved, the *paraklausithyron,* which, in the imitation of Tibullus, contains one of the most romantic lines of Latin poetry: "En ego cum tenebris totâ vagor anxius urbe"; there is the appeal to the night-lamp, whose repetition continues down to the elegy of André Chénier:

> Et toi, lampe nocturne, astre cher à l'amour.
> Sur le marbre posée, ô toi! qui, jusqu'au jour,
> De ta prison de verre éclairais nos tendresses,
> C'est toi qui fus témoin de ses douces promesses.

The gist of it all is in two perfect quatrains of Asclepiades himself:

Sweet is snow in summer for one athirst to drink, and sweet for sailors after winter to see the Crown of spring; but most sweet when one cloak hides two lovers, and the praise of Love is told by both;

and,

Let us drink an unmixed draught of wine; dawn is an handbreath; are we waiting to see the bedtime lamp once again? Let us drink merrily; after no long time yet, O luckless one, we shall sleep through the long night. [The words of Catullus: "Nox est perpetua una dormienda."]

From these two singers of Arcadia and of Samos and, of course, from other contributory sources proceeded the inspiration of the great body of epigrammatic literature which continues well down into the Byzantine Empire. Some of the writers were poets of fame, such as Callimachus and Philetas; some hid their obscurity under the forged names of Plato or another; others were grammarians, or philosophers, or men of the world—courtiers, perhaps, who took this method of summing up, half-seriously and half-jocosely, their lessons of disillusion. Many came from Asia, and were in no true sense of the word Greeks at all. In the first century before Christ, one of these writers, Meleager, who was born at Gadara (Ramoth-Gilead) of Northern Palestine, made a selected anthology of this literature so far as it already existed, adding a number of elegiac quotations from the older classical poets. Successive editors altered and enlarged the collection, until the Anthology, as we now have it with its thousands of epigrams, was formed in the late Middle Ages by scholars of Constantinople. The last shadowy name included is that of Cometas, called Chartularius, or Keeper of the Records, of the tenth century. None of his six epigrams possesses literary value, except the one beautiful pastoral couplet, in which, as Dr. Mackail says, "we seem to hear the very voice of ancient poetry bidding the world a lingering and reluctant farewell":

Dear Pan, abide here, drawing the pipe over thy lips, for thou wilt find Echo on these sunny greens.

Naturally the work of so many men during so many centuries comprises a variety of styles and ways of looking at life; yet the final impression, especially when so sympathetic a critic as Dr. Mackail has eliminated the superfluous, is singularly uniform. Beneath the ever-changing play of sentiment run two qualities, two ideas, that in their combination give the Anthology a peculiar flavour of its own—the sense of transitoriness and a certain indescribable kindliness or friendliness of spirit. There was in all these poets an unusual age-consciousness; the glory of Greece was behind them, and they wrote in a sort of crepuscle, awaiting the night. The past is always an insistent reality with men of imagination; its influence was incalculably strong in the most fervid periods of Greek creation; but in the declining pagan world it was present in a way almost incomprehensible to us. To one sailing in the Ægean Sea how many monuments of former greatness spoke on every coast—famous cities reduced to villages, proud States fallen into subserviency, memories of stirring battles. The temples were spoiled of their treasures, yet enough remained to show the nobility of an art now forever lost; the old plays were still produced on the stage, but they served only to mock the sterility of the present. These poets of the late Hellenic world were still in a way members of the ancient civilisation, they spoke the same language and worshipped, or named, the same gods; but what a gulf of impassable experience lay between them and their ancestors. It is not strange that the shadow of transi-

toriness enveloped all their thoughts. That feeling
indeed is universal to mankind and is never long
absent from poetry, but in the Anthology it has a
tone and pathos all its own. Homer felt it when he
put those great words into the mouth of one of his
heroes: "Ah, friend, if once escaped this battle we
were evermore to be ageless and deathless"; but then
follows the Homeric conclusion: "Now let us go forward, whether we shall give glory to another man, or
he to us." The feeling is latent in the epigrams of
Simonides on those who perished in the Persian war,
as in the two lines over the Spartan tomb at Thermo-
pylæ: "O passer-by, tell the Lacedæmonians that we
lie here obeying their orders"—but with it how much
else! The difference in the epigrams is all in the
moral. The will has been loosened and the foreboding of brevity leads not to greater resolve, but to
indulgence; and in the same way, in place of the boast
of immortality through duty performed—the "praise
that grows not old"—comes petulant indifference:

Straight is the descent to Hades, whether thou wert to go
from Athens or takest thy journey from Meroë; let it not vex
thee to have died so far away from home; from all lands the
wind that blows to Hades is but one.

That moral, which we have already seen in the
verse of Asclepiades, is sharpened in these lines of
Palladas, most disillusioned of all the epigrammatists:

All human must pay the debt [the Roman "morti debemur"],
nor is there any mortal who knows whether he shall be alive
to-morrow; learning this clearly, O man, make thee merry,
keeping the wine-god close by thee for oblivion of death, and
take thy pleasure with the Paphian while thou drawest thy
ephemeral life; but all else give to Fortune's control.

You may say that the conclusion, too, is common
to a large body of poetry outside of the Anthology.

So doubtless it is. You will find it, to go back to the
seventh century B.C., in the elegies of old Mimnermus;
it is the philosophy of Horace and, through him, of
men of the world generally. Yet if one reads these
poets and the epigrammatists side by side, one catches
a difference of note and emphasis, a something that
sets them in two separate classes. Perhaps it is the
suspicion of weariness in the diction of the epigrams
that renders them so distinct from Mimnermus, while
they lack that final adjustment of language which
makes of Horace's most questionable Epicureanism
almost a lesson in austerity. Only one who reads in
the original will quite understand such a distinction;
but there are other differences that inhere in the substance of the epigrams. One feels that to these later
moralists their very scepticism is something old and
long-ago experienced, and that so it involuntarily
passes into badinage, even when the intention is mocking and bitter. It is as if some guest at the banquet
table, when the fancy flagged, forgot himself so far
as to speak solemnly of the end of things, and another
were to rebuke him lightly:

All life is a stage and a game: either learn to play it, laying
by seriousness, or bear its pains.

(Is it accident that the very word "seriousness,"
σπουδή, is that which is naturally applied to the
classic literature of Greece, while game, παίγνιον,
was the technical term for these later expressions of
wit?) And then another after another of the guests
takes up the challenge:

Often I sang this, and even out of the grave will I cry it:
"Drink, before you put on this raiment of dust."

(How strangely the words prelude the thought of
FitzGerald's Omar; and so also the following:)

Give me the sweet cup wrought of the earth from which I was born, and under which I shall lie dead.

(But the Persian did not jest so amusingly as this wanton Greek:)

Must I not die? What matters it to me whether I depart to Hades gouty or fleet of foot? for many will carry me; let me become lame, for hardly on their account need I ever cease from revelling.

Day by day we are born as night retires, no more possessing aught of our former life, estranged from our course of yesterday, and beginning to-day the life that remains. Do not then call thyself, old man, abundant in years; for thou hast no share in what is gone.

(And the end of this fitting sequel to the old impressionism of Protagoras?—)

All is laughter, and all is dust, and all is nothing; for out of unreason is all that is.

(And yet not quite the end. Not laughter, but silence, awaited that world finally, as it awaited the banqueters:)

Thou talkest much, O man, and thou art laid in earth after a little; keep silence, and while thou yet livest, meditate on death.

For the spirit of resignation lies beneath all this laughter and incentive to joy. One is struck by the repetition here and there of the great motto of ancient Greece: *Think as a mortal;* and by the change in its meaning. The words are no longer, as they were in Pindar and Sophocles, and even in Demosthenes, a warning against the insolent pride, or *hybris,* that would storm the heavens, but a plea for ease: "Haste not, toil not; as thou canst, give, share, consume; think as a mortal." This humanity is merely an aspect of that accepted comfort of littleness which forms the compensation for the too clear perception of mutability. One feels this most strongly in the section of the Anthology headed *Religion,* for the very gods have shrunk in their dimensions, like the desires and ambitions of their worshippers. "Small to see am I, Priapus, who inhabit this spit of shore," begins one of the epigrams, and another, which Dr. Mackail entitles *Fortuna Parvulorum,* is still more pathetic in its humility:

Even me the little god of small things if thou call upon in due season thou shalt find; but ask not for great things; since whatsoever a god of the commons can give to a labouring man of this, I, Tycho, have control.

To me there is something deeply touching in this *little god of small things,* this turning from Olympus, so far away, to one of the *di minorum gentium,* and in this *ask not for great things.* And when destiny has done its worst, and the family is broken by calamity, the prayer of the survivor is still for the least consolation:

I wept the doom of my Theionoë, but borne up by hopes of her child I wailed in lighter grief; and now a jealous fate has bereft me of the child also; alas, babe, I am cozened of even thee, all that was left me. Persephone, hearken thus much at a father's lamentation; lay the babe on the bosom of its dead mother.

No English words can quite suggest the littleness and tenderness of that phrase in the last clause, *thes brephos.*

This is the cry that runs all through the Anthology; but the one thing passionately desired and prayed for, the one seemingly small boon, was beyond the giving of the great or the little gods. No wish is re-

peated so continually by these poets as the longing
for remembrance. All things are fleeting; nothing is
our own, not even this spark of life which is owed to
Death; but Oh, grant that after our going some inter-
position of human memory come between us and
utter obliteration! That longing is common, a com-
mon-place, if you will. The heroes of the Iliad felt
it in the underworld; and the pains of the lost in
Dante's Inferno are pointed by the dread of being
forgotten among the living. But the desire in this
fading pagan world is something different from these.
The braving of forgetfulness or the prayer for remembrance lies naturally at the heart of these poems,
which spring from the epitaph and the inscription. It
is not only that the dead cry to the living to be kept
from oblivion, but the living themselves beg a place
in the thought of strangers and passers-by: "Sit beneath the poplars here, wayfarer, when thou art
weary," runs the writing on a wayside tomb, "and
drawing nigh drink of our spring; and even far away
remember the fountain that Simus sets by the side of
Gillus his dead child."

In the end that comfort of little things and this
craving to be remembered are but signs of the coming
together of the sense of transitoriness and the spirit of
kindliness which mark the character of this whole
literature. Kindliness—yes, if any one word can
convey the innermost quality of these epigrams, it is
that. They are kindly in many subtle ways. It is
not only that friendship is directly celebrated, as in
the epigram of Callimachus so finely translated by
William Cory:

They told me, Heraclitus, they told me you were dead.
They brought me bitter news to hear and bitter tears to shed.
I wept as I remembered how often you and I
Had tired the sun with talking and sent him down the sky.

And now that thou art lying, my dear old Carian guest,
A handful of grey ashes, long, long ago at rest,
Still are thy pleasant voices, thy nightingales, awake;
For Death, he taketh all away, but them he cannot take—

it is not only this, but a feeling of friendliness with
the world at large pervades almost the whole Anthology. It explains the "charm of nature" (the
words actually occur in one of the epigrams) felt by
these writers in the protected valleys and wayside
fountains, as it exaggerates their disease at the salt,
estranging sea. It extends to the gods, who are very
near to help, as a human friend would be. Even
Pan, for a moment, is willing to leave his mountain
revels and come as the good physician:

This for thee, O pipe-player, minstrel, gracious god, holy
lord of the Naiads who pour their urns, Hyginus made as a
gift, whom thou, O protector, didst draw nigh and make
whole of his hard sickness; for among all my children thou
didst stand by me visibly, not in a dream of night, but about
the mid-circle of the day.

Among men the feeling of kinship is fostered both
by prosperity and misfortune. Does the sailor accom-
plish a safe voyage? Forthwith he records his thankfulness at some shrine of Poseidon, with a prayer for
general mercy: "Holy Spirit of the great Shaker of
Earth, be thou gracious to others also." Does he
perish by the way? Some stranger or comrade buries
him with an inscription which speaks at once his
desire of remembrance and his good-will towards
others: "Well be with you, O mariners, both at sea
and on land; but know that you pass by the grave of
a shipwrecked man." Scarcely any theme in the
Anthology is commoner than this plea of the shipwrecked or exiled traveller to the passer-by; it seems
to have been peculiarly welcome to the poet who
would enhance the comfort of the banquet by pictures

of distant toil and danger, and from this use it passed into the general repertory of the epigrammatists.

But I will not follow this note of kindliness through all its obvious and hidden manifestations. There is nothing entirely like it, I believe, to be found anywhere else, and more than any other quality it lends to the epigrams a beautiful and unique distinction. Its gentleness does not belong to the great pagan world, and might remind one rather of the new spirit of Christianity. So, when one reads the call to rest of Hermes to those "whose knees are tired with heavy toil," the temptation is strong to compare it with the words of Jesus, "Come unto me, all ye that labour and are heavy laden." But the similarity, it need not be said, is fallacious. There is no new-born faith underlying the mercy and friendliness of the Anthology, no mutual love binding together the children of a heavenly Father; nor, on the other hand, is there any touch of the mysticism, such as that in the *Rubáiyát,* which makes the whole world kin—and kind. The spirit is here rather the offspring of utter surrender to doubt, the brotherhood of those who have cut off the long hope and must find their comfort together and in the way of small things.

It should not, therefore, be supposed that the final impression of these epigrams is one of morose despondency. Rather, we rise from their perusal chastened in mood, but strangely heartened in endurance. The book is above all companionable, and has an insinuation of appeal that no other work quite possesses. Occasionally the word of bitterness escapes, or a phrase of less jocular satire; but these are quickly repressed as errors of taste against the occasion. Something of this is due to the origin of the epigram, but something also to the recollection of the proud civilisation of which these men were still the disinherited heirs. "Though thy life be fixed in one seat," writes an epigrammatist of the age of Augustus, "and thou sailest not the sea nor treadest the roads on dry land, yet by all means go to Attica that thou mayest see those great nights of the worship of Demeter; whereby thou shalt possess thy soul without care among the living, and lighter when thou must go to the place that awaiteth all." These poets, whose names for the most part mean so little to us, had partaken in memory of the *great nights* of Hellas, and, if the vision did not incite them to strenuous emulation, it at least made their soul lighter for the descending path—Θυμὸν ἐλαφρότερον. Even, at times, this serenity in the acceptance of fortune can imitate the nobler faith:

Me Chelidon, priestess of Zeus, an aged woman well-skilled to make libation on the altars of the immortals, happy in my children, free from grief, the tomb holds; for with no shadow in their eyes the gods saw my piety.

GEORGE GISSING

WHEN Gissing died at St. Jean de Luz, in 1903, broken down at the age of forty-six by years of toil and privation, he had begun to acquire in the world at large something of the reputation he had long possessed among a select circle. But it is to be feared that the irony of his later works, such as the posthumous volume of tales recently published,[1] may create a wrong impression of his genius among these newly won friends. For Gissing, more than most writers, underwent a change with the progress of time. His work in fact may be divided into three fairly distinct periods. Passing over the immature *Workers in the Dawn* (1880), we may mark off the first group of novels as beginning with *The Unclassed* (1884), and ending with *Born in Exile* (1892); between these two are *Isabel Clarendon, Demos, Thyrza, A Life's Morning, The Nether World, The Emancipation,* and *New Grub Street*. The second group, starting with *Denzil Quarrier* (1892), may be limited by *The Crown of Life* (1899), although the transition here to his final manner is more gradual than the earlier change. This second division embraces what are perhaps the best known of Gissing's novels—the *Year of Jubilee* and *The Whirlpool*—and here again there is danger of misunderstanding. These are

[1] *The House of Cobwebs and Other Stories*. By George Gissing. To which is prefixed *The Work of George Gissing*, an introductory study, by Thomas Seccombe. New York: E. P. Dutton & Co., 1906. Several of the most important of Gissing's earlier novels are not to be found in New York, either in bookshop or library; and, indeed, he cannot be said ever to have been properly published at all. By getting together a complete and decently printed edition of his works some enterprising publisher might benefit himself and the community.

books of undeniable power, comparable in some ways to Hardy's *Jude, the Obscure,* but pointed in the wrong direction, and not truly characteristic. One feels a troubling and uncertain note in all this intermediate work, done while the author, having passed beyond his first intense preoccupation with the warfare for existence, was still far from the fair serenity of his close. The greater Gissing is not to be found here, but in those tales which embody his own experiences in the cruel and primeval nether world of London—tales which together make what might be called the Epic of Poverty.

Poverty, the gaunt greedy struggle for bread, the naked keen reality of hunger that goads the world onward—how this grim power reigns in all Gissing's early novels, crushing the uninured dreamers and soiling the strong. It is the guiding power of *The Unclassed.* It casts its spume of disease and misery on the path of *Thyrza,*[1] that fragile Madonna of the slums, yet finds even here its pathetic voice of song:

A street organ began to play in front of a public-house close by. Grail drew near; there were children forming a dance, and he stood to watch them.

Do you know that music of the obscure ways, to which children dance? Not if you have only heard it ground to your ears' affliction beneath your windows in the square. To hear it aright you must stand in the darkness of such a by-street as this, and for the moment be at one with those who dwell around, in the blear-eyed houses, in the dim burrows of poverty, in the unmapped haunts of the semi-human. Then you will know the significance of that vulgar clanging

[1] It is a curious comment on the manufacture of books that *Thyrza,* which was published in 1887, has never been reprinted. I had to wait many months before I could pick up a secondhand copy, but my reward was great. It is a book of rare, poignant beauty. To the beginner in Gissing I should recommend this novel first.

of melody; a pathos of which you did not dream will touch you, and therein the secret of hidden London will be half revealed. The life of men who toil without hope, yet with the hunger of an unshaped desire; of women in whom the sweetness of their sex is perishing under labour and misery; the laugh, the song of the girl who strives to enjoy her year or two of youthful vigour, knowing the darkness of the years to come; the careless defiance of the youth who feels his blood and revolts against the lot which would tame it; all that is purely human in these darkened multitudes speaks to you as you listen.

A superb piece of imaginative prose, indeed, as Mr. Seccombe calls it, and significant of the music which Gissing himself wrested from the pathos of the London streets. The note rises in *Life's Morning* to tragic shrillness, making of it one of the most passionate stories in English of love striving against degraded associations. Again, in *New Grub Street,* it sinks to the forlorn plea of genius baffled by unremunerative toil and starved into despair. Those who care to know the full measure of agony through which the writer himself struggled, may find it portrayed here in the lives of the two unrecognized novelists. Only Gissing could tell how much of his own experience was poured into those "dwellers in the valley of the shadow of books"; how much of his fierce aspiration to paint the world as it really exists was expressed by the garret-haunting, hunger-driven Biffen; how often his breast, like Reardon's, swelled with envy of the prosperous, commercialised man of letters. "He knew what poverty means. The chilling of brain and heart, the unnerving of the hands, the slow gathering about one of fear and shame and impotent wrath; the dread feeling of helplessness, of the world's base indifference. Poverty! Poverty!" I am not sure that it is good to know these things even by hearsay, but for those who are strong in pity and fortified by resolve they have been written out once for all, ruthlessly, without mitigation.

More general, gathering up all the suffering and foulness and crime of want, embracing too the clear-eyed charity of strength that asks for no reward, is that terrible story of *The Nether World*. Here, most of all, Gissing is conscious of his grave theme. We have seen the pathetic joy of the children dancing to the simple music of the street organ; it may be well to compare with it a fragment of the Chapter *Io Saturnalia!* which describes a holiday of revelling at the Crystal Palace:

It is a great review of the People! On the whole how respectable they are, how sober, how deadly dull! See how worn-out the poor girls are becoming, how they gape, what listless eyes most of them have! The stoop in the shoulders so universal among them merely means over-toil in the work-room. Not one in a thousand shows the elements of taste in dress; vulgarity and worse glares in all but every costume. Observe the middle-aged women; it would be small surprise that their good-looks had vanished, but whence comes it that they are animal, repulsive, absolutely vicious in ugliness? Mark the men in their turn; four in every six have visages so deformed by ill-health that they excite disgust. . . .

A great review of the People. Since man came into being, did the world ever exhibit a sadder spectacle? . . .

On the terraces dancing has commenced; the players of violins, concertinas, and penny whistles do a brisk trade among the groups eager for a rough-and-tumble valse; so do the pickpockets. Vigorous and varied is the jollity that occupies the external galleries, filling now in expectation of the fire-works; indescribable the mingled tumult that roars heaven-ward. Girls linked by the half-dozen arm in arm leap along with shrieks like grotesque mænads; a rougher horse-play finds favour among the youths, occasionally leading to fisticuffs. Thick voices bellow in fragmentary chorus; from every side comes the yell, the cat-call, the ear-rending whistle; and as the bass, the never-ceasing accompaniment, sounds the myriad-footed tramp, tramp, along the wooden flooring. A fight, a scene of bestial drunkenness, a tender whispering between two lovers, proceed concurrently in a space of five square yards. Above them glimmers the dawn of star-light.

It is not strange that the witness and recorder of these things should have interposed the question: Did the world ever exhibit a sadder spectacle? Only one is surprised that to his memory, steeped as it was in classic history, the words of Pericles did not involuntarily arise: "Poverty is no bar. . . And our laws have provided for the mind an ever-recurring respite from toil by the appointment of public recreations and religious ceremonies throughout the year, performed with peculiar elegance, and by their daily delight driving away sordid care." How far we of the modern world have progressed from the philosophy of joy! We are not now at Athens, at the graves of those who died in battle for their native land, but in the harsher warfare of industrial London. And as a chorus above all the sounds of defeat and consternation rises the clamorous cry of "Mad Jack," like the prophesying of some Jeremiah of the slums:

"Don't laugh! Don't any of you laugh; for as sure as I live it was an angel stood in the room and spoke to me. There was a light such as none of you ever saw, and the angel stood in the midst of it. And he said to me: 'Listen, while I reveal to you the truth, that you may know where you are and what you are; and this is done for a great purpose.' And I fell down on my knees, but never a word could I have spoken. Then the angel said: 'You are passing through a state of punishment. You, and all the poor among whom you live; all those who are in suffering of body and darkness of mind were once rich people, with every blessing the world can bestow, with every opportunity of happiness in yourselves and of making others happy. Because you made an ill use of your wealth, because you were selfish and hard-headed and oppressive, and sinful in every kind of indulgence, therefore after death you received the reward of wickedness. This life you are now leading is that of the damned; this place to which you are confined is hell! There is no escape for you. From poor you shall become poorer; the older you grow the lower shall you sink in want and misery; at the end there is waiting for you, one and all, a death in abandonment and despair. This is hell—hell—hell!'" . . . Above the noise of the crowd rose a shrill, wild voice, chanting:

"All ye works of the Lord, bless ye the Lord; praise him and magnify him forever!"

It has seemed worth while to quote thus at length, because Gissing is one of the few English novelists whose trained and supple language makes itself felt in such extracts, and because his first lesson of life is shown in them so clearly. "Put money in thy purse," might seem to be the upshot of it all; "and again, put money in thy purse; for as the world is ordered, to lack current coin is to lack the privileges of humanity, and indigence is the death of the soul." It is a dubious philosophy, one which the writer's own heroic culture rebuked, and yet, what is it more than the modern rendering of Homer's δούλιον ἦμαρ—

> Jove fix'd it certain, that what ever day
> Makes man a slave, takes half his worth away?

But, waiving the point in ethics, there still remains the question of art: what profit is it, one asks, to paint in all its hideous colours this death of the soul, to forget the glad things of the world for its shadows, to deny Agamemnon and Achilles and choose Thersites for the hero of our tale? "Art, nowadays," Gissing replies boldly, "must be the mouthpiece of misery, for misery is the keynote of modern life." It is not entirely easy to reconcile such a theory with the judgment of Gissing's own riper years; for art, he came in the end to think, is "an expression, satisfying and abiding, of the zest of life." Certainly, it is this contrast between the misery and the zest of life, derived from the same materials, that makes the comparison between Dickens and Gissing so inevitable. Gissing felt it, and his *Critical Study* of Dickens is, as a result, a curiously ambiguous piece of writing; his intention is to praise, but he can never quite overcome his surprise and annoyance at the radical difference of Dickens' attitude towards poverty. And the same feeling crops out again and again in the earlier novels. Inextinguishable laughter were fittest, he says, musing on his own terrible nether world and thinking of the elder writer's gaiety, but the heart grows heavy. And elsewhere he blames the shallowness of Dickens, and calls on fiction to "dig deeper" into the substratum of life. The question thus posed exhibits one of the irreducible differences of artistic method. In my essay on Dickens I tried to show how he tended to portray his characters from the outside, without identifying himself with their real emotions. Here, on the contrary, we have a man whose ambition it was to strip off to the last rag those veils of melodrama and humour, which prevented Dickens from becoming a realist, and which, it may be added, he himself by native right possessed in large measure. He would not be waylaid and turned from his purpose by the picturesque grimaces of poverty, but would lay bare the sullen ugliness at its core; he would, in a word, write from the inside. The result of this difference of methods is too obvious to need attention here, but one rather curious detail I may point out. It has been observed that the people of Dickens indulge in a superhuman amount of drinking; wine and gin are elements of Gargantuan exhilaration. In Gissing's world, drunkenness is only a blind desire of escape from pain; and liquor, the rich man's friend, is the enemy always lying in wait to drag the needy to destruction.

Only by taking account of the sordid realities of Gissing's life can we understand the mingled attraction and repulsion exercised on him by the large joyousness and exulting pathos of Dickens in dealing with the nether world. Nothing, to be sure, in his career, was more depressing than the slavery of Dickens under "Murdstone and Grinby," but whereas Dickens rose almost at a bound to enormous prosperity, the life of Gissing was one of the tragedies of literature. Hints of that story are scattered through all his novels,—a youth cast from the country into the streets of London to earn a living as best he could, a period of storm and stress including a frantic attempt on fortune in the United States, years of starving at literary work, followed by years of broken health. He came out at the last into the light, but almost his friends might have pointed to him, as the people of Verona pointed to Dante, saying: "There goes one who has been in hell." Naturally a tone of bitterness, something of his own lack of vitality, if you will, crept into his work. He always wavered between the pathetic fallacy on the one hand of ascribing to the poor the distress of his own over-wrought sensitiveness and on the other hand hatred of a Destiny that inures its victims to their lot. "The man who laughs," he said, reproachfully, "takes the side of a cruel omnipotence." The words are suggestive. Not "cruel," but *unimplicated,* let us say, and accept the phrase as a mark of the greater art. It is because Dickens stands with the powers above and is not finally implicated in his theme, that he could turn it into an expression, satisfying and abiding, of the zest of life. And it is, on the other hand, just because Gissing cannot entirely rise above the "misery" he describes, that all his marvellous understanding of the human heart and his chastened style do not quite save his art in the end.

And yet, if his theory and practice must from the highest standard be condemned, it would be unfair to overlook the reservations that should go with even so strict a judgment. For though the zest of life be lacking in these novels, there is something in them that strangely resembles it. "How" he exclaims in one of his latest works—"how, in the name of sense and mercy, is mankind content to live on in such a world as this?" The question obtrudes itself upon the reader again and again, and slowly he becomes aware of the vast, dumb, tumultuous *will to live* that is struggling into consciousness through all these horrors and madnesses. The very magnitude of the obstacles, the unreason of endurance, is witness to the unconquerable energy of this blind will. What, after all, has been the substance of great literature, from the days when Sarpedon heartened Glaucus on the plains of Troy to the most modern singer of some soul divided against itself, but warfare, and again renewed war? And as one reads on in these novels of Gissing's, their plot begins to unfold itself as another and darker picture of the same battle. It is almost as if we were listening to the confused lamentation of a city besieged and captured by night, wherein the enemy is no invading army of Greece, but the more treacherous powers of hunger, and vice, and poverty:

Diverso interea miscentur mœnia luctu.

And there is another element which helps to relieve the depressing nature of Gissing's theme. Literature of the slums is not lacking in these latter days. Young men and women whose standards of life have been unsettled turn thitherward for some basis of reality and some reflected seriousness of emotion. In each of our large cities you will find a college settlement where a band of prurient souls sit at type-writing machines glutting a morbid ambition on the sorrows of the poor. Now, Gissing did not learn the meaning of poverty in any such fashion; there is, at all events, nothing of the dilettante in his work. He wrote, not from callow sympathy or patronising observation, but from his own deep experience; and, writing thus, he put into his account of the nether world the one thing commonly wanting to these pictures—the profound sense of morality. Through all these graphic, sometimes appalling, scenes one knows that the writer is still primarily concerned with the inner effects of poverty, and his problem is the ancient, insoluble antimony of the one and the many, the individual and the mass. Taken as a whole, the society he describes is the victim of circumstances. His philosophy is summed up in a gloomy determinism: "indigence is the death of the soul," and "misery is vice." And even where the instincts remain unsoiled, some hideous chance steps in to stunt the soul's growth:

It strengthened his growing hatred of London, a huge battle-field calling itself the home of civilisation and of peace. Battlefield on which the wounds were of soul, no less than of body. In these gaunt streets along which he passed at night, how many a sad heart suffered, by the dim glimmer that showed at upper windows, a hopeless solitude amid the innumerable throng! Human cattle, the herd that feed and breed, with them it was well; but the few born to a desire forever unattainable, the gentle spirits who from their prisoning circumstance looked up and afar, how the heart ached to think of them! Some girl, of delicate instinct, of purpose sweet and pure, wasting her unloved life in toil and want and indignity; some man, whose youth and courage strove against a mean environment, whose eyes grew haggard in the vain search for a companion promised in his dreams; they lived, these two, parted perchance only by the wall of neighbour houses, yet all huge London was between them, and their hands would never touch.

That is the philosophy of circumstance that rules over Gissing's world as a whole. But even here, as in that chorus of "Mad Jack" already quoted, the contradictory and less comprehensible law of morality makes itself heard at times; and when he touches the individual the sure insight of the artist asserts itself, and he orders his people not as automatons, but as characters moved by their own volition, and, though it may be in unaccountable ways, reaping as they have sown. The knot of fate and free-will is not always disentangled, there is no conventional apportioning of rewards and penalties such as Dickens indulged in at the end of his novels; but always, through all the workings of heredity and environment, he leaves the reader conscious of that last inviolable mystery of man's nature, the sense of personal responsibility. Had not he, George Gissing, been caught in the cruel network of circumstances, and had he not preserved intact the feeling that he was personally accountable? It is thus he attains by another road to something of the liberal enlargement of Dickens: the greatest art, it need scarcely be said, would combine both the free outlook of the older writer and the moral insight of the younger.

Those are the principles—the instinctive will to live and the law of moral responsibility—that saved the writer's tragic stage from insupportable dreariness; they furnished, also, the clue that in the end led the writer himself out of the labyrinth of doubtful questionings. But for a while it seemed as if they were to be lost, for it is not so much any lowering of literary skill as a change in these essential points that marks the transition from his first to his second period. Just what caused the alteration I cannot say. Possibly the long years of defeat began to shake his moral equilibrium; possibly the growing influence upon him of French and Russian fiction was to blame. Certainly the pride of English, what raises it, despite its deficiencies of form and ideas, to be the first of modern literatures, is the deep-rooted convention of moral responsibility. It is that which through all its romantic divagations joins English so closely to Greek; which would have made Socrates more at home with Dr. Johnson than with any other man of our world, and would have rendered Æschylus the most appreciative listener of Shakespeare—if such associations are not too fanciful. No one can sprinkle himself with the scented water of Anatole France or dabble in the turbid Slavic pool without hazarding the loss of that traditional sense; and there are signs that Gissing's mind for a time was bewildered by ill-digested reading.

The new spirit may be defined by a comparison of such novels as *The Nether World* from his first period and *The Whirlpool* from his second (the very names are significant), or as *Life's Morning* and *The Crown of Life*. In place of human nature battling with grim necessity, we now have a society of people contending against endless insinuations of tedium and vanity; in place of the will to live we meet a sex-consciousness, always strong in Gissing, but now grown to morbid intensity. And with this change comes a certain relaxing of moral fibre. The unconscious theme is no longer self-responsibility, or character in the strict meaning of the term, but a thousand vexatious questions of the day—anti-vivisection, anti-racing, anti-gambling, anti-hunting, anti-war, imperialism, the education of children, the emancipation of women, and, above all and more persistent than all, the thrice-dreary theories of marriage. The beginning of these may be traced back to *The Emancipated* (1890), written after he had been enabled by momentary success to visit Italy, the dream of his life. In that release from pressure his mind seems to have been left free to dwell on these problems resulting from the break-up of traditional obligations. But the core of the book is sound. "An educated woman, this," says Mallard, drawing the lesson of the heroine's life; "one who has learnt a good deal about herself and the world. She is 'emancipated,' in the true sense of the hackneyed word; that is to say, she is not only freed from those bonds that numb the faculties of mind and heart, but is able to control the native passions that would make a slave of her." And, indeed, it would be wrong to infer that the moral of his books is ever at bottom any other than this. In the full swing of his middle period he could close a novel with the ejaculation of his hero: "Now I understand the necessity for social law!" But one is aware, nevertheless, that conventions have grown irksome to him, and that his interest turns too much to the thronging, ambiguous problems of emancipation.

If the reading of modern Continental literature may be suspected of unsettling his inherited canons, his home-coming in the end was surely due in large measure to his devoted study of the classics. Strange as it may seem when one considers the topics he treated, there is scarcely a writer of the last century more thoroughly versed in Greek and Latin than Gissing, and that no doubt is the reason why the names of antiquity come to mind involuntarily when one tries to characterise his work. Through his struggle with poverty he commonly kept free of the pawnshop a few chosen books, Homer, Tibullus,

Horace, Gibbon, Shakespeare. Writing the memoirs of his life, at ease, and with a library at his command, he recalls his difficulties:

I see that alley hidden on the west side of Tottenham Court Road, where, after living in a back bedroom on the top floor, I had to exchange for the front cellar; there was a difference, if I remember rightly, of sixpence a week, and sixpence, in those days, was a very great consideration—why, it meant a couple of meals. (I once *found* sixpence in the street, and had an exultation which is vivid in me at this moment.) The front cellar was stone-floored; its furniture was a table, a chair, a washstand, and a bed; the window, which of course had never been cleaned since it was put in, received light through a flat grating in the alley above. Here I lived; here *I wrote.* Yes, "literary work" was done at that filthy deal table, on which, by the bye, lay my Homer, my Shakespeare, and the few other books I then possessed. At night, as I lay in bed, I used to hear the tramp, tramp of a *posse* of policemen who passed along the alley on their way to relieve guard; their heavy feet sometimes sounded on the grating above my window.

What a picture of the new Grub Street. One thinks of the deal table in Thoreau's hut at Walden on which a Homer lay, and one thinks, too, of Dickens in his comfortable study with his shelves of sham books. For most of his reading Gissing had to depend on public convenience:

How many days have I spent at the British Museum, reading as disinterestedly as if I had been without a care! It astounds me to remember that, having breakfasted on dry bread, and carrying in my pocket another piece of bread to serve for dinner, I settled myself at a desk in the great Reading-Room with books before me which by no possibility could be a source of immediate profit. At such a time, I worked through German tomes on Ancient Philosophy. At such a time, I read Appuleius and Lucian, Petronius and the Greek Anthology, Diogenes Laertius and—heaven knows what! My hunger was forgotten; the garret to which I must return to pass the night never perturbed my thoughts.

And Homer and Ancient Philosophy won the day. There was little occasion in the earlier novels to display this learning, yet here and there the author's longing for Rome and Italy breaks through, as in the passions of the apothecary's apprentice in *The Unclassed.* Then came the intellectual whirlpool. The release from that dizziness of brain shows itself first in a growing lightness of touch and aloofness from passion of all sorts. The novels and tales of the third period are chiefly distinguished by a tone of gentle and amused irony, in place of the satire of the middle group, and it is significant that the theme of *Will Warburton,* his last novel, is the same as that chosen by Biffen in the *New Grub Street* for the pronunciamento of rebellious realism—the life of a retail grocer. Only in the actual novel there is no realism at all as Biffen would have understood it, but the witty and mock-heroic story of a man of good birth who begins by selling groceries over the counter under an assumed name and ends by accepting his lot in all *gaieté de cœur*—so far had Gissing travelled from being at loggerheads with destiny. *Warburton* was written in Southern France when a moderate success had freed him from the hardest slavery of the pen, and when ill health had driven him from England. Here, too, he absolved himself from an ancient vow by composing, with all the artistry he possessed, a story of classical life—his *Veranilda*—and here he wrote that restrained and every way beautiful piece of self-revelation, *The Private Papers of Henry Ryecroft.*

There is nothing in the language quite like this volume of half-veiled autobiography. In the imagined quiet of a home in Devon, the part of England Gissing so passionately loved, he writes out his memories of toil and the reflections that come to him as the sum of his experiences. Here is no bitterness, no complaining; all the lesser problems that harassed him have solved themselves by simple vanishing; he returns to his early convictions, with the added ripeness of long meditation. He had used the life of the poor for his greatest creative work, and the question of the growing democracy is the only one that still abides with him in his repose. Everywhere he sees the decay of that natural instinct on which the morality of the world at large must always depend, and in its place an ever-widening spirit of interrogation which only unsettles and sets adrift. "I am no friend of the people," he exclaims, and the words come with a strange insistence from such a man. "As a force, by which the tenor of the time is conditioned, they inspire me with distrust, with fear. . . Every instinct of my being is anti-democratic, and I dread to think of what our England may become when Demos rules irresistibly. . . Nothing is more rooted in my mind than the vast distinction between the individual and the class." This doubt alone remained to annoy him, but with it he connected the other great movement of the day: "I hate and fear 'science' because of my conviction that, for long to come, if not for ever, it will be the remorseless enemy of mankind." To science he attributed the spread of that half-education which increases the powers of action while lessening the inhibitions of self-knowledge. It was from his close reading of the classics, I think, though he himself does not say so, came his notion of the one only salvation through the aristocratic idea, the essential idea of Greek literature:

The task before us is no light one. Can we, whilst losing the class, retain the idea it embodied? Can we English, ever so subject to the material, liberate ourselves from that old association, yet guard its meaning in the sphere of spiritual life? Can we, with eyes which have ceased to look reverently on worn-out symbols, learn to select from among the grey-coated multitude, and place in reverence even higher, him who "holds his patent of nobility straight from Almighty God"? Upon that depends the future of England.

The business of the novelist is with the realities of life, and not with hypotheses; yet one cannot leave Gissing without wishing that he had found strength and occasion to express in fiction these fundamental ideas of his maturity.

THOREAU'S JOURNAL

TWENTY volumes of Thoreau [1] make a pretty large showing for a man who had only a scant handful of ideas and, in particular, the thought of labouring through the fourteen volumes of the Journal, now for the first time published complete, may well appal the sturdiest reader. It cannot be denied that the bulk of these note-books have no interest except for the confirmed nature-worshipper, and, in part, I suspect, little even for him. Most of the memorable reflections and descriptive passages had already been transferred to the regular books and lectures; what remains is made up largely of trivial daily memoranda, often written down in the field, and then copied out at home for more convenient reference. But there are recompenses for the wary reader who has learnt the art of skipping; scattered at random through the pages he will discover fragments of magic description, shrewd bookish criticisms, glimpses of serene vision, the old familiar thoughts struck out in fresh language. Thus a certain largeness of outlook seems to be added to Thoreau's known feeling towards the humanitarians when we come across these words, written in 1842: "The sudden revolutions of these times and this generation have acquired a very exaggerated importance. They do not interest me much, for they are not in harmony with the longer periods of nature. The present, in any aspect in which it can be presented to the smallest audience, is always mean. God does not sympathise with the popular movements." And for description,

[1] *The Writings of Henry David Thoreau.* Walden Edition. Twenty volumes. Boston: Houghton Mifflin Co., 1906.

where will one turn for a more superbly Rabelaisian picture than this wassail scene of the woods:

And then the frogs, bullfrogs; they are the more sturdy spirits of ancient wine-bibbers and wassailers, still unrepentant, trying to sing a catch in their Stygian lakes. They would fain keep up the hilarious good fellowhsip and all the rules of their old round tables, but they have waxed hoarse and solemnly grave and serious their voices, mocking at mirth, and their wine has lost its flavour and is only liquor to distend their paunches; and never comes sweet intoxication to drown the memory of the past, but mere saturation and waterlogged dulness and distension. Still the most aldermanic, with his chin upon a pad, which answers for a napkin to his drooling chaps, under the eastern shore quaffs a deep draught of the once scorned water, and passes round the cup with the ejaculation *tr-r-r-r-r-oonk, tr-r-r-r-oonk, tr-r-r-r-oonk!* and straightway comes over the water from some distant cove the selfsame password, where the next in seniority and girth has gulped down to his mark; and when the strain has made the circuit of the shores, then ejaculates the master of ceremonies with satisfaction *tr-r-r-r-oonk!* and each in turn repeats the sound, down to the least distended, leakiest, flabbiest paunched, that there be no mistake; and the bowl goes round again, until the sun dispels the morning mist, and only the patriarch is not under the pond, but vainly bellowing *troonk* from time to time, pausing for a reply.

The scene was written while he was living on the banks of Walden, and afterwards copied, with a few unimportant changes, into his book. It is but one of a hundred examples showing how the essence of his diaries was pressed into that and his other works. It is an example, too, of the peculiarly happy inspiration that other poets besides Aristophanes have won from the sullen batrachian song. Thoreau returns to the same theme more than once. "There is the faintest possible mist over the pond holes," he writes six years later, "where the frogs are eructating, like the

falling of huge drops, the bursting of mephitic air-
bubbles rising from the bottom, a sort of blubbering
—such conversations as I *have* heard between men, a
belching conversation, expressing a sympathy of
stomachs and abdomens." The image of these
grotesque revellers haunts him, and has haunted
others, as if it were an obscene parody of the fabled
singing of the poets at the well of Hippocrene.

Et veterem in limo ranæ cecinere querellam—

the very word *querella* is sacred to the denizens of
Helicon.

Such isolated examples of wit and poetry we
stumble upon in the Journal, and take our reward
for pages of triviality. And, from another point of
view, by overlooking the question of immediate interest altogether, we may find a more solid profit
in these volumes. As a record written in large of
the life of which *Walden* expresses, so to speak, the
quintessential meaning, these private and garrulous
memoranda have a real value of corroboration. They
show the utter sincerity of the man; in their large
placid current we perceive the stillness of his nature,
and are further assured that his dramatic escape to
the woods was not a bit of posing, nor a calculated
exploit for "copy," but an experience quite harmonious with the tenor of his days. And this knowledge
is precious; for the distinction of Thoreau lies just
herein, that what other men were preaching, he lived.
In transcendental thought he was, if compared with
Emerson, thin and derivative, the shadow of a shadow; in power of description he excelled several of his
contemporaries only through greater precision of details—a questionable superiority; and he possessed not
a spark of Hawthorne's creative imagination. But
he had this one great advantage, that his words come

to us freighted with the conviction of experience. "There are nowadays professors of philosophy," he observes in defence of his Walden experiment, "but not philosophers. . . To be a philosopher is not merely to have subtle thoughts, nor even to found a school, but so to love wisdom as to live according to its dictates, a life of simplicity, independence, magnanimity, and trust. It is to solve some of the problems of life, not only theoretically, but practically."

For the student of the larger intellectual currents Thoreau offers a second advantage, which is made more conspicuous by the publication of the Journal. From his comparative poverty in original ideas and from the independence of his character we can see, better than in the case of Emerson or any other of the group, wherein the transcendentalism of Concord was an echo of the German school, and wherein it differed. No one has yet traced the exact channels by which the formulæ of romanticism migrated from Germany to New England, although it is known in a general way that the direct influence through translations in the American magazines and elsewhere was considerable. Moreover, most of the Concord scholars dabbled at one time or another in the German language. The strongest impulse, no doubt, came indirectly through Coleridge, Carlyle, and the other British Teutonisers, but once here it found a far more suitable soil than in England. Our people had just thrown off the strait-jacket of Puritan religion and were revelling in the always perilous consciousness of spiritual liberty. The situation in Germany at the time of the Romantic School was not altogether dissimilar. Lessing and the Titans of the *Sturm und Drang* had wrestled against the deadening tyranny of the Lutheran Church; they had discarded the for-

malism of French literary law, and with it pretty
much all sense of form whatever; they had, with the
help of Kant, broken down the official philosophy of
Leibniz and Wolff. On all sides resounded the
watchword of *Freiheit,* liberty—except in politics
where neither then nor now have the Germans, as a
people, reached any notion of individual liberty sub-
mitting to the discipline of self-imposed restraint,
without need of the strong hand of Government or
the bonds of socialistic regulation. So far as the aim
of the Storm and Stress can be described, it might
be called a rejection of the eighteenth-century principle of selection for that of university. The whole
of human nature should be embraced and developed,
and this development was to come through a setting loose of every impulse and passion of the breast
to run its full unhampered course. What that
career meant, the *Geniesucht,* the *Unendlichkeitsstreben,* the *ringende Titanenthum,* the *Emancipation
des Fleisches,* the *Seelenpriapismus*—may all be seen,
by whoever cares to read it, in such a work as Wil-
helm Heinse's *Ardinghello.* Out of this blind ferment of freedom came at last the spirit of a new and
more compact school, the cultus of the *Ich,* the romantic *I,* as formulated by Fichte, the Schlegels, Schleiermacher, and Schelling, and as practised by Tieck,
Novalis, and a small band of contemporaries.

German romanticism is often defined as a return
to mediæval ideals, and for a later period in the movement such a definition is fairly exact. And even in
the beginning, although such a master of the school
as Friedrich Schlegel preferred to call himself a Grecian, his interest in that land was mainly a sentimental nostalgia for some imagined home of
happiness in the past; whereas his kinship, vague at
first, and entirely unconscious, was rather with the

mediæval Church. Through all the years after the
Renaissance, the memory and habit of the Middle
Ages had run beneath civilisation like one of those
underground rivers, sending up its fountains here
and there, even in the disciplined years of the eighteenth century. And when at last the depths had
been broken up by the wild license of the Storm and
Stress, it reappeared at the surface, its old name forgotten and its current charged with many deposits
from its hidden pilgrimage. We are accustomed to
find the relationship between romanticism and the
Middle Ages chiefly in a common feeling of infinity,
in their *Unendlichkeitsstreben,* and this in a way is
true. But we must restrict the meaning of the word
closely. In the narrower acceptation, the Middle
Ages had less of the feeling than the centuries either
preceding or immediately following. There is more
of the infinite in Virgil's *loca nocte tacentia late* than
in Dante's vision of petrified eternity; there is more
of the infinite in Shakespeare than in all the mediæval
poets put together, more in Plato and Spinoza than in
all the intervening schoolmen. What the Middle
Ages really strove for was to combine the ideas of
personality and limitlessness; the human personality
was to be protracted unchanged through unending
periods of time, the deity was to be at once human in
nature and unbounded in power—a conception of the
world which could have arisen only when the feeling for the infinite as something positive in itself and
different from a mere quantitative limitlessness had
been lost. Necessarily such an effort to contain the
infinite within the vessel of the finite brought its
penalty—to some minds an unwholesome exaltation
and relaxing revery, to others, as to St. Augustine,
the anguish of mortal self-contradiction. This was
the burden of the *Confessions:* "How shall I call upon

my God, God and my Lord? For I call him into myself when I call upon him (*quoniam utique in meipsum eum vocabo, cum invocabo eum*). And what room is there in me, where my God may enter in, where God may enter in, God who made heaven and earth?" And this combat between the thought of a limited and an unlimited personality passed through the Middle Ages, disappeared for a time, and then returned to be absorbed and modified in the writings of the romantic school.

Only so can we understand the *Ich* which Fichte erected into that tortured system of philosophy, whose chief value is that it gave a backbone of rigid articulate logic to a body of otherwise flabby sentiment. The spirit of revolt is the beginning of the movement. Not only in art does the will or whim (*Willkür*) of the poet suffer no law over itself, as Friedrich Schlegel avers, but, more mystically, this liberty is necessary for the expansion of the I into the desired state of limitless self-satisfaction. Here is no true sense of infinity, nor yet much talk of God and the soul—these had withered away under the *Aufklärung*—but an attempt to account for the world by some juggling with the personal I and the not-I. In place of the mediæval contrast of a divine Person and a world created out of nothing by his fiat, Fichte substitutes a formula begotten of logic on lyricism. Bring together the logical law of identity (A = A, and not–A is not = A) and the craving of unrestrained egotism, and you get the romantic equivalent for mediævalism: God is replaced by the human personality, lifted as the transcendental I above the ordinary I of commerce and society, and the world is the not-I called into being as a field for its exercise and enjoyment.

Here is room for endless revery, for unbounded

exaltations, for insatiable self-tormentings. This I has in practice no concern with the reason, which is the faculty of defining and delimiting; it has no kinship with the will, which means self-restraint; it is the child of the feelings, which are essentially rebellious to limitations. So in religion there was a general repudiation of Luther and the Reformation, as the source of "a dry rational emptiness which leaves the heart to pine away." To Schleiermacher, the great preacher of the band, religion was neither reason nor morality, neither thought nor action, but an emotional contemplation of the universe by which the soul is thrown into a state of indistinguishing revery, and the I and the not-I swoon together into one. The religious feeling, he thought, should "accompany all the doings of a man as if it were a holy music; he should do all *with* religion, nothing *through* religion." And the aim of poetry was the same. It, too, should avoid all that is sharply defined, and should blend all the *genres* into a kind of ineffable music, appealing neither to the thought nor the will. "Poems which sound melodiously and are full of beautiful words, but without any sense or connection"—that, according to Novalis, is the consummation of art.

From the same source spring those peculiar accompaniments of the movement—the so-called romantic irony, the aloofness from society, the sacred idleness. Given this outreaching egotism, together with this contempt of limitations, and inevitably there arises an inner state which is the modern counterpart of St. Augustine's wrestling with the personality of God. Fichte might argue calmly about the world as not-I, but to the inflamed imagination of a Schlegel this division of nature was a disruption of self from self; it became the everlasting, uncompromising discord between the ideal and the real. The only escape from this anguish of dissatisfaction was to ascend into those towers of indifference from which the transcendental I might survey the life of mankind, even its own activities, with unconcerned irony. In art this is the quality by which the artist "appears to smile down upon his own masterpiece from the heights of his spirit"; in life it is the feeling which leads a man to move about in society as in an alien world whose concerns are to him nothing—a mere piece of "transcendental buffoonery." Hence the contempt of business and of the Philistines follows as a kind of seal set upon the romantic soul which is conscious of itself. It cultivates a divine idleness; the summons to loaf and invite one's soul came from over the sea long before the scandalous outbreak of Walt Whitman.

And the theatre of this vagrant aloofness was nature. To the wanderer in the field and on the mountain side, with his spirit bathed in the shifting glamour of colour and form, with no troublesome call upon his reason or his will, this visible music of nature might seem now to be spun like a dream from the depths of his own being and now to be absorbed in silence back into himself. Schelling had modified this mystic revery into a vast metaphysical parallelism. "The system of nature," he said, "is at the same time the system of our spirit"; and again, "Nature is the visible spirit, the spirit is invisible nature." And Novalis, to whom thought was "only a dream of the feelings," held that by a kind of transcendental "magic," to use his famous word, a man might juggle or shuffle spirit and nature together. In his *Lehrlinge zu Sais* romanticism received perhaps its purest expression. "At the well of freedom," says one in that book, "we sit and spy; it is the great magic-mirror wherein serene and clear the whole creation reveals itself; herein bathe the tender spirits and images of all natures, and here we behold all chambers laid open. . . And when we wander from this view into nature herself, all is to us well known, and without error we recognise every form. . . It is all a great scroll, to which we have the key." Whereto another prophet in the book replies in the language of Fichte, telling how a man is lord of the world, and how his I, brooding mightily over the abyss of mutable forms, reduces them slowly to the eternal order of its own law of being, *die Feste seines Ichs.*

Now, of the systematic romanticism of Fichte and Schelling there is little or nothing in the writings of our New England transcendentalists. Many similar ideas may be found in Emerson, but divested of their logical coherence; and as for Thoreau, "metaphysics was his aversion," says William Ellery Channing; "speculation on the special faculties of the mind, or whether the Not-Me comes out of the I or the All out of the infinite Nothing, he could not entertain." Nevertheless, in its more superficial aspects, almost the whole body of romanticism may be found reflected, explicitly or implicitly, in his Journal and formal works. He, too, had sat spying in the well of freedom, and the whole art and practice of his life were a pæan of liberty: "For a man to act himself he must be perfectly free." And this was his mission, to act himself, and to point to others the path of freedom. Calvinism had been discarded in Concord as Lutheranism had been by the romanticists at Berlin. There is little concern in Thoreau with God and the soul, but in its place a sense of individualism, of sublime egotism, reaching out to embrace the world in ecstatic communion. His religion was on the surface not dissimilar to Schleiermacher's mystical contemplation of the universe; "vast films of thought floated through my brain," he says on one occasion; and the true harvest of his daily life he pronounced "a little star-dust caught, a segment of the rainbow which I have clutched." This revery, or contemplation that spurned at limitations, passed easily into the romantic ideal of music—and that in a very literal, sometimes ludicrous, sense. A music-box was for him a means of consolation for the loss of his brother; a hand-organ was an instrument of the gods; and the humming wires on a cold day—his telegraph harp he called it—seemed to him to convey to his soul some secret harmony of the universe. "The wire is my redeemer, it always brings a special message to me from the Highest." This is the thought that occurs over and over again in the Journal. More particularly in one passage dated September 3, 1851, by Channing, and jumbled together from separate entries in the Journal, he expatiates on this modern harmony of the spheres:

As I went under the new telegraph wire, I heard it vibrating like a harp high overhead; it was as the sound of a far-off glorious life; a supernal life which came down to us and vibrated the lattice-work of this life of ours—an Æolian harp. It reminded me, I say, with a certain pathetic moderation, of what finer and deeper stirrings I was susceptible, which grandly set all argument and dispute aside, a triumphant though transient exhibition of the truth.

There is something bordering on the grotesque in this rhapsodical homage to a droning telegraph wire, but it might be paralleled by many a like enthusiasm of the German brotherhood. Nor was Thoreau unaware of this intrusion of humour into his ecstasy. Like Friedrich Schlegel, he indulges in the

romantic irony of smiling down upon himself and
walking through life as a *Doppelgänger*:

> I only know myself as a human entity; the scene, so to
> speak, of thoughts and affections; and am sensible of a certain
> doubleness by which I can stand remote from myself as from
> another. However intense my experience, I am conscious of
> the presence and criticism of a part of me, which, as it were,
> is not a part of me, but spectator, sharing no experience,
> but taking note of it; and that is no more I than it is you.
> When the play, it may be the tragedy, of life is over, the
> spectator goes his way. It is a kind of fiction, a work of the
> imagination only, so far as he was concerned.

How far this irony carried him in his hatred of
Philistinism and his aloofness from society, no reader
of his books need be told. The life of the business
man he compared to the tortures of an ascetic, and
the California gold-fever threw him into a rage of
disgust:—"going to California. It is only three
thousand miles nearer to hell. . . The gold of California is a touchstone which has betrayed the rot-
tenness, the baseness, of mankind." Nor did the
daily commerce of man with man come off much
better. He was not one who would "feebly fabulate
and paddle in the social slush." "I live," he says,
"in the angle of a leaden wall, into whose alloy was
poured a little bell-metal. Sometimes in the repose
of my mid-day there reaches my ears a confused
tintinnabulum from without. It is the noise of my
contemporaries."—Could an image be more sublimely
impertinent?

Often a passage in the Journal bears the stamp
of German romanticism so plainly upon it, that we
stop to trace it back in memory to Tieck or Novalis
or one of the followers of the earlier Storm and
Stress. Such are his scattered observations on child-

hood, on sleep, and the all-enveloping sacrament of silence; such is his constant thought of a new mythology which is to be the end of our study and our art—"all the phenomena of nature need to be seen from the point of view of wonder and awe. . . Men are probably nearer to the essential truth in their superstitions than in their science." These, I take it, are not cases of translation or plagiarism, but rather of that larger and vaguer migration of thought from one land to another. They show how thoroughly the transcendental philosophy of New England had absorbed the language and ideas of German romanticism, if not its inmost spirit.

And so, one may follow these movements step by step—through irony, aloofness, and sacred idleness, through their flowing in musical revery and communion with nature—and show how they develop on parallel lines always alike on the surface, yet always with some underlying difference more easily felt than named. And this difference is felt more strongly, is indeed then only to be understood, when we go back to that free individualism which is the root of all this varied growth. "Contemplation," says Schleiermacher in his second *Discourse,* "is and always remains something single, separate, the immediate perception, nothing more; to connect and bring together into a whole is not the business of the senses, but of abstract thought. So with religion: it is hers to abide by the immediate experience of the being and activity of the universe, by the individual perceptions and feelings; each of these is a work existing in itself without connection with others or dependence upon them. Of derivation and association religion knows nothing; of all things that may touch her, these are the most contrary to her nature. . . It is due just to this absolute individuality that the sphere of contemplation is so infinite." Here certainly—and we are at the very heart of German romanticism—is a doctrine which the wise men of Concord would have been the first to repudiate. "Infinity" to Schleiermacher was only another word for endless variety of particulars, amid which the soul of man, itself a momentary atom in the stream, moves in a state of perpetual wonder. The ideal of Emerson was that self-reliance by which the individual, shaking itself free from the mere conformity of manners and tradition, might rise to the community of the higher nature figured by him as the over-soul: "In all conversations between two persons, tacit reference is made as to a third party, to a common nature. That third party or common nature is not social, it is impersonal; it is God." And Thoreau represented friendship by the symbol of two lines divergent on the earth and converging together in the stars. I cannot find the equivalent of this in Schleiermacher. I find rather that, like the rest of the romantics, when he sought for the basis of a man's nature, he turned to pure emotionalism, the very power and faculty by which we are bound within the limits of our individuality. We have seen that to Schleiermacher "the essence of religion is neither thought nor action, but contemplation and feeling." Let us see in what colours he pictures this passive surrender of the soul to the impression of the world. Thus he continues in the *Reden:*

Only do not suppose—this is indeed one of the most dangerous errors—that religious contemplation and feeling at their beginning in the first activity of the soul (*des Gemüths*) are severed in any such way as they necessarily are in our discourse. Contemplation without feeling is nothing, and possesses neither the right source nor the right power; feeling without contemplation is likewise nothing: both are something only when and because they are originally one and unseparated. That first mysterious moment, which comes to us with every sensuous perception before contemplation and feeling have drawn apart, . . . fleeting is it and transparent, like the first exhalation wherewith the dew breathes upon the awakened flowers, demure and tender like the kiss of a virgin, holy and fruitful like the embrace of marriage. Nay, not *like* this, rather it *is* all this. Quickly and magically an appearance, an event, unfolds itself to a likeness of the universe. And so, as the beloved and ever-desired form takes shape, my soul flees to her, and I embrace her not as a shadow, but as the holy essence itself. I lie in the bosom of the infinite world; I am in that moment its soul, for I feel all its powers and its infinite life as my own. . . At the least jar the holy union is blown away, and then first Contemplation stands before me as a separate form; I gaze upon her, and she mirrors herself in the open soul as the image of the departing loved-one in the open eye of the youth. And now first feeling rises up from within him, and spreads like the blush of shame and desire over his cheek. This moment is the highest flowering of religion.

Could anything than this be more essentially at variance with the product of Concord? The nearest approach to it in substance is the hedonism of Pater as expressed in the *Conclusion* to his Renaissance studies. For what in the end is this religion of Schleiermacher's but that culture of the fleeting artistic impression which Pater taught: "Every moment some form grows perfect in hand and face; some tone on the hills or the sea is choicer than the rest; some mood of passion or insight or intellectual excitement is irresistibly real and attractive for us—for that moment only"? It is but the modern decking out of the ancient philosophical heresy of Heracleitus that all things move and flit away, which the English writer places as the motto of his essay. I would not be unappreciative of the great German divine, but I

cannot sever his unctuous preaching of emotionalism
from the actual emotions which ruled among the
coterie to whom his discourses were addressed.
When he turns from his image of the bridal of the
soul and the universe to the fable of Paradise, and
declares that only through the coming of Eve was
Adam enabled to lift his thoughts heavenward, when
he makes of love the only source of religion, he is, of
course, speaking within the acknowledged rights of
the preacher. Yet I cannot forget the morbid life of
Rousseau, from whom all this *Gefühlsphilosophie* is
ultimately derived; I remember more particularly
Heinse's yearning for some wilderness apart from the
world where he might, like a Platonic sage, pass his
life in saintly studies—with Laïs at his side.[1] I am
afraid of a religion which accords so easily with this
blending of Plato and Laïs, and which serves so well
a literature whose principle as announced by Tieck
was briefly this: "The decency of our common prosaic
life is unallowed in art; in these happy, pure regions
it is unseemly; it is among us even the document of
our commonness and immorality." I am Puritanic
enough to dislike and to distrust these confusions;
and it is because I do not find them in Thoreau that
I can turn to him after reading much in the *roman-
tische Schule* with a sense of relief, as one passes from
a sick-chamber to the breath of the fields. Concord
is remote and provincial in comparison with the
Berlin and Jena of those days; it lacks the universality and culture of those centres; above all, it lacks
the imposing presence of a Goethe and a Schiller,

[1] This conjunction of Plato and Laïs is taken up from the
decadence of Greece itself. The Pseudo-Platonic epigram is
well known: "I Laïs who laughed exultant over Greece, I who
held that swarm of young lovers in my porches, lay my mirror
before the Paphian; since such as I am I will not see myself,
and such as I was I cannot."

who, however loosely, were still connected with the romantic brotherhood; but it possessed one great off-set—character.

"Life shall be the living breath of nature," might have been the motto of Thoreau as it was of a great German. He, too, went out to find the God of history in nature, inasmuch as man is but a part of the whole, a brother to the worm—but the ways of their search led them far asunder. We have seen how on the surface the mystical revery of Novalis's *Lehrlinge zu Sais* is akin to the ideals of Thoreau: yet follow the two to the end. We shall see one of the scholars of Sais journeying through a tropical clime to the shrine of Isis; we shall see him in an ecstasy before that veiled goddess of nature; "then lifted he the light, gleaming veil, and—Rosenblüthchen sank into his arms." It is only Heinse's Plato and Laïs, or Schleiermacher's Adam and Eve if you will, under other names. There is a taint of sickliness in all this. It corresponds too well to the "heavenly weariness" of Novalis himself, as he might be found at the grave of his Sophie, vowing himself to death for lofty en-sample of love's eternal faithfulness, and in a short while after discovering his religion incarnate in an-other woman.

Now there was no Laïs in Thoreau's life, no sen-timental identification of a dead Sophie with a living Julie, and above all, no rapturous embrace of both together in the person of the goddess of nature. It may even be granted that the absence of primitive human emotion is so pronounced in his diaries as to render them thin and bloodless. To lay bare the sources of this difference between Thoreau and Novalis it would be necessary to analyse a score of influences silently at work beneath the surface of his culture—the inheritance of Puritian religion, denied

indeed, but still making any real return to mediævalism impossible; the British notion of practical individualism expressed in the philosophy of Adam
Smith; the lesson of Wordsworth's austerity in the
devotion to nature; the spirit of fine expectancy derived from the poets of the seventeenth century, who
were Thoreau's chief mental nourishment; the incalculable force of Emerson's personality. It comes at
the last chiefly to this: the freedom of the romantic
school was to the end that the whole emotional nature
might develop; in Thoreau it was for the practice
of a higher self-restraint. The romantics sought for
the common bond of human nature in the *Gemüth,*
Thoreau believed it lay in character. In the *Gemüth*
(the word is untranslatable; heart, with the con-
notation of sentiment, mood, revery, is the nearest
equivalent) Schleiermacher found the organ of religion to the absolute exclusion of the reason and the
will; there Novalis looked for the inspiration of all
art; communion with nature was desirable only because in her, too, might be discovered "all the varia-
tions of an endless *Gemüth*"; and to this organ of the
individual person was reduced in reality the high-
sounding *Ich* of Fichte. *Gemüth*—character, *Gefühl*
—conduct; in that contrast lay the divergence between German and New England transcendentalism.
"What are three-score years and ten hurriedly and
coarsely lived to moments of divine leisure in which
your life is coincident with the life of the universe?"
asks Thoreau in his Journal; but he adds as a cor-
rective: "That aim in life is highest which requires
the highest and finest discipline." Man's life, he
says elsewhere, "consists not in his obedience, but his
opposition, to his instincts," and genius was to him
another name for health. This was his resolution
and his prayer:

I pray that the life of this spring and summer may ever lie fair in my memory. May I dare as I have never done! May I persevere as I have never done! May I purify myself anew as with fire and water, soul and body! May I gird myself to be a hunter of the beautiful, that nought escape me! May I attain to a youth never attained! I am eager to report the glory of the universe; may I be worthy to do it; to have got through with regarding human values so as not to be distracted from regarding divine values. It is reasonable that a man should be something worthier at the end of the year than he was at the beginning.

And so, despite its provincialism and its tedium, the Journal of Thoreau is a document that New England may cherish proudly. It is the mirror of a life, the record of romanticism striving to work itself out in actual character, and shows thus, as clearly as the far greater writings of Emerson, wherein the originality of the Concord school really lies. The dangers of transcendentalism are open enough—its facile optimism and unballasted enthusiasms—dangers to the intellect chiefly. Any one may point at the incompatibility of Thoreau's gospel with the requirements of society. To follow him, as to follow Walt Whitman, a man must needs shun the responsibilities of the family and State, and walk in solitary ways. Yet, withal, there is brave inspiration in the scornful independence of this botanising vagabond. For the motto of his Journal one might choose the familiar lines of Matthew Arnold:

> For most men in a brazen prison live,
> Where, in the sun's hot eye,
> With heads bent o'er their toil they languidly
> Their lives to some unmeaning taskwork give,
> Dreaming of nought beyond their prison-wall.

.　.　.　.　.　.　.

And the rest, a few,
Escape their prison and depart
On the wide ocean of life anew.
There the freed prisoner, where'er his heart
Listeth, will sail;
Nor doth he know how there prevail,
Despotic on that sea,
Trade-winds that cross it from eternity.
Awhile he holds some false way, undebarr'd
By thwarting signs, and braves
The freshening wind and blackening waves,
And then the tempest strikes him. . . .
And he too disappears, and comes no more.

Put out of mind the wild hurtling words Thoreau
was so fond of uttering, forget the ill taste into which
his narrower circumstances often led him, and there
remains this tonic example of a man who did actually
and violently break through the prison walls of rou-
tine, and who yet kept a firm control of his career.
If his aim was to refine his senses so that, like an
Æolian harp, he might quiver in response to every
impression of mountain and field and river, at least
he sought for this refinement by eliminating all the
coarser and more relaxing emotions of his breast; by
disciplining his will into harmony with the pure and
relentless laws of universal being. And if the terms
of his practical philosophy may be traced back
through the German romanticists to Rousseau's ideal
of a return to nature, yet his sympathetic knowledge
of hard savage life among the Indians and the tradition of New England's struggle with the wilderness
kept him, always in act and generally in words, from
sentimental softening of the reality.

Perhaps, in the end, what remains in the mind of
the reader is the sense of constant expectancy that
plays on almost every page of his works. "Is not

the attitude of expectation somewhat divine?" he asks in one of his letters, and always it is morning with him. The clearest expression of this buoyancy of the dawn may be found in the account of *A Walk to Wachusett*, but it is never long absent from the Journal and was a characteristic of his daily life. He walked the fields like one who was on the alert for some divine apparition, and Mr. M. D. Conway has observed that a strange light seemed to shine on his countenance when abroad. This, too, is a trait of the romantic spirit, no doubt; but its quality in Thoreau does not point to Germany. It came to him in part from his birth in a new land, and it was strengthened by his familiarity with the English poets of the seventeenth century. In the works of Henry Vaughan more particularly you will find this note of expectation, rising at times to a cry of ecstasy for which there is no equivalent in the later American. I think of Vaughan as travelling his quiet rounds in his Silurian hills, with an eye open to every impression, and a heart like Thoreau's always filled with the waiting wonder of the dawn. If his mood strikes deeper than Thoreau's, it is because, coming before the romantic worship of the individual, he never cut himself off from the Church and State, but moved in the greater currents of tradition.

CHESTERFIELD

A LIFE of Lord Chesterfield [1] devoted almost exclusively to the political career of that arbiter of elegancies might seem to promise an oddly distorted portrait. Yet we may find our profit in Mr. Craig's well-meant, if carelessly composed, work. It will at least do something to modify the contemptuous ignorance which passes commonly for a judgment of his lordship, and which, for one reason or another, has overtaken most of the men who fought in the Opposition to that right British master, Sir Robert Walpole. And a sober consideration of his career brings also a new element into our opinion of his Letters. We are likely to look with more lenience on his reiterated preaching of politeness and superficial address when we remember that in active life he himself played an honourable and manly part. The second member of his favourite motto, *Suaviter in modo, fortiter in re,* assumes a just proportion to the first by a comparison of his acts with his words.

Philip Dormer Stanhope, the fourth Earl of Chesterfield, came of a distinguished house, so ancient that he could safely ridicule the vanity of birth by setting up portraits of Adam and Eve de Stanhope in his family gallery, and by calling it, in one of his *World* papers, "the child of Pride and Folly, coupled together by that industrious pander Self-love." He was born in St. James's Square, London, in 1694. His father, the third Earl, seems to have been more distinguished by stubbornness than any other quality;

---

[1] *Life of Lord Chesterfield.* An Account of the Ancestry, Personal Character, and Public Services of the Fourth Earl of Chesterfield. By W. H. Craig. New York: John Lane Co 1907.

being a strong Jacobite, he punished his heir's Hanoverian tendencies by cutting his allowance down to five hundred pounds a year, and, for his other traits, we may suppose that Swift exaggerated a little when he wrote: "If it be old Chesterfield, I have heard he was the greatest knave in England." The son lived not at home, but with his maternal grandmother, the excellent Marchioness of Halifax,[1] who indulged his bent and kept him out of school until, at the age of eighteen, he was entered at Trinity Hall, Cambridge. Here apparently he combined the studious and the rakish life, with a predominance of the former. At any rate, he steeped himself in the Classics, and began that discipline in the precise use of language which made him one of the first masters of English. His method of study he explained later to his son: "So long ago as when I was at Cambridge, whenever I read pieces of eloquence (and indeed they were my principal study), whether ancient or modern, I used to write down the shining passages, and then translate them as well and as elegantly as ever I could; if Latin or French, into English; if English, into French." At nineteen he left the university, if we may believe his own words, as precious a pedant as ever went up to London: when he talked best, he talked Horace; his wit was to quote Martial, and his notion of a fine gentleman to follow Ovid. He never forgave the university for sending him out with this tincture of scholasticism, and his unrelenting rancour inclines one to believe that his accounts of a blundering start in society are not a commonplace fiction for pointing a moral. And indeed, as

---

[1] It has been remarked that in intellect and temperament he was more of a Savile than a Stanhope, and a comparison of his writings with those of his grandfather, the first Marquis of Halifax, fully confirms the observation.

his perfected manners were the polish of a sensitive egotism, it is natural that his entrance upon the world should have been marked by a bashful self-consciousness. He would not permit his son to go either to Cambridge or Oxford. His letters speak of the universities always with hatred and contempt, and one of his journalistic portraits of a boor repeats the theme: "As he had resided long in college, he had contracted all the habits, prejudices, the laziness, the soaking, the pride, and the pedantry of a cloister, which after a certain time are never to be rubbed off."

It need not be said that Chesterfield soon rubbed off his *mauvaise honte* by contact with the world. For some years he served in the lower house of Parliament with indifferent success. At the age of thirty-one he succeeded to the earldom by the death of his father, and began his real career, being better fitted by temperament and education for influence among the Lords than among the Commons. Two periods of his political activity stand out prominently: his mission as ambassador to The Hague from 1728 to 1732, and his vice-royalty of Ireland in 1745-46; in both which offices he showed undoubted ability. At The Hague, where the tangled dynastic relations of Europe were debated, he kept his head and maintained the honour of England—and no man could do more. To Ireland he gave for eight memorable months a happy government, showing a peculiar sympathy for that tormented people. Some of his best-known witticisms come from Dublin, and his wit, together with his firm tolerance, was an important element in his success. "I would much rather," he once said, "be distinguished and remembered by the name of the *Irish Lord-Lieutenant* than by that of Lord-Lieutenant of Ireland." Again, at a critical moment, when the Castle officials brought him word in the morning that "the people of Connaught were actually rising," he first gravely consulted his watch and then replied with composure: "Well, it is nine o'clock, and certainly time for them to rise; I therefore believe your news to be true." Nor did he lose his interest in the people after his return. Throughout his later correspondence with Irish friends he was constant in his support of the paper and linen manufactures, by which he hoped the country could be brought to efficient independence.

In the interval between his residence at The Hague and in Dublin he was, until Walpole's downfall in 1742, a member of the cabal which led the Opposition and gave hostility to that minister the name of Patriotism. Chesterfield's part in the political game was an active, but not the leading, one. He had neither the virulent pen nor the personal weight of Bolingbroke; he could not intrigue with the trimming Pulteney, or contend against the domineering, gusty Carteret; but he wrote and spoke much, and took his part in the harrying of the great Parliamentary boar. After his return from Ireland, he was for a while Secretary of State in the Broad-bottom ministry of the Pelhams, but gradually dropped out of the arena into the quiet of a valetudinary old age that fluttered between the magnificent library of Chesterfield House in South Audley Street and his gardens and *Babiole* at Blackheath. "I am now, for the first time in my life," he writes to an old friend in 1753, "impatient for the summer, that I may go and hide myself at Blackheath and converse with my vegetables *d'égal à égal,* which is all that a deaf man can pretend to. . . The place agrees with my health and becomes my present situation. It employs my eyes, my own legs, and my horse's agreeably without having any demand upon my ears, so that I almost forget sometimes I have lost them." As for the library in his city house, it was one of the spectacles of London, and still exists, little changed. In 1845, a writer in the *Quarterly Review* thus described,

What [Chesterfield] boasted of as "the finest room in London"—and perhaps even now it remains unsurpassed—his spacious and beautiful library, looking on the finest private garden in London. The walls are covered half-way up with rich and classical stores of literature; above the cases are, in close series, the portraits of eminent authors, French and English, with most of whom he had conversed. Over these and immediately under the massive cornice, extend all round in foot-long capitals the Horatian lines:

Nunc veterum libris. Nunc somno et inertibus horis.
Ducere solicitæ jucunda oblivia vitæ.

On the mantelpiece and cabinets stand busts of old orators, interspersed with voluptuous vases and bronzes, antique or Italian, and airy statuettes in marble or alabaster of nude or semi-nude opera nymphs.

Stoic we may believe the oblivion of the half-cloistered wit, deaf and broken in health, to have been, but *jocund* never. "Physical ills," he writes, "are the taxes laid upon this wretched life; some are taxed higher, and some lower, but all pay something. My philosophy teaches me to reflect how much higher, rather than how much lower, I might have been taxed." And again: "I read a good deal, and vary occasionally my dead company. I converse with grave folios in the morning, while my head is clearest and my attention strongest; I take up less severe quartos after dinner; and at night I choose the mixed company and amusing chit-chat of octavos and duodecimos. *Je tire parti de tout ce que je puis;* that is my philosophy; and I mitigate, as much as I can, my physical ills by diverting my attention to other objects." It is the *savoir vieillir*, the bland resignation of the man of the world, such as we meet in page after page of the letters of Horace Walpole, like Chesterfield, old and gouty. "Visions," wrote Walpole, "are the consolation of life; it is wise to indulge them, unless one builds on them as realities. Our dreams are almost at an end! Mine are mixed with pain; yet I think it does not make me peevish. I accept with thankfulness every hour in which I do not suffer. I am not impatient for the moment that will terminate both anguish and cheerfulness, and I endeavour to form my mind to resigning the first with gratitude, and the latter with submission." The visions of Chesterfield, we may fancy, were more solid than those of the epicure of Strawberry Hill. He had seen the great world, and knew men and manners. From those perpetual friends, his books, he could turn to living memories of Mr. Addison and Mr. Pope, in whose company, as he wrote, he used to feel in society as much above himself as if he had been with all the princes in Europe. The quarrels and reconciliations of those mighty wits, no doubt, he reflected upon much, as also upon the coarser battles of the politicians, including the relentless Lord Bolingbroke. Much, too, he must have thought of the flutter of more effeminate society, and of his own reputation as the glass of form, given so grudgingly by his rivals, won with such pains to himself. There was a world of recollections to occupy the gouty and somewhat lonely old gentleman in his chair.

We can almost see him in his library by his garden window, a frail and uncomely figure, the eyes, beneath the bushy high-arched brows, large and touched with pain; the mouth small and lifted in a half-kindly, half-cynical smile; the chin heavy, but rounded to a point. So Gainsborough painted him, and so the face appears, not without nobility and power, in most of the memoirs of the day. But the voice was shrill and the body curiously awkward. Plain-speaking George II. calls him a "dwarf baboon," and handsome Hervey, Pope's "white curd of ass's milk," who has no love for his person or respect for his morals, will not even allow dignity to the countenance:

With a person as disagreeable as it was possible for a human figure to be without being deformed, he affected following many women of the first beauty and the most in fashion; and, if you would have taken his word for it, not without success; whilst in fact and in truth he never gained any one above the venal rank of those whom an Adonis or a Vulcan might be equally well with, for an equal sum of money.[1] He was very short, disproportioned, thick, and clumsily made; had a broad [it is narrow in the portraits], rough-featured, ugly face, with black teeth [he alludes himself to this defect], and a head big enough for a Polyphemus. One Ben Ashurst, who said few good things, though admired for many, told Lord Chesterfield once that he was like a stunted giant—which was a humorous idea and really apposite. Such a thing would disconcert Lord Chesterfield as much as it would have done anybody who had neither his wit nor his assurance on other occasions; for though he could attack vigorously, he could defend but weakly, his quickness never showing itself in reply, any more than his understanding in argument.

[1] The same insinuation may be found elsewhere. But Hervey was, perhaps, a little embittered by the somewhat scandalous ballad to his lovely wife, attributed conjointly to the Earls of Chesterfield and Bath:

"The Muses, quite jaded with rhyming,
    To Molly Mogg bid a farewell;
But renew their sweet melody, chiming
    To the name of dear Molly Lepel!

"Bright Venus yet never saw bedded
    So perfect a beau and a belle,
As when Hervey the handsome was wedded
    To the beautiful Molly Lepel!" . . .

Lord Hervey's report of this encounter with Ben Ashurst might be used as a simile of the Parliamentary contest between Chesterfield and Sir Robert. And in other respects the description is something more than gossip; it helps to explain the exaggerated insistence upon form and manner in a man who could leave nothing to nature, but must win his reputation entirely by art. We must remember always that the great Earl, in writing to an ungainly son, had had also his own ungainliness to overcome. And we must remember, too, that his passionate interest in the son's

Complimentary enough, but the sting comes later. Chesterfield's marriage to Melusina de Schulemburg, daughter of George I. and the Duchess of Kendall, neither young nor attractive, but rich, was as prosaic as possible, but there is a hint of romance in the story of Fanny Shirley, whom in his younger years he saw enough of at Twickenham to start the sly tongue of gossip a-wagging. Charles Hanbury Williams, the licensed satirist of society, put them into limping verse:

> "Says Lovel—-There were Chesterfield and Fanny,
>   In that eternal whisper which begun
>   Ten years ago, and never will be done."

To Chesterfield was accredited (though it was more likely from the hand of Thomas Phillips) the ballad upon her, "When Fanny, blooming fair," which Horace Walpole had parodied:

> "Here Fanny, 'ever blooming fair,'
>   Ejaculates the graceful prayer;
>   And 'scaped from sense, with nonsense smit,
>   For Whitfield's cant leaves Stanhope's wit."

There are several allusions to her pitiable old age in Walpole's Letters: "'Fanny, blooming fair,' died yesterday of a stroke of palsy. She had lost her memory for some years, and remembered nothing but her beauty and not her Methodism. Being confined with only servants, she was continually lamenting, 'I to be abandoned that all the world used to adore!' She was seventy-two."—Such strange gleams of pathos shine through the wit of that period.

ambition arose in part from a feeling that his own career had fallen short of what his powers promised. He had held office and had won respect as a speaker in Parliament, yet his actual weight in the Government, or against it, was never equal to his capabilities; and of this he seems to have been painfully conscious. We may give various reasons for this partial thwarting of his hopes, but the truth probably lies in Hervey's caustic words:

> Lord Chesterfield was allowed by everybody to have more conversible entertaining table-wit than any man of his time; his propensity to ridicule, in which he indulged himself with infinite humour and no distinction, and with inexhaustible spirits and no discretion, made him sought and feared, liked and not loved, by most of his acquaintance; no sex, no relation, no rank, no power, no profession, no friendship, no obligation was a shield from those pointed, glittering weapons, that seemed to shine only to a stander-by, but cut deep in those they touched. . . . I remember two lines in a satire of Boileau's that fit him exactly:
>
> > Mais c'est un petit fou qui se croit tout permis,
> > Et qui pour un bon mot va perdre vingt amis.
>
> And as his lordship, for want of principle, often sacrificed his character to his interest, so by these means he as often, for want of prudence, sacrificed his interest to his vanity.[1]

The fact is his lordship was not much liked or trusted. From the King down he made men feel the inferiority of their minds, and this, in an age when

---

[1] Compare Burnet's portrait of Halifax: "He was a man of a quiet and ready wit: full of life and very pleasant; much turned to satire. He let his wit run much on matters of religion, so that he passed for a bold and determined atheist; though he often protested to me he was not one; said he believed there was not one in the world. . . . The liveliness of his imagination was always too hard for his judgment. A severe jest was preferred by him to all arguments whatsoever." Lord Dartmouth gives him the same character.

politics were so completely personal, was in itself enough to ruin him. And, besides, he did not play the game. Bribery and corruption were the tools of administration used notoriously by Walpole, as they were in turn by the protesting Patriots; now Chesterfield would not take a bribe, and is one of the few men who came out of public life with clean hands. So much was to his honour and not against his influence; but he had an uncomfortable way of failing to see that other men might pocket their rewards and still be honest within the acknowledged rules of the sport. He lacked apparently the first requisite of political *savoir vivre,* and in this he was coupled with Lord Carteret: "They both of them, too, treated all principles of honesty and integrity with such open contempt that they seemed to think the appearance of those qualities would be of as little use to them as the reality, which must certainly be impolitic, since always to ridicule those who are swayed by such principles was telling all their acquaintance, 'If you do not behave to me like knaves, I shall either distrust you as hypocrites or laugh at you as fools.'" After following Chesterfield's career in all its details and allowing credit to his incorruptibility and his occasional efficiency, one still returns, unfairly it may be, to the judgment of Horace Walpole on reading his Letters: "Yet in all that great character what was there worth remembering but his *bons mots?* . . . from politics he rather escaped well, than succeeded by them:"— so dangerous is the reputation for wit.

As a maker of epigrams, rather than as a statesman, he moves through the records of the age, and it should seem that people looked for his inevitable witticism at every occurrence in the government or society. So Mrs. Montagu sends to her husband "an admirable *bon mot* of Lord Chesterfield's" on the perplexities of

George III. just come to the throne: "He said the King was in doubt whether he should burn Scotch coal [Bute], Pitt coal, or Newcastle coal." And Horace Walpole, as part of the regular news of the day, writes to Horace Mann, "two new *bon mots* of his lordship much repeated, better than his ordinary." At another time, after relating an outrageously wicked retort to Mrs. Ann Pitt, Chatham's sister, he breaks out: "What gaiety and spirit at seventy-five, and how prettily expressed! It contains the cheerfulness of the wars of the Fronde in France."

On one occasion Lord Chesterfield left the retirement of his library and gardens, and what he then accomplished was the proudest achievement of his life. In 1582 Gregory XIII. had reformed the calendar, and all the countries of Europe, except England, Russia, and Sweden, had adopted the New Style. As a consequence, there were in Chesterfield's day two different methods of reckoning dates, an inconvenience which had been impressed upon him by the difficulties of correspondence during his embassy to The Hague. In 1751 he had a bill introduced in Parliament by which the year henceforth should begin the 1st January, instead of the 25th March, and the eleven superfluous days should be voided by calling the 3d September, 1752, the 14th. Superstition, habit, and the embarrassment of altering contract dates combined to oppose the bill, but with the aid of Henry Pelham, who was prime minister, and of the Lord Chancellor Macclesfield, it was passed in the end. He was fond of repeating the story of the triumph to his son in that vein of didactic modesty so peculiarly his own. March 18, O. S., 1751, he wrote:

I was to bring in this bill, which was necessarily composed of law jargon and astronomical calculations, to both of which

I am an utter stranger. However, it was absolutely necessary to make the House of Lords think that I knew something of the matter, and also to make them believe that they knew something of it themselves, which they do not. For my own part, I could just as soon have talked Celtic or Sclavonian to them as astronomy, and they would have understood me full as well; so I resolved to do better than speak to the purpose, and to please instead of informing them. I gave them, therefore, only an historical account of calendars, from the Egyptian down to the Gregorian, amusing them now and then with little episodes; but I was particularly attentive to the choice of my words, to the harmony and roundness of my periods, to my elocution, to my action. This succeeded, and ever will succeed: they thought I informed, because I pleased them; and many of them said that I had made the whole very clear to them, when God knows, I had not even attempted it. Lord Macclesfield, who had the greatest share in forming the bill, and who is one of the greatest mathematicians and astronomers in Europe, spoke afterwards with infinite knowledge and all the clearness that so intricate a matter would admit of; but as his words, his periods, and his utterance, were not near so good as mine, the preference was most unanimously, though most unjustly, given to me.

After this incursion into public life, he returned to valetudinarian ways, preparing himself with tranquil stoicism for the end, ever ready with a jest or a sententious fling at destiny. He reminds one of Franklin, without Franklin's great body and without his imperturbability. "Not so loud," he replied to one who accosted him in the street walking with a friend. "The fact is that Tyrawley and I have been dead these two years, only we don't wish it to be generally known." It is like Franklin's "I seem to have intruded myself into the company of posterity, when I ought to have been abed and asleep." Eight years before his death he was in a mood to write to his son: "I feel the beginning of the autumn, which is already very cold; the leaves are withered, fall apace, and seem to intimate that I must follow them; which I shall do without reluctance, being extremely weary of this silly world." Everybody knows his last words—they are classic—spoken when the *valet de chambre* opened the curtains of his bed and announced his old and well-tried friend: "Give Dayrolles a chair." That act of formal courtesy should be added to the illustrations of Pope's ruling passion strong in death.

He died 24 March, 1773, leaving the tradition of his wit to be taken up by such lesser men as George Selwyn, Richard Brinsley Sheridan, and Sydney Smith.

Lord Chesterfield's letters are divided into two distinct collections, those to various correspondents on Political and Miscellaneous topics and those To his Son on Education. They are alike in the dry light, the almost pitiless clarity of intelligence, which they throw upon all the affairs of life, but in other respects they are naturally diverse. One is impressed in the general collection by the shrewd understanding of men and movements which again and again predicts the shifting political combinations of the age. Nor did he fail to observe the larger currents of national destiny, as in his insight into the condition of France, the clearest expression of which occurs, however, in a letter to his son: "In short, all the symptoms which I have ever met with in history previous to great changes and revolutions in government, now exist and daily increase in France." With this insight goes an irresistible impulse to elucidate and advise; there is, in fact, just a touch of the schoolmaster, strangely compounded with the fine gentleman, in his inveterate didacticism. In his friendships generally, few but enduring, he maintains a kind of discreet enthusiasm, rising in the correspondence with one or two French ladies to a really exquisite gallantry. Was ever a prettier compliment turned than that by which he made his desire to conform his dates to those of Madame de Monconseil the cause of reforming the British calendar? The whole letter (11 Avril, V. S., 1751) should be read in connection with that to his son a month earlier, to see with what refinement of address he turns the same notable act to the uses of pedagogy and courtesy. There is the proud self-effacement of the good teacher in the one, as of the courtly gentleman in the other: "Mais enfin voilà votre style établi ici. Voyez par là comment le public ignore presque toujours les véritables causes des évènements; car il ne vous soupçonne pas d'entrer pour quelque chose dans celui-ci."

But it is the long series of letters to his son that have made the name of Chesterfield to be a living symbol. No legitimate children were born to him, but while at The Hague he had formed a *liaison* with a certain Madame du Bouchet, governess in a wealthy Dutch family, who followed him to England and lived there quietly on an allowance during his life. In 1732, their son, Philip Stanhope, was born. In the care of this boy the father and the pedagogue combined in Chesterfield to produce an overpowering anxiety; and never was legitimate child trained and pushed in the world with such unwearied assiduity. He was educated under the best masters and then sent, with a "bear-leader," to the Continent for years to be ripened and *décrotté*. Parliament and diplomacy were both opened to him, but in the end, owing in part to the stigma of his birth and in part to an invincible clumsiness of manner, he proved little better than a failure. In 1768 his death revealed the fact that he had been secretly married to a lady, who made profit of the connection by selling the Earl's treasured letters to her husband for £1575. They were pub-

lished in 1774, to the scandal of the family and of
England.

In truth, few men dared at the time to defend these
extraordinary documents. Horace Walpole was
shocked by their naked candour. "A most proper
book of laws," he calls them, "for the generation in
which it is published"; they have "reduced the folly
and worthlessness of the age to a regular system."
But all the world read them, even though, like John
Wesley, they were horrified at the picture of this cunning libertine "studiously instilling into the young
man all the principles of debauchery, when he himself
was between seventy and eighty years old." Dr. Johnson, with more vigour than justice, had already, in his
terrible satire of the patron, held Chesterfield up to
contempt, and now he flung upon the author of the
Letters a hideous phrase which no amount of pallia-
tion can ever quite obliterate. These things occurred
towards the end of the century, when the age was in a
somewhat repenant mood for its sins. Having become
established in virtue, the world to-day can afford to
be a little more lenient—and just. For really the
manners taught by Lord Chesterfield were not those
of a dancing master, nor the morals—what Dr. Johnson was permitted to call them. There is enough to
excuse without any such distortion of the truth as this,
and, for the most part, Chesterfield's morals are very
much those of his age.

Nor would it be just to condemn his frankness of
expression on the principle of *pueris reverentia*. It
must be remembered always that they were written to
an illegitimate son, to whom the preaching of rigid
virtue would imply either repentance or hypocrisy on
the part of the writer, and Chesterfield was neither
repentant nor hypocritic. It must be remembered
also that they were never intended for publication,

and this for their literary as well as their moral qualities. Their greatest fault as compositions is a certain monotony arising from endless repetition of the same theme, very useful in pressing home the desired lesson, but rather irksome when the Letters are read together. Their chief excellence is their style, for which our admiration must be heightened by knowing they were entirely unpremeditated. To one who takes pleasure in the sheer mastery of a difficult artistic medium, the language of Lord Chesterfield must be a continual wonder and joy. He had not the measured eloquence of Bolingbroke, the gravity of Dr. Johnson, the naïve grace of Goldsmith, the homely elegance of Cowper, or the idiomatic ease of Gray; his style lacks colour and magnetism; but he had other qualities which make his Letters on the whole the finest models of English of the mid-eighteenth century, beside which most writing in our tongue seems to wallow unwieldy. It is distinguished for precision, unfaltering directness, and a kind of splendid clearness. It cannot be judged from specimens, for its effect depends on sustained balance of tone; there are no purple patches. To read it is to feel such an exhilaration as comes from watching the swift, thin motion of a foil in the hand of a skilled fencer—and the foil has no button. We have seen how he trained himself as a stylist while at college, but his real masters were the great French writers, whom he knew personally and imitated, and by whom he was in turn looked upon as *l'homme le plus spirituel des trois royaumes.* He had helped to introduce Voltaire and Montesquieu to British philosophy and government, and had filched from them the mysteries of French prose. His English is thoroughly idiomatic, but there is not the slightest jar in passing from his letters in that language to those in French scattered through the collection.

And from France also he borrowed another trait. Englishmen are not frank, or, perhaps, not logical. There is grossness and plain-speaking aplenty in their letters throughout the eighteenth century, but it is sheer naughtiness; they rarely deny the convention of morality. Now Chesterfield was French in conforming his standards with his acts. One finds extremely little of the contemporary coarseness in his Letters, but they accept unreservedly and, indeed, unblushingly inculcate the practical code of society as he knew it. They are overwhelmingly honest, honest in a far higher sense than can be applied, for instance, to the garrulous self-revelation of a Pepys, or to the portrait of a creature of impulse like Tom Jones. Here, if anywhere, the man of the world, the *honnête homme,* as he then was, and as, at heart, he still is, stands exhibited; there is something almost sublime in the dry unshrinking light cast upon him. And if much must be reprobated in that character, much also is admirable and at all times worthy of imitation. He was the late product of an art which has virtually passed from the world. We are concerned to-day about our duties and our pleasures, and about the means of making life efficient; but who is concerned to mould his life into an artistic design? We write enormously of all the mechanical arts, but where is to be found a modern treatise on the one supreme art of living? It did not use to be so, as any one knows who has read the literature of the Renaissance.

It would carry me too far, even if I had the material at hand, to trace the development of this conception of life as one of the fine arts. There are hints of it in Xenophon and Horace and other writers of antiquity, but its real origin would be found in the engrafting of the classical sense of decorum on the mediæval ideal of chivalry. Petrarch's sonnets and letters may be regarded as the opening of the voluminous literature that sprang up on the subject, and the *Decameron,* with its bravely ordained delights against the background of the mortal plague, started its course in fiction.[1] From these sources the art became gradually defined and specialised, reaching its climax in Castiglione's elaborate dialogue on the training of *The Courtier,* certainly one of the richest fruits of the Italian genius. The art came over seas to England with the rest of the Renaissance, and soon made itself felt in literature. Lyly's *Euphues* is at the head of the new *genre,* that book, to follow the title page, "Very pleasant for all Gentlemen to reade, and most necessary to remember: wherein are contained the delights that Wyt followeth in his youth by the pleasauntnesse of Love, and the happynesse he reapeth in age, by the perfectnesse of Wisedome." *The Faerie Queene* is the flower of the school in England, with its confessed attempt "to fashion a gentleman or noble person in vertuous and gentle discipline" by uniting "the twelve private morall vertues" of Aristotle with the graces of chivalry. There is a long drop from *The Faerie Queene* to Peacham's *Compleat Gentleman* (1622), but the ideal, *ut in honore cum dignitate vivamus,* is still in view, and we are preparing for Chesterfield in such passages as this:

There is no one thing that setteth a fairer stampe upon Nobility than evennesse of Carriage, and care of our Reputation, without which our most graceful gifts are dead and dull, as

[1] The very tone and colour of its gayer aspect are given by Boccaccio in the stately language of his Introduction: "Io giudicherei ottimamente fatto che noi, . . . fuggendo come la morte i disonesti esempli degli altri, onestamente a' nostri luoghi in contado, de' quali a ciascuna di noi è gran copia, ce ne andassimo a stare: e quivi quella festa, quella allegrezza, quello piacere che noi potessimo, senza trapassare in alcuno atto il segno della ragione, prendessimo."

the Diamond without his foile; for hereupon as on the frontispice of a magnificent Pallace, are fixed the eyes of all passengers, and hereby the height of our Iudgements (even our selves) is taken.

The Civil War left scant leisure or appetite for discoursing on delicate points of conduct, and the Restoration brought back with it all the froth of France without the substance. It remained for the dull and boorish court of Hanover to smother vice in vulgarity, and it was nothing to Chesterfield's discredit that both George II. and Caroline feared and detested him; indeed, his passionate pleading for refinement of manners may best be understood by reading Hervey's record of the family doings at St. James's and Hampton Court.

These Letters of Lord Chesterfield to his son, then, are to be taken as a part, and perhaps the most valuable part, of that literature of Courtesy which began at the first dawn of the Renaissance. But it must not be supposed that in cultivating the art of life he meant to belittle the need of a substantial foundation. On the contrary, their whole aim was to prepare the boy for an efficient career as a statesman, not without the spur of generous service to his country. They insist upon strenuous study, although my Lord would avoid the pedantry of the universities; they declare again and again that nothing can be accomplished without application and that habit of attention which is as much the lesson of the world as of the closet. The first letter of the collection, written in French to the lad when he was only seven years old, is a disquisition in little on the necessity of cultivating eloquence, ending with the observation: *"Nascitur Poeta, fit Orator: c'est-à-dire, qu'il faut être né avec une certaine force et vivacité d'esprit pour être Poète; mais que l'atten-*

tion, la lecture, et le travail suffisent pour faire un Orateur." In other words, the young Stanhope was already destined for Parliament. Nor is morality, as the writer understood it, neglected; he was earnest in trying to set the boy *à l'abri des grandes écueils de la jeunesse,* and was not ashamed to warn him from the evils of gambling by his own example; for play, he had to admit, had been his one ruling and wasteful passion.

But it is true that towards the end these precepts become rather implicit in the letters than openly taught, and that the *fortiter in re* appears to be forgotten too often in the *suaviter in modo;* the end is swallowed up in the means. It happened that the young man developed a disposition studious and serious to excess, with little care for the graces, so that his Mentor felt obliged to lay special emphasis on all this side of education. The basis of Chesterfield's theory and something of his insight into the workings of human nature can be seen from a few quotations taken somewhat at random:

I would wish you to be a Corinthian edifice, upon a Tuscan foundation; the latter having the utmost strength and solidity to support, and the former all possible ornaments to decorate.

A proper secrecy is the only mystery of able men; mystery is the only secrecy of weak and cunning ones.

A man of the world must, like the chameleon, be able to take every different hue; which is by no means a criminal or abject, but a necessary complaisance, for it relates only to manners and not to morals.

Smooth your way to the head through the heart. The way of reason is a good one; but it is commonly something longer, and perhaps not so sure.

Knowledge may give weight, but accomplishments only give lustre; and many more people see than weigh.

Never seem wiser, nor more learned, than the people you are with. Wear your learning, like your watch, in a private pocket; and do not pull it out and strike it, merely to show that you have one.

It is hard to say which is the greater fool, he who tells the whole truth or he who tells no truth at all. Character is as necessary in business affairs as in trade. No man can deceive often in either.

Have a real reserve with almost everybody, and have a seeming reserve with almost nobody; for it is very disagreeable to seem reserved, and very dangerous not to be so.

Good-breeding carries along with it a dignity that is respected by the most petulant. Ill breeding invites and authorises the familiarity of the most timid.

When a man of sense happens to be in that disagreeable situation, in which he is obliged to ask himself more than once, *What shall I do?* he will answer himself, Nothing. When his reason points out to him no good way, or at least no way less bad than another, he will stop short and wait for light. A little, busy mind runs on at all events, must be doing; and, like a blind horse, fears no dangers, because he sees none.

If a fool knows a secret, he tells it because he is a fool; if a knave knows one, he tells it wherever it is his interest to tell it.

Distrust all those who love you extremely upon a very slight acquaintance, and without any visible reason. Be upon your guard, too, against those who confess, as their weaknesses, all the cardinal virtues.

I have often thought, and still think, that there are few things which people in general know less, than how to love and how to hate. They hurt those they love, by a mistaken indulgence—by a blindness, nay, often a partiality to their faults. Where they hate, they hurt themselves, by ill-timed passion and rage.

Remember, there are but two *procédés* in the world for a gentleman and a man of parts: either extreme politeness or knocking down.

Whoever is in a hurry shows that the thing he is about is too big for him. Haste and hurry are very different things.

I, who have been behind the scenes, both of pleasure and business, and have seen all the springs and pullies of those decorations which astonish and dazzle the audience, retire, not only without regret, but with contentment and satisfaction. But what I do, and ever shall, regret, is the time which, while young, I lost in mere idleness and in doing nothing. . . . Do not imagine that by the employment of time I mean an uninterrupted application to serious studies. No; pleasures are, at proper times, both as necessary and as useful; they fashion and form you for the world; they teach you characters, and show you the human heart in its unguarded minutes. But then remember to make use of them. I have known many people, from laziness of mind, go through both pleasure and business with equal inattention; neither enjoying the one nor doing the other; thinking themselves men of pleasure because they were mingled with those who were, and men of business because they had business to do, though they did not do it. Whatever you do, do it to the purpose; do it thoroughly, not superficially. *Approfondissez:* go to the bottom of things.

The sure characteristic of a sound and strong mind is to find in everything those certain bounds, *quos ultra citrave nequit consistere rectum.* Those boundaries are marked out by a very fine line, which only good sense and attention can discover; it is much too fine for vulgar eyes. In manners, this line is good breeding; beyond it, is troublesome ceremony; short of it, is unbecoming negligence and inattention. In morals, it divides ostentatious puritanism from criminal relaxation; in religion, superstition from impiety; and, in short, every virtue from its kindred vice or weakness.

Good-breeding, and good-nature, do incline us rather to help and raise people up to ourselves, than to mortify and depress them; and, in truth, our private interest concurs in it, as it is making ourselves so many friends, instead of so many enemies.

Having mentioned laughing, I must particularly warn you against it; and I could heartily wish that you may often be seen to smile, but never heard to laugh while you live.

There is nothing reprehensible in all this, and Chesterfield's insistence on the minutest points of good-breeding—an insistence which cannot be conveyed to the reader by particular quotations—can be censured only when it is coupled with the cynical distrust of human nature which he learned from Rochefoucauld and La Bruyère and from living society. Undoubtedly his instruction sometimes leads to the conclusion that men are either knaves or fools, either deceiving or deceived by means of the mere semblance of things. The art of living has thus, despite his protests to the contrary, an ugly tendency to transform itself into a masque of imposture. His second great maxim, *volto sciolto e pensieri stretti,* is at times not far removed from Machiavelli's system of moral strategy, or, if we wish to remain within Great Britain, from such an adaptation of the system as this by Francis Bacon: "Have openness in fame and repute, secrecy in habit; dissimulation in seasonable use, and a power to feign if there be no remedy; mixture of falsehood is like alloy in coin of gold and silver which may make the metal work better." The most notorious and most unpardonable lapses of this kind in Chesterfield occur when he touches on the relation to women. At times he lays himself open to Wesley's charge that he taught pure debauchery, yet his worst immorality is not so repulsive as the cynicism which he adopts frankly as a part of his system. What is to be said of such a passage as this?—

As women are a considerable, or at least a pretty numerous part, of company; and as their suffrages go a great way towards establishing a man's character in the fashionable part of the world (which is of great importance to the fortune and figure he proposes to make in it), it is necessary to please them. I will, therefore, upon this subject, let you into certain *arcana,* that will be very useful for you to know, but which you must, with the utmost care, conceal, and never seem to know. Women, then, are only children of a larger growth; they have an entertaining tattle, and sometimes wit; but for solid, reasoning good-sense, I never in my life knew one that had it, or who reasoned or acted consequentially for four-and-twenty hours together. . . A man of sense only trifles with them, plays with them, humours and flatters them. . . They love mightily to be dabbling in business (which, by the way, they always spoil); and being justly distrustful, that men in general look upon them in a trifling light, they almost adore that man, who talks more seriously to them, and who seems to consult and trust them: I say, who seems; for weak men really do, but wise men only seem to do it.

Here, I think, my Lord falls below the code of honour of his age, and fortunately for his reputation there are not many passages in which he so heartlessly makes a prey of human weaknesses. In general he rather inculcates a refined practice of gallantry, coupling with it a sort of moral prudence and fastidiousness:

The gallantry of high life, though not strictly justifiable, carries, at least, no external marks of infamy about it. Neither the heart nor the constitution is corrupted by it; neither nose nor character lost by it; manners possibly improved.

I may be excused if I do not attempt to bring together the passages in which my Lord initiates his son into these practices of "high life," although his instruction, all things considered, is not so shocking to me as perhaps it ought to be. Love, or gallantry if you choose, was with Chesterfield only a chapter in the larger art of living—*Disce bonas artes, moneo, Romana iuventus*—and if it may seem to verge more on Ovid's *Ars Amandi* than on Petrarch's bastard Platonism (which Plato would have been the first to repudiate), it still contains the virtue of discipline and the graces of delicate choice. It may be something less than "strictly justifiable"—so far my Lord would go in apology—but we are forced to admit that the ages when life has seemed most noble and beautiful have commonly accepted this *ars amandi* as a necessary part of their code, and that a denial of the code has too

often meant (as some would think it means to-day)
a retention of their vice with a loss of their grace.

At least the lessons of Chesterfield were the practice
of society in his day, if not in all days, and in the end
our indignation reduces itself to Walpole's disgust at
seeing the frailty of mankind clothed in high authority.   There is an inevitable injustice in writing about
Chesterfield, for the more questionable side of his
morality somehow assumes an importance out of all
proportion to its real place. Only long familiarity
with his Letters can acquaint one with their better
wisdom and their brave and unfailing acceptance of
human conditions.   It is depressingly easy to lay bare
the snares to virtue they contain, whereas only here
and there will any reader clearly apprehend and make
his own that supreme art of living of which they are
the last and most honest exhibition.   We shall do well
to take leave of him in a few words from the *World,*
in which he shows the better and more genuine side
of his system:

> To sacrifice one's own self-love to other people's, is a short,
> but I believe, a true definition of civility: to do it with ease,
> propriety, and grace is good-breeding.   The one is the result
> of good nature; the other of good sense, joined to experience,
> observation, and attention.

His letters may be said to present the Sir Charles
Grandison of life as it is really lived.

SIR THOMAS BROWNE

WITH the din of battles and marchings in our ears, with the wrangle of plots and counter-plots worrying our memory, it is hard to realise the uneventful life of a provincial physician, like that of Sir Thomas Browne, during the Civil War and the Commonwealth; so easily deafened are we by the clamour of history. He was born in London, 19 October, 1605, his father being a mercer in the parish of St. Michael-le-Quern. His education was at Winchester, where he was admitted as a scholar in 1616, and at Broadgates Hall, Oxford, Dr. Johnson's college (afterwards called Pembroke), where he was matriculated as fellow-commoner in 1623. He obtained the bachelor's degree in 1626, and proceeded master three years later. Soon after this he is on the Continent, studying at the famous medical schools of Montpellier and Padua, and completing his course at Leyden, where the new chemical therapeutics was taught by the celebrated Van Helmont, in opposition to the botanical method still in vogue among the Italians. In 1633 we find him back in England, established at Halifax in Yorkshire. Four years later, at the invitation of friends, he transfers his practice to Norwich, and in this Norfolk home the remainder of his life flows busily and prosperously. He had in his youth written rather scornfully of matrimony: "I never yet cast a true affection on a woman, but I have loved my friend as I do virtue, my soul, my God"—and worse than that; but in 1641 he married a woman who appears to have been as notable a housewife and as devoted a mother as she was eccentric in spelling. Of their ten (or eleven) children, four lived to a considerable age; one, Edward, became a famous traveller, a popular London physician, and a member of the Royal Society. The correspondence that passed between this son and the father is preserved in part, and is as honourable to the learning as to the character of both. In 1671 King Charles, then in Norwich, knighted the father as the most distinguished citizen of the town. Eleven years later, at the age of seventy-seven, on his birthday, our erudite and kindly physician went to his rest—but not "to the iniquity of oblivion."

He was in a way but an amateur author, and his first book was printed without his consent; yet there is no writer of English prose whose name has greater assurance of that immortality of fame he mocked at, and whose eloquence is more certain to be remembered among the "wild enormities of ancient magnanimity." Before coming to Norwich he had for his own pleasure written out his meditations on the problem of science and religion which was then troubling the conscience of men, and the manuscript book, after the fashion of the day, had been lent among his friends and occasionally transcribed. One of these copies fell into the hands of Andrew Crooke, a London publisher, who in 1642 issued it piratically as the *Religio Medici*. Now happens a curious incident in the book-world of that age, told with great gusto by Mr. Edmund Gosse in his life of the author. Sir Kenelm Digby, the eccentric philosopher who may be likened to Browne himself with a strong tinge of charlatanism added, was then for political reasons confined in Winchester House. There, late one evening, he received a letter from Lord Dorset recommending the newly published treatise. Without delay he sent out for a copy, and the next morning reported on the work to his friend:

This good-natured creature [*Religio Medici*] I could easily persuade to be my bedfellow, and to wake with me as long as I had any edge to entertain myself with the delights I sucked from so noble a conversation. And truly, my Lord, I closed not my eyes till I had enriched myself with, or at least exactly surveyed, all the treasures that are lapped up in the folds of those few sheets.

Not content with expressing his enthusiasm thus privately, Sir Kenelm set himself immediately to write and afterwards to publish an elaborate critique of the work. On hearing of this project Browne wrote to him, saying that the book had been printed surreptitiously and was full of errors, and begging him to hold back his criticism until a correct impression could be got out. This authorised text was issued by Crooke in 1643. Its effect was extraordinary. There were at least fourteen editions printed during the author's lifetime, not to mention the discussions, favourable and hostile, it provoked. Twice it was translated into Latin and thus attracted much attention among Continental scholars. As early as 1644, Guy Patin, the witty physician of Paris, was celebrating it in letters to his friends:

Un petit livre nouveau intitulé *Religio Medici* fait par un Anglais et traduit en Latin par quelque Hollandais. C'est un livre tout gentil et curieux, mais fort délicat et tout mystique; l'auteur ne manque pas d'esprit; vous y verrez d' étranges et ravissantes pensées. Il n'y a encore guère de livres de cette sorte.

Browne's next work, the *Pseudodoxia Epidemica* or *Vulgar Errors* (published in 1648), was an attempt, half-hearted it must be said, to apply the new scientific methods to the inveterate superstitions about animals, plants, and stones that had originated for the most part in some hoary antiquity, had been gathered together in Pliny's *Natural History* and so transmitted

through the Middle Ages, and had taken on fresh
vitality with the euphuistic movement of the Renaissance. Nothing followed this treatise for ten years,
when there appeared in a single volume his *Hydrio-
taphia,* a mystical rhapsody on death suggested by the
unearthing of a number of burial urns at Old Wal-
singham, and *The Garden of Cyrus,* which, beginning
with Xenophon's description of trees laid out in
groups of five like the figure X (⦂), goes on, as
Coleridge said, to find "quincunxes in heaven above,
quincunxes on earth below, quincunxes in the mind
of man, quincunxes in tones, in optic nerves, in roots
of trees, in leaves, in everything." This *Cyrus-Garden*
is, in fact, about as nondescript a piece of Pythagorean
madness as ever bewildered the wits of man; yet even
here, lost in a quincuncial labyrinth of words, there
are wandering snatches of Browne's entrancing music, as in that paragraph on the adumbrations of religion, or in that other which explains why "Providence
hath arched and paved the great house of the world
with colours of mediocrity." And the conclusion, who
shall forget it?—written down, we fondly suppose,
when the author, rising from his finished manuscript,
looked out at the stars that were never far from his
thoughts, and beheld the five faintly glimmering
Hyades now at midnight dropping to the horizon:

But the Quincunx of Heaven runs low, and 't is time to close
the five ports of knowledge; We are unwilling to spin out
our awaking thoughts into the phantasms of sleep, which often
continueth precogitations; making Cables of Cobwebs and
Wildernesses of hansome Groves. . . Though Somnus in Homer
be sent to rouse up Agamemnon, I find no such effects in the
drowsy approaches of sleep. To keep our eyes open longer
were but to act our Antipodes. The Huntsmen are up in
America, and they are already past their first sleep in Persia.
But who can be drowsy at that hour which freed us from

everlasting sleep? or have slumbering thoughts at that time, when sleep itself must end, and as some conjecture all shall awake again?

It is this swift extravagance of analogy that never fails to stir our sleeping faculties of wonder, however often we return to Sir Thomas Browne. In his books, as on the stage of *Faust,* the imagination is a winged thing to which space and time are a jest:

> So schreitet in dem engen Bretterhaus
> Den ganzen Kreis der Schöpfung aus.

After this volume of 1658 there was silence until his death. Then a number of his miscellaneous tracts and letters were published posthumously, but among them nothing of great interest save the lingeringly-cadenced *Letter to a Friend,* with its ecstatic pathos, and the paragraphs collected under the title of *Christian Morals,* grave with an old man's warnings from "the pedagogy of example," wavering between admiration of "this courtly and splendid world!" and amazement to behold its inhabitants in their "haste or bustle unto ruin."

More than most writers Sir Thomas Browne was influenced by a single idea dominant in his age. The two aspects of that idea were rationalism and science, for which the early years of the century had prepared the way and which the latter years were to see fully developed. From the many workers who laid the foundation of science three names may be selected as variously typical: Bacon its prophet, Descartes its theoriser, and Aldrovandus its practical examplar. All three were conscious of the radical break with the past involved in the new idea. "The only clue and method," wrote the Englishman in the Preface to his *Great Instauration,* "is to begin all anew, and direct our steps in a certain order, from the very first perceptions of the senses"; and at the end of the path he described as in a prophetic vision the race of discoveries, sprung from the nuptial couch of the mind and the universe, which should fulfil the wants and vanquish the miseries of mankind. How deliberately Descartes swept, or tried to sweep, his brain free of the cobwebs of tradition, need not be told; he too had his vision, not so much of the future, as of the present universe revolving like some monstrous engine, wheel within wheel, all whose intricate motions could be explained by purely mechanical laws. And already Aldrovandus, in his garden at Padua, had seen, imperfectly no doubt, the necessity of rewriting the whole book of natural history from actual observation. The fruition of the movement, so far as England is concerned, began in the year 1662, when Charles II., himself a curious observer of physical experiments, chartered the Royal Society. In a few years Newton and Locke, the acknowledged fathers of the eighteenth century, were to complete the theory of natural law and extend its sway over mankind, the one by his investigations of universal motion, the other by his analysis of the human understanding.

Now the significance of Sir Thomas Browne lies in the fact that he was at once by intellect a force in the forward movement and by temperament a reactionary. How clearly he has caught the new method of study and how lovingly he nevertheless dallies with the witchery of the old learning, may be seen by any one who is willing to read through his formidable treatise of *Vulgar Errors*. His professed purpose is to take the magical and fantastic legends about natural objects one by one, and show their incompatibility with reason and observation; yet it is evident withal that his heart is not entirely in his thesis. No doubt he often employs the obvious means of discrediting a myth by direct experiment. Thus it is commonly believed "that a kingfisher hanged by the bill sheweth in what quarter the wind is by an occult and secret propriety." Browne is not content with declaring it repugnant to reason "that a carcase or body disanimated should be so affected with every wind as to carry a conformable respect and constant habitude thereto"; he will in an open chamber suspend a dead kingfisher with untwisted silk and thereby satisfy himself of the fabulosity, as he would call it, of the story. That is good science. But at other times he is satisfied to meet the traditional unreason of signatures and final causes with arguments from abstract probability and inherent propriety which are really a part of the mythology he would explode; and this when a simple experiment or observation lies close to his hand.

But this ambiguity of method strikes deeper than a mere uncertainty in rectifying individual errors. In his introductory chapters Browne undertakes a general purgation of the faculties, which suggests somewhat vaguely Bacon's analysis of the fourfold fallacy besetting the understandings of men. "The first and rather cause of common error is the common infirmity of human nature," begins the *Pseudodoxia*, with, possibly, a direct reminiscence of the Baconian idols that are "inherent in human nature and the very tribe or race of man." For the idols of the den, or those incalculable dispositions of the individual which cause the spirit of man to be "variable, confused, and as it were actuated by chance," Browne gives a scornful chapter on the "erroneous inclination of the people," who being, in the eyes of this fastidious royalist, "a farriginous concurrence of all conditions, tempers, sexes, and ages, it is but natural if their determinations be monstrous and many ways inconsistent with

truth." In place of the idols of the theatre and of the
market there follows a somewhat confused survey of
the misapprehensions and false deductions, together
with the misleading adherence to authority, which it
is the more specific purpose of the treatise to expose
for here, in the blind submission to the past, as he
says, lurks "the mortallest enemy unto knowledge and
that which hath done the greatest execution upon
truth." His whole treatise is thus professedly an essay
such as Bacon or Descartes would have approved, to
shake off the accumulated burden of antiquity, yet it
becomes clear as he proceeds that his interest is quite
as much in amassing this legendary lore as in exhibit-
ing its errors. His scholarship is half of a kind with
that of Burton's *Anatomy of Melancholy* and Cud-
worth's *Intellectual System,* taking the form of a huge
commonplace book wherein the quantity of the cita-
tions is the first concern of the scholar and their relation to his argument only the second. His hankering
goes out after the mistress he discards. A composite
of Bacon and Burton in equal parts would make a
good formula for the author of the *Pseudodoxia.*

Nor does this ambiguity end with Browne's halting
between the claims of the past and the present. It
was not merely the shackles of tradition in matters
external which the new scholarship would throw
away; it would invade the ancient sanctuaries of the
heart also, and for the humility of religious faith substitute its own pride of investigation. The end of that
movement was not unapparent even to the men involved in its triumphant progress. Not a few of them
foresaw and dreaded what seemed to them a limiting
of man's higher life under the rationalising tendency
of science and deism; and the middle of the seventeenth century, in the years before the dominion of
Newton and Locke, shows a number of writers who

revolted against the threatened tyranny, either by denying its dictates or by accepting them and twisting them to other conclusions. Pascal sought to avert the danger by a revival of Augustinian doctrine tempered with the intuitions of the imagination. Henry More undertook to involve the ancient sombre faith together with the coming optimistic deism within a cloud of Neo-Platonic mysticism. Bunyan belonged to the extreme wing of Protestantism which disguised its participation in the new philosophy and its lessening spirituality by a rigid discipline of intellectual and moral dogmatism. Our Norwich physician, half unconscious no doubt of his position and with the Briton's usual incapacity of logic, was led by the insubordinate faculties of the poet within him to another door of escape. Coming back to England from the Continental schools where the militant ideas were already far advanced, he felt a troubled uneasiness of conscience, and in his *Religio Medici* undertook to establish himself in a safe compromise. As the title of the book implies, the problem presented itself to him immediately as the need of reconciling orthodoxy and the materialism of the new medicine; and so he begins:

> For my Religion, though there be several Circumstances that might persuade the World I have none at all, as the general scandal of my Profession, the natural course of my Studies, the indifferency of my Behaviour and Discourse in matters of Religion, neither violently Defending one, nor with that common ardour and contention Opposing another; yet, in despite hereof, I dare, without usurpation, assume the honourable Style of a Christian.

Such is his thesis, but religion, as Pascal and Bunyan understood it and as his orthodox enemies were not slow to observe, receives scant attention from his wandering mind, while his boasted tolerance towards

the creed of Catholic, Jew, or Pagan is next of kin to
indifference. In effect his work takes its place, a
splendid place, among the innumerable protests of the
imagination against the imperious usurpations of science. The freedom of fancy which had wantoned in
every arbitrary and impossible combination of natural
objects—

> Humano capiti cervicem pictor equinam—

such license was becoming impossible for a trained
intellect, as Browne himself had proved in his *Vulgar
Errors.* If the spirit were to maintain its liberty
against the encroachments of a fatalism which would
reduce the circle of a man's life to a mere wheel spinning for an hour in the vast unconscious mechanism
of the world, it must be by the assertion of another
principle distinct from and unmoved by the levers of
physical energy. Bacon, and more definitely Descartes,
had indeed granted this immaterial law, but—*quæ
supra nos nihil ad nos;* they were pleased to leave it in
the sphere of the lofty inane, with no hold upon the
heart and actions of men, with no answer to the cry
of the bewildered conscience, with no root in human
experience—an empty figment of the reason or a sop
to quiet the barkings of the Church. What they
lacked essentially, and what Sir Thomas Browne supplied, was the religious imagination, as later it was to
be defined by Coleridge—the faculty, that is, by which
we unite the broken and dispersed images of the
world into an harmonious poetic symbol. There is in
the unrestrained use of this religious imagination, as
in all liberty, a danger of evaporation into a vague and
insubstantial mysticism, and such a tendency was in
the end to wreck the magnificent intellect of Coleridge; but as a protest against a greater and more common peril it had its beautiful advantages. Certainly

in their investigation of the law of nature the new men of science and reason in Sir Thomas Browne's day did not sufficiently recognise that these solid-seeming phenomena are but the shadow, too often distorted and misleading, of the greater reality which resides within the observer himself, and obeys its own law. In their haste they lost the power of subjecting the less to the greater reality, of associating the outer with the inner, and thus of finding through the many that return to the one which was the *esemplastic* function of the imagination.[1] They followed too well the precept of Bacon: "The understanding must not therefore be supplied with wings, but rather hung with weights, to keep it from leaping and flying."

It is, I know, a part of our present-day eagerness for obliterating distinctions to deny any incompatibility between science and religion, as between science and poetry. And in a way no doubt science has its own worship and its own imaginative domain. Who can be insensible to the exaltation that must come from tracking nature into her secret reserves? who has not felt that exaltation when the mind opens to

---

[1] *Biographia Literaria*, chaps. x. and xiii.: "'*Esemplastic. The word is not in Johnson, nor have I met with it elsewhere.*' Neither have I. I constructed it myself from the Greek words, εἰς ἕν πλάττειν, to shape into one."—"The IMAGINATION then, I consider either as primary, or secondary. The primary IMAGINATION I hold to be the living Power and prime Agent of all human Perception, and as a repetition in the finite mind of the eternal act of creation in the infinite I AM. The secondary Imagination I consider as an echo of the former, co-existing with the conscious will, yet still as identical with the primary in the *kind* of its agency, and differing only in *degree*, and in the *mode* of its operation. It dissolves, diffuses, dissipates, in order to recreate; or where this process is rendered impossible, yet still at all events it struggles to idealise and to unify. It is essentially *vital*, even as all objects (*as* objects) are essentially fixed and dead."

the thought of illimitable dynamic law? And always there is the residuum of mystery at the end of our actual vision, intensified it may be by the slow-groping security of our approach. There is the imagination of science as of religion. Some minds may dwell in one and the other of these alternately, or even confuse them together; but in their essence they are distinct. If we were to define these two *genera* scholastically, we should say that the scientific imagination is quantitative, the religious qualitative. Thus Lucretius, impressed by the almost infinite divisibility of matter and the impossibility of conceiving any ordered relation among so many parts, sees in vision the innumerable atoms hurtling blindly towards some centre of space, all obeying, so far as the shock of other atoms permits, some incalculable whim of diverse motion, and after countless changes of combination cohering for a moment in the forms of this world. Such a vision is the carrying to a quantitative extreme of the chance and individualism that, to a first glance at least, seem to control the momentary meetings and separations of men and things. It is, without the introduction of any new quality, the utmost visible extension of our feeling of that which Cæsar called "Fortune whose whim governs mankind." Of the same kind quantitatively is the development of the sense of order in things, as seen in another mood, to a universal scheme of nature, typified so graphically by the legend of Newton's deducing the law of gravitation from the fall of an apple. There must be a powerful excitement of the imagination, an almost overwhelming magnitude of vision, in this exercise of the scientific faculty; we know how profoundly Newton himself was stirred by the grandeur of his discovery. There is in it also, we must admit, something disquieting to most minds when they enter into themselves to reflect on this dominance of nature, whether it be in the direction of un-governed chance or of inevitable regularity. The melancholy, if not the madness, of Lucretius is well known:

> O miseras hominum mentes, O pectora cæca!
> Qualibus in tenebris vitæ quantisque periclis
> Degitur hoc ævi quodcumquest!

(O wretched minds of men, O blind hearts! in what shadows of life, in how great perils, is passed this little term of being!)

Nor is there less significance in the anxious awe of Herbert Spencer at the contemplation of those un-soundable gulfs of space through which his law of irresponsible evolution extended its sway.[1] These are the nostalgias of impersonal science.

Now, what I have called the qualitative imagination, religious or poetic, may show itself in the same mind with the quantitative, but it always implies the addition of a new element. Thus in Lucretius side by side with his vision of endless ruthless motion is the conception, or at least the passionate desire, of a calm which may remove him entirely outside of the world's despotic chance. When, in the exordium to his second book, he breaks into that magnificent praise of the *sapientum templa serena,* the lofty and serene places whence the wise may look down dispassionately on the wanderings of men and their restless seekings and cruel ambitions, it is no mere separation from toiling mankind for which he prays, but a retreat of religion within his breast where he may take refuge from the terror of these wild aberrations carried into the very being and mechanism of the universe. It was thus, in the superb expression of this longing for a faith which

[1] It was both the man of science and the man of religion in Pascal that expressed the same dread.

his reason would not admit, that he may be said to have denied divinely the divine. Newton also turned from his contemplation of inexorable natural law to the most orthodox and childlike confidence in Providence and the medley of Hebraic prophecy. We are apt to forget that besides his *Principia* he wrote an exposition of Daniel and the Apocalypse. Lucretius, intellectually a man of science, emotionally a poet, seeks relief in pure negation, and balances annihilation against the world. Newton apparently never tried to connect the spheres of science and of religion or saw any difficulty in embracing both at once; his dualism of nature and deity was of that mechanical sort which is possible only when a man has not stopped to realise his ideas in actual human experience.

Sir Thomas Browne, it is needless to say, stands far below Lucretius in emotional vigour and as a man of science is not to be named with Newton; but in his method of escape from an overweening naturalism he has a place of his own in the long battle of the spirit. In him the witness within does not speak in the Lucretian voice of magnificent denial, nor is it, like Newton's, a mere echo of a past faith, but makes itself heard in every act of the intelligence. Always there is present the sense of something other and different lurking beneath natural law and peering out at the observer with strange enticements; and this to him was the great reality. He is one of the purest examples of the religious imagination severed from religious dogma or philosophy; dualism with him takes the form of an omnipresent and undefined mystery involving, and sometimes dissolving, the fabric of the world. There is, one must repeat, in this romantic wonder, setting itself above the systematic intellect and the governing will, an insidious danger, which in

ater times we have seen degenerate into all kinds of
awless and sickly vagaries. Undoubtedly, the works
of Sir Thomas Browne are already lacking in solid
content, and verge into the pure emotionalism of
music; yet they are saved in the end by the writer's
sturdy regularity of life and by the great tradition
which hung upon the age. Wonder with him was a
wholesome elation of spirit, substituting dreams, it
may be, for the laws of the solid earth, but still a
tonic and not a narcotic to the law of character.
"Now for my life," he exclaims in the most famous
passage of his *Religio,* "it is a miracle of thirty years,
which to relate were not a history but a piece of poetry,
and would sound to common ears like a fable; for the
world, I count it not an inn but an hospital, and a
place not to live but to die in. The world that I
regard is my self; it is the microcosm of my own
frame that I cast my eye on; for the other, I use it but
like my globe, and turn it round sometimes for my
recreation." Here, if I may repeat, is no harsh opposition of spirit and matter, but an attempt to interpret
and estimate the law of nature by the law of a man's
inner life. For this protest of the pure imagination
against an all-invading rationalism the book was carried over Europe, accepted the more readily because
the window of escape into the *O altitudo* was opened
by one who had standing in the schools of the new
science.

Browne was no systematic philosopher, nor is the
Religio Medici constructed on a rigid argument—far
from it. Yet, with all its fantastic divagations and its
quaint confessions, this desire to restate facts in accordance with the author's "solitary and retired imagination" is never long absent and gives it a strong
unity of effect. "The whole creation is a mystery,"
he says; ". . . a dream or mock-show, and we all

therein but pantaloons and antics"; rather: "in thi
mass of Nature there is a set of things that carry i
their front, though not in capital letters yet in steno
graphy and short characters, something of divinity
which to wiser reasons serve as luminaries in the
abyss of knowledge, and to judicious beliefs as scale
and roundles to mount the pinnacles and highes
pieces of divinity. . . This visible world is but a pic
ture of the invisible, wherein as in a portrait thing
are not truly but in equivocal shapes, and as they
counterfeit some more real substance in that invisibl
fabric." Theology itself is saved for Sir Thomas by it
appeal to the soaring imagination:

As for those wingy Mysteries in Divinity, and airy subtletie
in Religion, which have unhinged the brains of better heads
they never stretched the *Pia Mater* of mine. Methinks ther
be not impossibilities enough in Religion for an active faith
the deepest Mysteries ours contains have not only been illus
trated, but maintained, by Syllogism and the rule of Reason
I love to lose myself in a mystery, to pursue my Reason to a
O altitudo! . . . Where there is an obscurity too deep for ou
Reason, 't is good to sit down with a description, periphrasi
or adumbration; for by acquainting our Reason how unable
is to display the visible and obvious effects of nature, it be
comes more humble and submissive unto the subtleties of Faith
and thus I teach my haggard and unreclaimed reason to stoo
unto the lure of Faith.

It was inevitable that such a mind, groping in th
bowels and anatomies of nature for a justification o
faith, should have been fascinated by that myster
which, while extending the claims of materialism t
their logical consummation, startles the observer by it
horrible *reductio scientæ ad absurdum.* The repor
of the unearthing of some old mortuary vessels wa
therefore, only the accidental cause that set our autho
off in wild pursuit of the paradox which finds in th

absolute negative of death the affirmation of omnipotent mystery. Through all the pedantries of the *Urn-
Burial,* with its notes on funeral customs jumbled together from every conceivable source, it is the glimpse
of these mockeries of reason, breaking through the
stiff language ever and anon with shrill eloquence,
that keeps the interest of the reader alert. What is
human pride before this imperious scoffer? "Now
since these dead bones have already outlasted the living ones of Methuselah, and in a yard underground,
and thin walls of clay, outworn all the strong and
specious buildings above it, and quietly rested under
the drums and tramplings of three conquests; what
prince can promise such diuturnity unto his reliques?"
—"The iniquity of oblivion blindly scattereth her
poppy, and deals with the memory of men without
distinction to merit of perpetuity."—"And therefore
restless inquietude for the diuturnity of our memories
unto present considerations seems a vanity almost out
of date and superannuated piece of folly."—"But man
is a noble animal, splendid in ashes and pompous in
the grave, solemnising nativities and deaths with
equal lustre, nor omitting ceremonies of bravery, in
the infamy of his nature." Thus paradox swallows
paradox until at the end of the book, as all readers
know, these tongues of eloquence leap together like
the flames bursting upward from a funeral pyre, and
the grinning contradiction of the tomb is lost in "the
metaphysics of true belief."

Once again, in his *Letter to a Friend,* Browne takes
up the theme of death; and again, as he tells of watching by the bed-side of the young man who is fading
away visibly into the invisible darkness, it is the
strangeness of the miracle that absorbs him. He could
not go to cure the body of a patient, he says elsewhere,
without losing his profession in concern for the man's

soul; but one interest of his own he must always take with him—his inquisitive research into the paradox of living and dying. Thus his *Letter to a Friend,* with its lingering absorption in the present mystery creeping upon the world before the very eyes of the watcher like an all-obliterating shadow out of the infinite, may be regarded as a complement to the *Urn-Burial,* with its rhapsody on the memorials of the past. Together they would seem to say: Look hither and lay aside vain pretensions; there is no science of death.

Other writers, especially in more recent times, have undertaken to express this constant dualism of knowledge and wonder, of reason and mystery, which it was the main business of eighteenth-century philosophy to deny, but none with the same magnificent impetuosity as Sir Thomas Browne. Something of his power was due to the age, something to the solidity of his training; but still more to the imaginative burden of his language. Of style in one sense he possesses indeed little; unless sustained by poetic emotion, he is never safe from floundering in the most awkward verbiage. He is, more perhaps than any other author in English, dependent for his fame on purple patches. But at its best there is I know not what excellence of sound in his language, a melody through which we seem to catch echoes of other-worldly music that lift the hearer into an ecstasy of admiration. He has, as he himself might say, transfused into words the magic of that Pythagorean numerosity which forever haunted his understanding:

It is my temper, and I like it the better, to affect all harmony; and sure there is music even in the beauty, and the silent note which *Cupid* strikes, far sweeter than the sound of an instrument. For there is a music where ever there is a harmony, order or proportion; and thus far we may maintain the music of the Spheres: for those well-ordered motions, and regular paces, though they give no sound unto the ear, yet to the understanding they strike a note most full of harmony. Whosoever is harmonically composed, delights in harmony; which makes me much distrust the symmetry of those heads which declaim against all Church-Music. For my self, not only from my obedience, but my particular Genius, I do embrace it: for even that vulgar and Tavern-Music, which makes one man merry, another mad, strikes in me a deep fit of devotion, and a profound contemplation of the first Composer. There is something in it of Divinity more than the ear discovers: it is an Hieroglyphical and shadowed lesson of the whole World, and creatures of God; such a melody to the ear, as the whole World well understood would afford the understanding. In brief, it is a sensible fit of that harmony, which intellectually sounds in the ears of God. I will not say with *Plato,* the soul is an harmony, but harmonical, and hath its nearest sympathy unto Music: thus some whose temper of body agrees, and humours the constitution of their souls, are born Poets, though indeed all are naturally inclined unto Rhythm.

It is not easy to discover the secret of these harmonies in the words of Sir Thomas Browne himself, for his manner varies from page to page. At times, especially in his earlier works, the language is brief and direct, built up on the simplest Anglo-Saxon roots. More often it has a touch of exotic strangeness, due principally to the excess of Latin. "He has many *verba ardentia,*" said Dr. Johnson, "forcible expressions, which he would never have found, but by venturing to the utmost verge of propriety; and flights which would never have been reached, but by one who had very little fear of the shame of falling." There is undoubtedly a risk in this constant recourse to Latin idioms as may be seen in many of his imitators. Dr. Johnson, who is known to have modelled his style on Browne's, was able to attain by this means a gravity that raises the commonplace almost to the sublime; but other writers only sank with its weight.

Whole passages in *The Seasons,* for instance, halt and stumble as if loaded with foreign chains. Browne himself, we may suppose, employed this exotic style, as did Milton and others of that age, primarily because his reading was so much more in Latin than in English that these outlandish terms came to him more promptly than their home equivalents. But there is also at times an artistic consciousness that the note of surprise was better obtained by unusual words, and the desired richness of harmony more fully developed. I do not know whether the musical difference of the Anglo-Saxon and classical elements in our tongue has been analysed, but to me they seem in the hands of a master to be related to each other as a pure tone is to one rich in harmonics. There is, to one at least whose mind is much charged with reading, a full and complex effect from the sonorous Latin words due to countless half-remembered associations, comparable to the overtones that give the note of the violin its pathetic appeal. Almost always we catch these echoes of the past in the language of Sir Thomas Browne when most characteristic; they are heard clearly in such a passage as this, in the *Letter to a Friend:*

And altho' he had no Opinion of reputed Felicities below, and apprehended Men widely out in the Estimate of such Happiness; yet his sober Contempt of the World wrought no *Democritism* or *Cynicism,* no laughing or snarling at it, as well understanding there are not Felicities in this World to satisfy a serious Mind; and therefore to soften the Stream of our Lives, we are fain to take in the reputed Contentations of this World, to unite with the Crowd in their Beatitudes, and to make ourselves happy by Consortion, Opinion, or Co-existimation: for strictly to separate from received and customary Felicities, and to confine unto the Rigor of Realities, were to contract the Consolation of our Beings unto too uncomfortable Circumscriptions.

That may sound at first merely quaint, if not cumbrous; yet to the attentive ear what subtle harmonies unfold themselves. To understand the force of this deliberate Latinisation, consider for a moment the contrast of the words *felicity* and *happiness* that stand so close together. The Saxon word is direct, strong, simple, with the associations of the common homely feelings of the day. But in that thrice-repeated *felicities* there is I know not what magic accumulation of meaning from the hopes and desires and disappointments of many peoples through many ages. I hear, as it were a deep undertone, the grave reflection of Virgil's *Felix qui potuit rerum cognoscere causas.* I hear the pathetic phrase of Boëthius, thinking of his own fall from felicity and of the waning world: *Fuisse felicem et non esse.* That phrase, I recall, was caught up by Dante and placed in the mouth of his Francesca da Rimini: *Che ricordarsi del tempo felice*—"there is no greater woe than to remember in pain the time of felicity"; and from Dante it has passed into the emotional life of Europe. Echoes of the word come to me from great passages in Spanish and French, and last of all the plea of dying Hamlet to his friend:

> If thou didst ever hold me in thy heart,
> Absent thee from felicity awhile,
> And in this harsh world draw thy breath in pain.

Can any one fail to perceive the lingering sweetness and manifold associations of the word *felicity* here as it is contrasted with the quick, stinging Saxon words that follow? Such was the music of the emotions sought and obtained by Sir Thomas Browne in the passage quoted. To vary the metaphor, his cunning use of Latin words affects the ear like the hearing of some majestic fugue, in which the melody, taken up by voice after voice, is repeated and varied and inter-woven until the listener by the long accumulation of sound is rapt out of the solid world into mystic ad-miration.

And of the man Thomas Browne himself, the dreamer of these haunting fugues, what shall be said? As I read his meditations on life and death it seems to me I am in communication with one of the few happy men of this world. I do not mean that there was any cheap illusion in his mind. "Place not the expectation of great happiness here below," he writes near the end of his life, "or think to find heaven on earth; wherein we must be content with embryon-felicities and fruitions of doubtful faces." But more almost than any other Englishman he was able to transform the hard perception of facts into a calm and continuous delight of wonder. The visions of the night, in which he seems to have been so fortunate, were but the freer realisation of the dream that filled his waking hours:

Let me not injure the felicity of others, if I say I am as happy as any: *Ruat cœlum, Fiat voluntas tua,* salveth all; so that whatsoever happens, it is but what our daily prayers desire. In brief, I am content, and what should providence add more? Surely this is it we call Happiness, and this I do enjoy; with this I am happy in a dream, and as content to enjoy a happi-ness in a fancy, as others in a more apparent truth and reality. . . . And surely it is not a melancholy conceit to think we are all asleep in this World, and that the conceits of this life are as mere dreams to those of the next, as the Phantasms of the night, to the conceits of the day. There is an equal delusion in both, and the one doth but seem to be the emblem or picture of the other; we are somewhat more than our selves in our sleeps, and the slumber of the body seems to be but the waking of the soul.

That is, if you please, the very tongue and utterance of a confirmed disillusion; yet it is, in men of his temperament, out of this brave appropriation of vanity, and out of this alone, that reflection rises into its own station of content. Only thus, to use the language of Dr. Henry More, was he able to sound "the sweetest and most enravishing musical touches upon the melancholised passions."

Nor must this mood of Sir Thomas Browne be regarded as a sullen withdrawal from the world of common activities; there was nothing personal in his melancholy, and his disillusion was consistent with a noble conquest of fortune. By profession and character he was led to hold aloof from the civil tumult that stormed over England until his fifty-fifth year. Yet there was nothing cowardly in his inaction, and indeed it was by the waiting sobriety of such men as he that his country was finally saved and made sound. His sympathies were openly with the royalist cause, and at least once he defied Parliament by refusing to contribute to the fund for reducing Newcastle. Apart from politics he must have been one of the busiest men of his age, combining with rare completeness the happiest traits of the amateur and the professional. He was greatly learned, yet carried his erudition as a plaything. He was deeply religious, yet without bigotry or intolerance; a man of science abreast with the movement of the times, yet a maker of magic dreams; a witness of tremendous events, yet undisturbed in his private pursuits; a wide traveller, yet satisfied with the provincial circle of Norwich; an observer of nature and inveterate collector of curiosities, yet an adept in immaterial mysticism; a man of countless interests and engagements, yet carrying with him always the peace of a conscious self-recollection. Honours came to him with the years, and from the first to last he practised the supreme art of friendship. Especially, as age grew upon him, he renewed his hold upon life by sympathy with the young men who came to him as to a master in the new learning and one skilled in the musical interpretation of doubt. So many men famous in thought and action seem to us, as we search narrowly into their hearts, to have suffered some inner thwarting and discontent, that there is always a charm in turning back to the confessions—and all his works are successive chapters of self-revelation—of one who found inviolable happiness in the wisdom of the imagination. And we are assured that, if we knew him even more intimately, we should not find these springs of content lacking, and that, if we had preserved to us the diary which apparently he kept in order to "annihilate not the mercies of God by the oblivion of ingratitude," we should the more abundantly admire the miracle of his daily life. That precious journal is lost, but we have at least one glimpse into his habits, no wise miraculous, indeed, but homely and pleasant to remember, from another diarist. On the 17th of October, 1671, John Evelyn made this record of a visit to Norwich:

Next morning I went to see Sir Tho. Browne (with whom I had some time corresponded by letter, tho' I had never seen him before). His whole house and garden being a paradise and cabinet of rarities, and that of the best collection, especially medals, books, plants, and natural things. Amongst other curiosities Sir Thomas had a collection of the eggs of all the fowl and birds he could procure, that country (especially the promontory of Norfolk) being frequented, as he said, by several kinds which seldom or never go farther into the land, as cranes, storks, eagles, and variety of water-fowl. He led me to see all the remarkable places of this ancient city, being one of the largest, and certainly, after London, one of the

noblest of England, for its venerable cathedral, number of
stately churches, cleanness of the streets, and buildings of flint
so exquisitely headed and squared as I was much astonished
at. . . . The suburbs are large, the prospects sweet, with other
amenities, not omitting the flower gardens, in which all the
inhabitants excel.

SHELLEY

IN confessing that he wrote his life of Shelley[1] as a middle-aged man for others of his class, Mr. Clutton-Brock forgot to reckon with the wit of his youthful reviewers; and yet, if by middle-age he means the experience of life, what right, after all, has Shelley or any other darling of the Muses to be exempt from that censure? The biographer's real fault is rather an amazing ingenuousness in trying to ride at once the horses of both youth and maturity. On one page he analyses *Prometheus Unbound* as a drama of a single event, and that causeless, acted by characters who drift about aimlessly and know not who they are or what relation they bear to one another: that is the critical attitude of mature common-sense. It is the audacious enthusiasm of youth when in a later passage he insists that the author of this drama proves himself an "intellectual poet." This same double-dealing appears when in one place he asserts that Shelley's ideas and emotions underwent little change; and then, a few pages after, with a covert allusion to Matthew Arnold, declares that the poet "was not a vapid angel singing silly hymns; but a man who only learnt to live well and write well by sharp experience." Now, Shelley is "a being prophetic of some higher state to which mankind shall attain, and unfit for this life only because he was fit for a better"; elsewhere, his Paradise is pronounced "a mere impossibility, an incongruous mixture of present pleasure of the flesh with imagined delights of the spirit."

I do not quote these acrobatic feats of criticism because I wish to ridicule Mr. Clutton-Brock's book,

[1] *Shelley: The Man and the Poet.* By A. Clutton-Brock. New York: G. P. Putnam's Sons, 1909.

which is as a whole a fairly illuminating piece of work; but because they are so characteristic of our modern way of dealing with facts and tendencies. Look, for instance, into Miss Vida Scudder's school edition of the *Prometheus,* with its long Introduction —not a very wise production, perhaps, but significant as a woman's conception of a peculiarly feminine genius and as a specimen of what commonly, no doubt, passes in courses of literature. You will there find that the drama "has a noble and organic unity," although, while the second act is the most wonderful thing "in the whole cycle of English song," the third "drops into bathos" and is "weak, sentimental, empty." The poem as a whole is "a work of resplendent insight," yet its interpretation of evil—that is, the very heart of its theme—is "hopelessly superficial," and man is depicted in it as "a creature of no personality, scarcely higher, except for his æsthetic instincts, than an amiable brute."

After all, these knights and ladies of the romantic pen seem to discover in Shelley traits pretty much like those which they so magnificently disdain Matthew Arnold for dilating upon. Nor is Arnold's criticism the only field of their inconsistent attack. Mr. Clutton-Brock cites for reprobation a long passage from Hazlitt's *Table Talk;* yet most of what the old bludgeoner says can, with some change of emphasis, be matched in the modern biographer's own pages. In like manner Miss Scudder puts the ancient reviewers in the stocks to show by comparison how wise we since have grown. She quotes from *Blackwood's* of September, 1820, and from the *Quarterly Review* of October, 1821:

In short, it is quite impossible that there should exist a more pestiferous mixture of blasphemy, sedition, and sensual-ity, than is visible in the whole structure and strain of this poem [*Prometheus*], which, nevertheless, and not withstanding all the detestation its principles excite, must and will be considered by all that read it attentively, as abounding in poetical beauties of the highest order. (*Blackwood's.*)

In Mr. Shelley's poetry, all is brilliance, vacuity, and confusion. We are dazzled by the multitude of words which sound as if they denoted something very grand or splendid: fragments of images pass in crowds before us; but when the procession has gone by, and the tumult of it is over, not a trace of it remains upon the memory. The mind, fatigued and perplexed, is mortified by the consciousness that its labour has not been rewarded by the acquisition of a single distinct conception. (*Quarterly.*)

Really, with the best will in the world, I cannot see that Miss Scudder differs so much from the reviled reviewer of *Blackwood's,* except that she seems to feel no indignation against an author whose sense of evil is "hopelessly superficial." Nor does Mr. Clutton-Brock stand very far from the *Quarterly* when he says that "in a story there should be some relation of cause and effect, otherwise it will not hold together; in *The Revolt of Islam* there is none"; and admits that "in its very absurdity it shows the character of Shelley's mind." The chief difference is that Mr. Clutton-Brock apparently thinks it quite a small matter if a long and professedly philosophical poem leaves the reader perplexed and without any distinct conception of what it is all about.

Now these names represent no isolated paradox of taste, but the almost constant current of criticism from Shelley's own day to this. Their dilemma is due, I think, to a fact which his contemporary critics held, if anything, too belligerently in view, and which his modern worshippers commonly allow and then deliberately forget—that his was a genius fine and impressionable, meant by nature for the perception and utterance of rare truths, but marred in its very essence by the obliquity of Time. His work is a confirmation in a way of his master Godwin's theory—though contrary in direction to his master's wish—that education is a power to shape the destinies of man. The value of Mr. Clutton-Brock's biography lies in the clearness and frankness with which he unravels Shelley's motives and ideas; and this value is enhanced, perhaps, by the biographer's sympathy, paradoxical indeed, but so profound as to make him in the end deny utterly the logic of his premises. But we need not go to the commentators on Shelley's life to discover the influences that worked upon him. Sufficient testimony may be found in his own Letters, which have just been brought together and excellently edited by Roger Ingpen.[1] The new material here offered is slight, but the collection has the merit of setting the recently discovered letters to Elizabeth Hitchener—and others less important—in their proper place in the full correspondence. I do not see how any open mind can go through these letters without feeling that Shelley was powerfully affected by the prevailing forces of the age (which is commonly conceded), and that his character and poetry suffered a certain perversion from this influence (which is often conceded and denied in the same breath).

Those directing forces were the twin spirits—if they were not one power in dual manifestation—of revolution and romanticism. The revolutionary spirit, whether for weal or for ill, had breathed upon all the finer minds of the age, and indeed not upon the minds of that age alone. But the impulse that came to

[1] *The Letters of Percy Bysshe Shelley.* Collected and edited by Roger Ingpen. Two volumes. New York: Charles Scribner's Sons, 1909.

Shelley was not merely revolt against tyranny, or even
the wanton itch for change—*neoterism,* as the ancients
called it. That kind of political excitement may or
may not have a perverting effect upon a poet. Milton
lived in such a time of upheaval; and if the excess
and bad taste that here and there mar his later works
are attributable to the harsh pride of rebellion, it left
his genius sound at heart, perhaps even strengthened
the wings of his fierce aspiration. But with Shelley
revolution meant the fluttering of an opaque and
dizzying flag between the poet's inner eye and the
truth of human nature. He was peculiarly the child
of his age, betrayed by his own feminine fineness of
nature, and lacking that toughness of fibre, or residue
of resistant prose, which made Byron and Wordsworth
followers but not altogether the victims of the ever-
despotic Hour. With a child-like credulity almost
inconceivable he accepted the current doctrine that
mankind is naturally and inherently virtuous, needing
only the deliverance from some outwardly applied
oppression to spring back to its essential perfection.
With Rousseau the perverting force had been property. With Shelley it was more commonly personified
as Jehovah or Jove,

> Foul tyrant both of Gods and Human-kind.

Shelley was a pretty wide reader of Greek, and it
may be that in writing his drama on this creed he not
only had in mind the *Prometheus Bound* of Æschylus, but for a remote analogy to his personification of
evil went back to Homer's blind *atê,* which Zeus
cast upon the minds of those who were doomed to sin.
And in so far as he did this he would only have voiced
a universal and unreasoning sentiment of the human
heart; for Achilles was but the type of us all, when in

the stress of bewilderment he cried out against the government of the world:

> It is thou, father Zeus, that givest to men the great passions of evil (μεγάλας ἄτας).

But Zeus was to Homer at least a living being, whereas Shelley's Jehovah is merely a symbol of a power in human nature tremendously energetic, yet, if you seek it, nowhere to be found. And Shelley, when he made of man's bewildered outcry a rigid philosophy and principle of action, might have remembered also the words of Zeus (to which Pope has given so amusing an anti-Calvinistic twang):

> Perverse mankind! whose wills created free,
> Charge all their woes on absolute decree;
> All to the dooming gods their guilt translate,
> And follies are miscall'd the crimes of fate.

To Shelley's old detractor of *Blackwood's* (when religion was a fairly serious concern) his philosophy was "pestiferous blasphemy"; his modern academic admirer merely disregards it as "hopelessly superficial." To me, I confess, it is chiefly unliterary, destructive, that is to say, of that self-knowledge out of which the great creations and the magnificent joys of literature grow. The importance of Shelley's Letters also is largely derived from their confirmation of this critical attitude by their betrayal of the same force at work in his conduct. It is not that he was by nature base or sensual or cruel; on the contrary, his life was ennobled by many acts of instinctive generosity, and his feelings were normally fine. Nevertheless, there was some flaw at his heart, some weakness of overweening self-trust, which exposed him to the most insidious poison of the age, and in the final test left him almost inhuman. "In all Shelley did," wrote his wife after his death, "he, at the time of doing it, believed himself justified to his own conscience." The words have been used by Matthew Arnold as a text; they would have been still truer to character if to "at the time" Mrs. Shelley had added "and always." Opinions may differ in regard to Shelley's culpability towards his first wife, Harriet Westbrook, although no chivalrous mind, I think, can read his letters at the time of his elopement with her and, later, of his desertion of her for another woman, without feeling a touch of resentment at his self-absorption and his complete assumption of righteousness. And resentment deepens into detestation at his letters written when the abandoned woman, a pitiable thing no matter what her fault, drowned herself in the Serpentine. On the day he heard the news, or possibly the day after, he wrote to Harriet's supplanter:

Everything tends to prove, however, that beyond the shock of so hideous a catastrophe having fallen on a human being once so nearly connected with me, there would, in any case, have been little to regret. Hookham, Longdill, every one does me full justice; bears testimony to the upright spirit and liberality of my conduct to her. There is but one voice in condemnation of the detestable Westbrooks. If they should dare to bring it before Chancery [they did dare, and nothing derogatory to them transpired], a scene of such fearful horror would be unfolded as would cover them with scorn and shame.

Little to regret, save the shock to his nerves of so unpleasant an event. Mr. Clutton-Brock observes that Shelley did not do himself "full justice in this letter." He did not, for he was by birth neither maniac nor brute; but he wrote on that day a lurid comment on the effect upon individual character of revolutionary Pharisaism; nor did his sentiments change with time, for in a letter to Southey four years later he wrote of the event in the same vein. The malignant reviewer of *Blackwood's* called those principles "pestiferous"; Miss Scudder rebukes the reviewer and styles them "superficial." Perhaps it is more critical to reflect merely that, as Mrs. Shelley said, the poet's verse was inspired by the passions of his private life, and that the horrors threatened in *Prometheus* against the "foul tyrant both of Gods and Human-kind" sprang from precisely the same source as the imprecations upon the Westbrooks. "I have confidence in my moral sense alone," said Shelley once in a letter to Leigh Hunt; "but that is a kind of originality."

With that moral self-complaisance went another trait, if indeed it was not merely a different aspect of the same influence. By Shelley each emotion as it arose in his breast was accepted as justified in itself, without pausing to consider its cause or consequence. The full meaning of this emotionalism can be grasped only by a long view into the past. To the great writers of the seventeenth century human nature was a thing to distrust as containing tendencies of ruinous evil. "Men naturally know no Good," said Jeremy Taylor, voicing the constant opinion of his age, "but to please a wild, undetermined, infinite Appetite." But along with this fear of undisciplined nature, went a belief in the efficacy and virtue of certain supernatural emotions, in an infinite appetite that was not wild and indetermined—in enthusiasm.

The following age—and this was the whole force of Deism, one of the most important movements in history—brought about a complete reversal of this position. The very titles of the leading publications show the change: Dr. Clarke writes on *The Unchangeable Obligations of Natural Religion;* Wollaston elaborates his *Religion of Nature Delineated;* Butler preaches *Upon the Natural Supremacy of Conscience,* etc., etc. But this rehabilitation of nature, for which the eighteenth century, and particularly England of that age, laboured so assiduously, was based, in the earlier years, on a constant distinction: nature was used almost without deviation as a synonym of reason; and strong emotion, or enthusiasm, was condemned as contrary to nature and perilous. Pages might be filled with utterances of deists and even of the opponents of Deism on this head, but nothing, perhaps, can be found more characteristic and inclusive than the simple words of the Rev. Nicholas Carter to his daughter Elizabeth, the learned translator of Epictetus: "You seem extremely fond of her [Mrs. Rowe's] writings. I have seen some that have in them a tincture of enthusiasm. 'T is proper to caution you not to read them with too much pleasure. Enthusiasm grows upon us insensibly." I doubt if more of the eighteenth century was ever summed up in a few unpretentious sentences. In that distrust of free emotion lay the strength of the time, the power that made its belief in nature ancillary to its belief in order and subordination (*cf.* Butler's *Sermons* and Dr. Johnson's conversation *passim* on subordination); here, too, lay the cause of its limitation, for this dread of enthusiasm cut off the great inspirations of the preceding age as well as the disturbing passions. The fascination of the century for the student is to watch the rise of this hated spirit of enthusiasm through all obstacles to the surface. The word was long repudiated even by those who were bringing back its force; so Wesley cries out: "The reproach of Christ I am willing to bear; but not the reproach of enthusiasm." Who can measure all that has passed in the inner life of man between the timidity of Dr. Carter and the bold utterance of Shelley in the preface to *The Revolt of Islam:* "It is the business of the poet to communicate to others the pleasure and the enthusiasm," etc.?

There is expressed the elevation and the power of the romantic renaissance; the peril of the movement lies in the fact that with its return to seventeenth-century enthusiasm it retained the eighteenth-century acceptance of nature, but now without restriction, thus leaving to itself no inner check.

All the revolutionary poets of England were affected by the same emotional philosophy, however their practice was modified by other principles. Wordsworth proclaimed it in his worship of the "impulse from the vernal wood," but with an admixture of Puritanic asceticism which made of it a kind of passive discipline. Byron possessed with it a saving self-reproach and cynicism. In Keats it was qualified by an æsthetic humility which rendered him in the end curiously docile to tradition. Few things are more significant in the romantic poetry of England than the change in Keat's versification from the license of his rhymed couplets in *Endymion* to the almost Drydenian regularity of *Lamia*. Whether or not that change will appear altogether a profit, it must be admitted that no such organic development can be discovered in Shelley; nor in his correspondence will you find anything comparable to the long letter of Keats to Reynolds (3 May, 1818) in which he questions the very principles of his poetic theory. "The thought of such discipline," wrote Keats himself to Shelley, "must fall like cold chains upon you." Shelley, indeed, grew in metrical skill and power of expression, but from first to last his procedure was essentially unaltered: his *Prometheus* is only *Queen Mab* writ large; his *Epipsychidion* re-echoes in firmer strain the vagaries of *Alastor*. Always his philosophy, whether magnified into a shadowy mythology or expressed in human drama, whether it be the love or hate of Prometheus or his own relation to mankind, is the voice of enthusiasm, of unreasoned emotion.

It would not be profitable to follow out all the workings of that emotionalism, but one aspect of it shows so curious a link between the man and the poet as to deserve emphasis. Critics have commented on Shelley's extraordinary faculty of self-deception in regard to his friends, who so often were angels of light when first they appeared to him under the radiance of his own imagination, and demons of malevolence when they came to be known as real men and women having wills at variance with his. This form of delusion was not due merely to the inexperience of youth, for at the end of his life in Italy he was subject to the same revulsion, if not so violently expressed, towards such friends as the Gisbornes. But the classic example (classic as being so perfect an expression of a trait common to all the Rousseauistic tribe) is in the letters to Miss Hitchener. These have been for some time known in manuscript, and have forced even the most ardent romanticists to admit a certain weakness in their hero. A few years ago they were printed in a separate edition, but the full weight of their testimony is best understood by reading them as they are now incorporated by Mr. Ingpen in the general correspondence.

Elizabeth Hitchener was a young school-mistress with whom Shelley became acquainted shortly before his marriage to Harriet Westbrook. Her notions were liberal and her fancy ardent; "an *esprit fort,*" Medwin called her; "ceruleanly blue," who "fancied herself a poet." After his marriage Shelley began to send her letters in the most rhapsodical vein of adulation. She is the sister of his soul: "I look up to you," he exclaims, "as a mighty mind. . . I anticipate the era of reform with the more eagerness as I picture to myself *you* the barrier between violence and renovation"; with his brain and his heart she constitutes the

Trinity of his Essence; she must leave all and come to live with him and Harriet—"nothing shall prevent our eternal union in the summer"; and to defer to the opinions of those who foresee scandal in such a union is to sacrifice "to the *world!* to the swinish multitude, to the indiscriminating million, to such as burnt the House of Priestley, such as murdered Fitzgerald," etc. Well, this female paragon closed her school, and joined the young married couple in July of 1812; in November of the same year she had left them, and Shelley is soon writing to his friend Hogg of "the Brown Demon, as we call our late tormentor and school-mistress. . . She is an artful, superficial, ugly, hermaphroditical beast of a woman." To another friend he describes her as "a woman of desperate views and dreadful passions, but of cool and undeviating revenge."

Do not these fragments of correspondence offer a curious comment on the statement of Mr. Clutton-Brock that most of the characters of the *Prometheus* are "so abstract that we do not even know who they are"; and again that *The Cenci,* which deals with human beings, is even "far more unreal" than the *Prometheus,* which is professedly allegorical? As Shelley judged his friends from the immediate emotions they aroused in him, or from some fanciful association with the emotion dominant in his mind, without a care for the various and real springs of action in himself or them, so he created his poetical characters.

I am aware that my criticism of Shelley may seem harsh and prosaic, yet I am really saying nothing which cannot be confirmed by the words of Mr. Clutton-Brock, and in fact by the views, less openly avowed perhaps, of the more whole-hearted Shelley-ans. It is scarcely doing a violence to draw such support even from a critical work like Arthur Symons's *Romantic Movement,* which is written with the avowed purpose of exalting the work of Blake and Coleridge and Shelley as the final criterion of poetry. Mr. Symons does indeed look upon Shelley as an enchanter who "never mistakes the images which he calls up for realities," but, with that extraordinary contradiction which dogs all such critics, he adds immediately that the *Prometheus* is "a cloudy procession of phantoms, seen in a divine *hallucination.*" Even more significant is that strangely-fated essay on Shelley by the late Francis Thompson. Dithyrambic praise has never poured itself out in more intoxicated language than in some of these paragraphs:

It [*Prometheus Unbound*] is unquestionably the greatest and most prodigal exhibition of Shelley's powers, this amazing lyric world, where immortal clarities sigh past in the perfumes of the blossoms, populate the breathings of the breeze, throng and twinkle in the leaves that twirl upon the bough; where the very grass is all a-rustle with lovely spirit-things, and a weeping mist of music fills the air. The final scenes especially are such a Bacchic reel and rout and revelry of beauty as leaves one staggered and giddy; poetry is spilt like wine, music runs to drunken waste. The choruses sweep down the wind, tirelessly, flight after flight, till the breathless soul almost cries for respite from the unrolling splendours.

Yet these closing scenes are "nevertheless the artistic error of the poem"; yet Shelley wrote "with some misdirected view to truth"; yet in religion and morals "his methods were perniciously mistaken"; yet "his theory was repulsive but comprehensible"; and "the spell on which depend such necromantic castles is some spirit of pain charm-poisoned at their base." That charm-poisoned spirit was nothing less than the peculiar romantic illusion of the Revolution which ignored the native impulse of evil, ever lurking in the heart of man, ready to leap forth when its chains are shaken, and which valued the emotions in accordance with their mere spontaneity and intensity.

If, notwithstanding these admissions, the true Shelleyan still cherishes the *Prometheus* and *The Revolt of Islam* as great and beautiful powers in the intellectual world, the issue becomes a matter of emphasis, or, rather, of exclusions in taste. What really appeals to the romantic idealist in the spirit of these poems, in their total effect, is a kind of elusive, yet rapturous, emanation of hope devoid of specific content. The poet may look upon the world of living men with perverted gaze, but his truth is faith in the future; he is "a being prophetic of some higher state to which mankind shall attain"; and from the intoxication of this sheer hope the destinies of mankind become like the vision of the chariots of the Hours:

> In each there stands
> A wild-eyed charioteer urging their flight.
> Some look behind, as fiends pursued them there,
> And yet I see no shapes but the keen stars:
> Others, with burning eyes, lean forth, and drink
> With eager lips the wind of their own speed,
> As if the thing they loved fled on before,
> And now, even now, they clasped it. Their bright locks
> Stream like a comet's flashing hair: they all
> Sweep onward.

There is at least something in this that seems dynamic, a power to make man

> . . . hope till Hope creates
> From its own wreck the thing it contemplates.

And indeed it is on this power, without account of its direction, that Mr. Clutton-Brock bases his admiration; to him Shelley "in his worst errors . . .

was far more admirable and less mischievous than those who persuade us to submit to the mere mechanism of life by their own comfortable submission to it." Shall we, then, end here? The right comparison, I maintain, is not with those sunk in the comfortable mechanism of life, but rather with those strong poets of the true romance, who can hope and still maintain the balance of common-sense. I am bold to assert that this surrender to hope without thought of the thing it contemplates is possible only to a mind which has, in a sense, been debauched by false ideas and vain reading; that a mind deeply nourished on the true poets may for a time and by a sort of self-violence suffer itself to become inflated with this wind of vanity, but cannot long forget the actual outcome of that spirit in the poet's own life and its sterility or falseness in dealing with the actual motives of mankind. It is no sufficient answer to say that the veritable content of Shelley's hope is love, for the scope of this emotion is left as vague, if not as morbid, as the other. It is a long hope to build on the power which "makes the reptile equal to the God"; nor will that power convey much satisfaction to the heart that has sustained itself on the *amor* of Catullus in this world or on that of Dante in the visionary spheres. Love without a true understanding of evil is meaningless.

Or it may be that your Shelleyan eschews philosophy and ideas altogether, caring only for the poet's musical evocation of beauty. To such a one, as to Francis Thompson, the *Prometheus* is like a magical incantation, under the spell of which forms of fleeting iridescent loveliness float before his dream-open eyes:

> Dim twilight lawns, and stream-illumined caves,
> And wind-enchanted shapes of wandering mist.

That is an innocent and blissful kind of inebriation, very desirable, no doubt, in a world too much given to seeking its escape from prose in quite other and baser ways; but he who indulges therein should beware of speaking of this phantom realm as if it were peopled with ideas. There is a beauty of dreaming and a beauty of waking; they are sisters both and daughters of the gods, but only one is acknowledged on Olympus. If you desire to know them apart, read in the *Prometheus* of the voices that emanate from those wind-enchanted shapes:

> Canst thou imagine where those spirits live
> Which make such delicate music in the woods?
>
> .   .   .   .
>
> 'Tis hard to tell:
> I have heard those more skilled in spirits say,
> The bubbles, which the enchantment of the sun
> Sucks from the pale faint water flowers that pave
> The oozy bottom of clear lakes and pools,
> Are the pavilions where such dwell and float
> Under the green and golden atmosphere
> Which noon-tide kindles thro' the woven leaves;
> And when these burst, and the thin fiery air,
> The which they breathed within those lucent domes,
> Ascends to flow like meteors thro' the night,
> They ride on them, and rein their headlong speed,
> And bow their burning crests, and glide in fire
> Under the waters of the earth again.

Read that and then recall Adam's account to Eve of the music that haunted the woods of Paradise:

> How often from the steep
> Of echoing hill or thicket have we heard
> Celestial voices to the midnight air . . .

The change is a transition from dreaming to the sober certainty of waking bliss; from a bubble-blown phantasmagoria to the ecstasy of intellectual beauty.

The fact is that if you press the meaning from all but the very few unreasoning worshippers of Shelley, you will find that they regard his long poems, organically conceived, as sublime failures, and that they really cherish him for the strains of lyric ecstasy caught up in the amorphous mass. That is fair criticism, and a man may pass over much in the waiting expectation for those scattered strains of music,

> Clear, silver, icy, keen, awakening tones
> Which pierce the sense and live within the soul.

Of Shelley, taken merely as the author of a group of lyrics, brief in compass, but exquisite in melody and feeling, quite another account might be given than this I am writing. Here, whether in independent songs or in short strains that can be detached from their context without any mark of incompleteness, here, when he expresses a purely personal joy or sorrow, love or regret, his genius suffers no let or thwarting; it is even strengthened by that romantic acceptance of the emotions. That is the Shelley of the young man's and the maiden's passionate admiration:

> Music, when soft voices die,
> Vibrates in the memory—
> Odours, when sweet violets sicken,
> Live within the sense they quicken.
>
> Rose leaves, when the rose is dead,
> Are heap'd for the beloved's bed;
> And so thy thoughts, when Thou art gone,
> Love itself shall slumber on.

But it is necessary to add that even this wonderful lyric vein is subject at times to a kind of defeat from excess of the very power that produced it. *Adonais* is commonly reckoned, and no doubt is, the most perfect of his longer lyrics; yet the best stanzas of that poem, those that contain lines which have sung themselves into the memory of the world, are almost always always marred by lapses into the vague and inane. There is no greater stanza in the elegy than the forty-fifth:

> The inheritors of unfulfilled renown
> Rose from their thrones, built beyond mortal thought,
> Far in the Unapparent. Chatterton
> Rose pale, his solemn agony had not
> Yet faded from him; Sidney, as he fought
> And as he fell and as he lived and loved
> Sublimely mild, a Spirit without spot,
> Arose; and Lucan, by his death approved:
> Oblivion as they rose shrank like a thing reproved.

The literary inspiration of those lines (and in pointing to this I mean no disparagement of Shelley's originality) is clearly born from a kind of mystical blending of Virgil's

> Heu, miserande puer! si qua fata aspera rumpas,
> Tu Marcellus eris—

and of Milton's

> So were I equall'd with them in renown.

There are lines in Shelley's stanza—the first and the eighth, particularly—which are in no wise diminished by this association with two of the most celebrated passages in literature; yet a comparison of the stanza as a whole with the full parts of the *Æneid* and *Paradise Lost* shows quite as clearly the weakness of Shelley. It is inconceivable that Virgil or Milton should have held so loose a rein on his genius as to sink from "The inheritors of unfulfilled renown" to the vapid "Far in the Unapparent," or should have dropped immediately from the magnificent directness of Shelley's eighth verse (which rings like Lucan himself when most Roman) to the vague allegory of oblivion shrinking reproved.

It would not be difficult to extend this kind of criticism to a considerable number of Shelley's most admired lyrics—to show, for instance, that the throbbing and tumultuous music of the great *Ode to the West Wind* straggles here and there to unmelodious conclusions, chiefly because the poet—like all his English compeers—disdained the inherent laws of the *terza rima* as these are exemplified in the works of Dante and the lesser Italian masters of the measure. There is no other metre in which it is so imperative to mould the thought to the pauses of the rhythm, under penalty of letting the rhymes hang as an impertinence instead of a support; but this lesson none of the English poets learned, and least of all was Shelley capable of such wise docility.

Nevertheless, granted that *Adonais* may occasionally descend into bathos, if it contains also images of pure and radiant beauty, why not give ourselves to these, and pass the errors by? Doubtless that is the part of wisdom, so far as it is feasible; but here again we are blocked by certain insurmountable exclusions of taste. There is a pleasure, the highest critical joy, in the perfection and harmonious unity of such work as Milton's *Lycidas,* and he who has trained his mind to respond to that joy has by the very process rendered himself sensitive to false and obtrusive notes. He simply cannot read the stanza quoted from *Adonais* without suffering from the spirit of perversity at work within it. It is true, no doubt, that there are blemishes—occasional awkwardnesses of execution, failures of the imagination, even lapses of taste of a kind—which may not affect essentially our attitude towards an extensive work of art; but they are not the faults which throw a suspicion of obliquity or vanity upon the very sources of the artist's inspiration.

These, I say, are the inevitable exclusions of taste.

If a man avers that the thorough appreciation of *Lycidas* does not exclude for him an unmarred pleasure in Adonais, I can only suspect that he has never felt the full force of the former. This is by no means to say that the enjoyment of Milton deadens a man to all lower forms of literature. The commonplace or the small may in its own sphere be commendable and may afford a true relish to the finest palate; and, indeed, one of the functions of criticism is to set forth and so far as possible rescue from oblivion the inexhaustible entertainment of the lesser writers. But the humble is another thing than the false, the false is noxious just in proportion to the elevation of the genius to which it adheres. There is nothing mutually exclusive in the complete enjoyment of both Milton and Crabbe; it is at least questionable whether the same man can heartily admire both Milton and Shelley.

THOMAS HENRY HUXLEY

IN a world that is governed by phrases we cannot too often recur to the familiar saying of Hobbes, that "words are wise men's counters, they do but reckon by them; but they are the money of fools"; and so to-day, when the real achievements of science have thrown a kind of halo about the word and made it in the general mind synonymous with truth, the first duty of any one who would think honestly is to reach a clear definition of what he means when he utters the sanctified syllables. In this particular case the duty and difficulty are the greater because the word conveys three quite different meanings which have correspondingly different values. Positive science is one thing, but hypothetical science is another thing, and philosophical science is still another; yet on the popular tongue, nay, even in the writings of those who pretend to extreme precision, these distinctions are often forgotten, to the utter confusion of ideas.

By positive science I mean the observation and classification of facts and the discovery of those constant sequences in phenomena which can be expressed in mathematical formulæ or in the generalized language of law; I mean that procedure which Huxley had in mind when he said that science is "nothing but trained and organized common sense, differing from the latter only as a veteran may differ from a raw recruit: and its methods differ from those of common sense only so far as the guardsman's cut and thrust differ from the manner in which a savage wields his club." Now for such a procedure no one can feel anything but the highest respect—respect which in the lay mind may well mount to admiration and even to awe. He has but a poor imagination who cannot be stirred to wonder before the triumphs over material forces gained by methods of which he can confess only humble ignorance; and beyond these visible achievements lies a whole region of intellectual activity open to the man of science, but closed and forever foreign to the investigator in other kinds of ideas. I am bound to insist on the fact that I have no foolish desire to belittle the honours of science in its practical applications, and that I can in a way estimate its rewards as an abstract study, however far the full fruition of the scientific life may lie beyond my reach.

Positive science, thus defined as that trained observation which brings the vision of order out of disorder, system out of chaos, law out of chance, might seem splendid enough in theory and useful enough in practice to satisfy the most exorbitant ambition. But it must be remembered that a law of science, however wide its scope, does not go beyond a statement of the relation of observed facts and tells us not a word of what lies behind this relationship or of the cause of these facts. Now the mind of man is so constituted that this ignorance of causes is to it a constant source of irritation; we are almost resistlessly tempted to pass beyond the mere statement of law to erecting a theory of the reality that underlies the law. Such a theory is an hypothesis, and such activity of the mind is hypothetical science as distinguished from positive science. But we must distinguish further. The word hypothesis is used, by the man of science as well as by the layman, in two quite different senses. On the one hand, it may mean the attempt to express in language borrowed from our sensuous experience the nature of a cause or reality which transcends such experience. Thus the luminiferous ether is properly an hypothesis: by its very definition it transcends the reach of our perceptive faculties; we cannot see it, or feel it in any way; yet it is, or was, assumed to exist as the cause of known phenomena and its properties were given in terms of density, elasticity, etc., which are appropriate to material things which we can see and feel. On the other hand, the word hypothesis is often taken to signify merely a scientific law which belongs to the realm of positive science, but which is still to be established. Confusion would be avoided if we employed the term scientific conjecture for this second, and proper, procedure, and confined the use of the term hypothesis to the former, and as I think improper, procedure. To make clear these distinctions let me give an illustration or two. The formula of gravitation merely states the regularity of a certain group of known phenomena from the motion of a falling apple to the motion of the planets about the sun. When this formula first dawned on the mind of Newton, it was a scientific conjecture; when it was tested and proved to conform to facts, it became an accepted scientific law. Both conjecture and accepted law are strictly within the field of positive science. But if Newton, not content with generalizing the phenomena of gravitation in the form of a law, had undertaken to theorize on the absolute nature of the attraction which caused the phenomena of gravitation,[1] he would have passed from the sphere of positive science to that of hypothetical science. So when Darwin, by systematizing the vast body of observations in biology and geology, showed that plants and animals develop in time and with the changes of the earth from the simplest forms of animate existence to the most complex forms now seen, and thus gave precision to the law of evolution, he was working in the field of positive science: he changed what had been a conjectured law to a generally accepted law. But

[1] On this point compare Berkeley, *Siris*, §§ 245-250.

when he went a step further and undertook to explain the cause of this evolution by the theory of natural selection or the survival of the fit, he passed from positive to hypothetical science.

In my essay on Newman I found it convenient to classify the minds of men figuratively in an inner and an outer group. In the outer group I placed the two extremes of the mystic and the sceptic, and in the inner group the non-mystical religious mind and the non-sceptical scientific mind. These two classes of the inner group differ in their field of interest, the one being concerned with the observation of spiritual states, the other with the observation of material phenomena; but they agree in so far as the former passes from the facts of his spiritual consciousness to the belief in certain causes conceived as mythological beings and known by revelation, while the latter passes from the facts of his material observations to the belief in certain causes conceived as hypotheses and known by inference. Hypotheses, in other words, are merely the mythology, the *deus ex machina,* of science, and they are eradicated from the scientific mind only by the severest discipline of scepticism, just as mythology is eradicated from the religious mind by genuine mysticism. I am aware of the danger of inculcating such an eradication. As for most men to take away the belief in their gods as known realities would be to put an end to their religion, so, it may be objected, to take away these hypotheses would be to endanger the very foundations of science. Yet, even if scientific hypotheses, in consideration of human frailty, may have their use just as mythologies have their use, I still protest that they are not necessary to scientific discovery, as is proved by the great example of Newton. I believe, though my temerity may only be equalled by my ignorance, that they have oftener introduced confusion into pure science than they have aided in the discovery of new laws or in the broadening of known laws; and I am confirmed in this belief by the present state of biology. Darwin's law of evolution has remained virtually unshaken and has, I suppose, been the instigation of innumerable discoveries; but, so far as I may judge from my limited reading in the subject, Darwin's hypothesis of natural selection and the survival of the fit has on the one hand been seriously and widely questioned as a cause sufficient to account for evolution, and on the other hand has led to speculation to find a substitute for it which in wildness of theorizing and in audacity of credulousness can only be likened to the intricacies of religious scholasticism.

The condemnation of hypothetical science as dangerous to integrity of mind is no new thing. Even in the seventeenth century Joseph Glanvill saw how surely the enthusiasm engendered by the foundation of the Royal Society would lead to vain hypotheses. In his *Scepsis Scientifica* he sets forth their nature and forestalls Hume's destructive analysis of our notion of causality, with strong warning that the man of science should not "build the *Castle* of his intellectual security, *in the Air of Opinions.* . . Opinions [he adds, meaning hypotheses] are the Rattles of immature intellects. . . *Dogmatizing* is the great disturber both of our *selves* and the *world* without us." In the next age Bolingbroke, in his *Essays Addressed to Mr. Pope,* argued the question of the limits of human knowledge and the fallacies of hypothetical theorizing with a clearness and penetration which would have made that work one of the bulwarks of English philosophy, were it not for my Lord's disdain of the rules of composition and the tediousness of his endless repetitions, and were it not above all for his own inconsistency in urging the most colossal of all hypotheses, that of universal optimism. In particular he takes up, more than once, the common plea that hypothese are useful, whether true or not.

It will be urged, perhaps, as decisive in favor of hypotheses [he observes], that they may be of service, and can be of no disservice to us, in our pursuit of knowledge. An hypothesis founded on mere arbitrary assumptions will be a true hypothesis, and therefore of service to philosophy, if it is confirmed by many observations afterwards, and if no one phænomenon stand in opposition to it. An hypothesis that appears inconsistent with the phænomena will be soon demonstrated false, and as soon rejected.

In reply he shows by example how hypotheses have kept men from the right path of investigation and how they have been maintained (what rich and even ridiculous examples he might have produced from our age) after they have been proved inconsistent with facts and common sense. "The fautors of hypotheses would have us believe that even the detection of their falsehood gives occasion to our improvement in knowledge. But the road to truth does not lie through the precincts of error." Now, it is true that neither Glanvill nor Bolingbroke distinguished between the legitimate use of scientific conjecture and the illegitimate use of hypotheses, but they had chiefly in mind, I think, not the mere formulation of law but the attempt to penetrate into ultimate causes.

The chief fault of hypotheses, however, lies not in the entanglement of pure science among perilous ways and in the lifting up of the scientific imagination to idolatrous worship, as it were, of the *chimæra bombinans in vacuo,* but in the almost irresistible tendency of the human mind to glide from hypothetical science into what I have called philosophical science, meaning thereby the endeavour to formulate a philosophy of life out of scientific law and hypothesis. An hypothesis may be proclaimed by the man of science as a purely subjective formula for a group of phenomena, and as a confessedly temporary expedient for advancing a little further in the process of bringing our observations under the regularity of law; the man of science may pretend verbally to a purely sceptical attitude towards his transcendental definitions, but in practice this scepticism almost invariably gives way to a feeling that the formula for causes is as real objectively as the law of phenomena which it undertakes to explain, and to a kind of supercilious intolerance for those who maintain the sceptical attitude practically as well as verbally, or for those who build their faith on hypotheses of another sort than his own. Hence the hostility that has constantly existed between those who base their philosophy of life on intuition and the humanities and those who base it upon scientific law and hypothesis. At the very beginning of the modern scientific movement this antagonism made itself felt, and, as religion had then the stronger position in society, took the form of apologetics on the part of science. In what may be called the authorized *History of the Royal Society,* Bishop Sprat undertook to allay the suspicions that had immediately arisen against the chartered organization of experimental science. With specious sophistry he argued that the "new philosophy" would never encroach on the established system of education in the humanities. He admitted the natural alliance between science and industry against the feudal form of government, but asserted that science in this was only a handmaid of the times.

Nor ought our *Gentry* [he declares] to be averse from the promoting of *Trade,* out of any little Jealousy, that thereby they shall debase themselves, and corrupt their Blood: For they are to know, that *Trafic* and *Commerce* have given Mankind a higher Degree than any Title of *Nobility,* even that of *Civility* and *Humanity* itself. And at this time especially above all others, they have no reason to despise *Trade* as below them, when it has so great an influence on the very *Government* of the World. In former Ages indeed this was not so remarkable.

Primarily, however, Sprat, as a prelate in good standing, contended that religion stood in no danger from the deductions of the new philosophy:

I do here, in the beginning, most sincerely declare, that if this Design [of the Royal Society] should in the least diminish the *Reverence,* that is due to the *Doctrine of Jesus Christ,* it were so far from deserving *Protection,* that it ought to be abhorr'd by all the *Politic* and *Prudent;* as well as by the devout Part of Christendom. . . With these Apprehensions I come to examine the *Objections,* which I am now to satisfy: and having calmly compar'd the Arguments of some devout Men against *Knowledge,* and chiefly that of *Experiments;* I must pronounce them both, to be altogether inoffensive. I did before affirm, that the *Royal Society* is abundantly cautious, not to intermeddle in *Spiritual Things.* . . So true is that Saying of my Lord Bacon, *That by a little Knowledge of Nature Men become Atheists; but a great deal returns them back again to a sound and religious Mind.* In brief, if we rightly apprehend the Matter, it will be found that it is not only Sottishness, but Prophaness, for Men to cry out against the understanding of *Nature;* for that being nothing else but the Instrument of God, whereby he gives Being and Action to *Things:* the *Knowledge* of it deserves so little to be esteem'd impious, that it ought rather to be reckon'd as *Divine.*

It may seem a little illogical in the good Bishop first to apologize for science as having no finger in *Spiritual Things* and then to exalt it as a bulwark against atheism, but such an inconsistency is very human, and it is an example of the almost irresistible tendency of the mind to use its own specific form of knowledge as a criterion of all knowledge. The vacillation between apology and presumption introduced by the historian of the Royal Society has persisted to this day, and in essay after essay of Huxley's you will find the modern president of the Society maintaining on one page the self-limitations of positive science and on another page passing from hypothesis to a dogmatic philosophy, here rebuking those who confound the domains of scientific and spiritual law and there proclaiming science as a support of what he deems true religion. Much that he wrote was directed to temporary questions, and to open his volumes may seem even now to breathe the dust of battles fought long ago and rendered meaningless by the advance of time; but in reality, though their outer form may change, the disputes in which he engaged have not yet been settled as he so fondly believed they were, and can never be settled unless a sullen apathy be taken for assent.

Certainly Huxley, looking back from his quiet retirement at Eastbourne over his long and belligerent career, might be justified in thinking that victory was altogether the reward of his laborious life. He had had no other regular instruction than what he received for a couple of years in the semi-public school at Ealing of which his father was assistant master, and what he gained from lectures in Sydenham College, London, and at Charing Cross Hospital. In 1846, at the age of twenty-one, he was appointed surgeon to H.M.S. *Rattlesnake* which was bound for a long surveying cruise in the Torres Straits. After four years in the Far East he returned to England, with a large experience in zoölogical and ethnological work, and with no immediate prospects of advancement. His first experience in London was embittered by governmental delays and neglect, but in 1851 he was elected a Fellow of the Royal Society, receiving the Gold Medal the next year, and in 1854 he was appointed professor of natural history at the School of Mines. After that honours and offers came to him in rapid succession. He could not be tempted to leave London, where he felt himself at the centre of things, but in 1872 he accepted the position of Lord Rector of Aberdeen University, since this office afforded him an opportunity for exerting an influence on national education without giving up his residence in the capital. In 1883 he was chosen president of the Royal Society, and in 1892, in lieu of a title which he would not accept, he was raised to the Privy Council. It is not insignificant of his position in England that, on the occasion of kissing hands with the other Councillors at Osborne, when he snatched an opportunity for obtaining a close view of the Queen, he found Her Majesty's eyes fixed upon himself with the same inquisitiveness.

But the most sensible triumphs were no doubt those that came to him in public as the recognized spokesman of the new philosophy, and of these, two of a personal sort, gained at Oxford, the very citadel of the forces leagued against him, must have been peculiarly sweet. Every one knows of his famous tilt with Wilberforce at the meeting of the British Association at Oxford in 1860. It was just after the publication of *The Origin of Species,* and the Bishop of Oxford thought it a proper occasion to demolish the rising heresy with argument and ridicule. The lecture-room was crowded, the clergy being massed in the centre of the audience, and the very windows being packed with ladies who encouraged the champion of religion with their fluttering handkerchiefs. The Bishop spoke for an hour, assuring his hearers that there was nothing in the idea of evolution, and then, turning "with a smiling insolence" to Huxley who was sitting on the platform, "begged to know, was it through his grandfather or his grandmother that he claimed his descent from a monkey." At this Huxley is said to have struck his hand upon his knee, and to have exclaimed to his neighbour, "The Lord hath delivered him into mine hands." Then, as the event was described in *Macmillan's Magazine,* he "slowly and deliberately arose. A slight, tall figure, stern and pale, very quiet and very grave, he stood before us and spoke those tremendous words—words which no one seems sure of now, nor, I think, could remember just after they were spoken, for their meaning took away our breath, though it left us in no doubt as to what it was." According to Huxley's son and biographer the most accurate report of the concluding words is in a letter of John Richard Green:

I asserted—and I repeat—that a man has no reason to be ashamed of having an ape for his grandfather. If there were an ancestor whom I should feel shame in recalling it would rather be a *man*—a man of restless and versatile intellect—who, not content with an equivocal success in his own sphere of activity, plunges into scientific questions with which he has no real acquaintance, only to obscure them by an aimless rhetoric, and distract the attention of his hearers from the real point at issue by eloquent digressions and skilled appeals to religious prejudice.

Again, at another meeting of the British Association at Oxford, in 1894, Huxley appeared as a champion of Darwinism against the insinuations of Lord Salisbury, who, in his speech as president, spoke with delicate irony "of the 'comforting word, evolution,' and, passing to the Weismannian controversy, implied that the diametrically opposed views so frequently expressed nowadays threw the whole process of evolution into doubt." [1] But things were not what they had been. The ready and vociferous applause was for the prophet of Darwinism, and Huxley, instead of repelling sarcasm with invective, now conscious of his triumphant position and of the courtesy due to one who as Prime Minister had only two years before honoured him with the Privy Councillorship, was compelled to veil "an unmistakable and vigorous protest in the most gracious and dignified speech of thanks." It was his last public appearance on any important occasion, a proper and almost majestic conclusion to his long warfare. He died on June 29 of the following year, having just completed his threescore and ten. By his direction three lines from a poem by his wife were inscribed on his tomb-stone:

> Be not afraid, ye waiting hearts that weep;
> For still He giveth His belovèd sleep,
> And if an endless sleep He wills, so best.

Better, if he could have known them, would have been the words spoken only the other day by the Vice-Chancellor of Cambridge at the great dinner given at the university on the occasion of Darwin's centenary:

I claim as a theologian—and I see representatives of law, music, and letters, and many other sciences and arts present—that only one spirit animates us all, and I should beg that we might be included in the term "naturalists."

Now to Huxley more than to any other one man in England is due this victory, seeming to some so complete and final; he more than any other one man

---

[1] Professor H. F. Osborn in *Transactions of the N. Y. Acad. Sci.*, vol. xv.

stood in the nineteenth century for the triple power of positive and hypothetical science and of philosophical science in the form of naturalism. Of his work in positive science I am incompetent to speak, but I can at least say that it was important enough to give him honourable standing among investigators and to clothe his popular utterances with authority. His great opportunity came with the publication of *The Origin of Species* when he was thirty-four years old, and for the remaining thirty-six years of his life he was the valiant and aggressive champion of evolution and the Darwinian hypothesis against all comers, whether they were mighty men of the Church or of Parliament. He was, so to speak, the Plato to the Socrates of the new philosophy, applying its premises to every department of life. His power in this field was conditioned by his knowledge of science and of philosophy, but it depended also on his consummate skill in the use of language. To read his essays, which deal so magnificently with old disputes and forgotten animosities, is to feel—at least a literary man may be pardoned for so feeling—that here is one of the cunning artificers lost to letters, an essayist who, if he had devoted his faculties to the more permanent aspect of truth, might have taken a place among the great masters of literature. Certainly in sarcasm and irony he had no superior, unless it was Matthew Arnold, whom, indeed, he in many superfical respects resembles. He had, no doubt, easy material in the bishops, and the epithet *episcopophagous,* which he pleasantly coined for himself, tells the story of that contest in a word. Better material yet was afforded by Gladstone when, rushing in where bishops feared to tread, he undertook to uphold the cosmogony of Genesis as scientifically correct. Whatever one's attitude towards philosophical science may be, one can acknowledge a feeling of unreserved glee in seeing that flabby, pretentious intellect pricked and slashed in such masterly fashion. Satire like the following is never old:

In particular, the remarkable disquisition which covers pages 11 to 14 of Mr. Gladstone's last contribution [to the *Nineteenth Century*, January, 1886] has greatly exercised my mind. Socrates is reported to have said of the works of Heracleitus that he who attempted to comprehend them should be a "Delian swimmer," but that, for his part, what he could understand was so good that he was disposed to believe in the excellence of that which he found unintelligible. In endeavouring to make myself master of Mr. Gladstone's meaning in these pages, I have often been overcome by a feeling analogous to that of Socrates, but not quite the same. That which I do understand has appeared to me so very much the reverse of good, that I have sometimes permitted myself to doubt the value of that which I do not understand.

That is the true joy of battle, that keeps the wrangling of ancient days forever young:

> Full of the god that urged their burning breast,
> The heroes thus their mutual warmth express'd.

In the case of Huxley himself there is no question of what we understand and what we do not understand. All in his writing is that of peculiarly lucid quality which is an argument in itself, for we are prone to accept the canon that what is clear must be true. Yet there is a distinction. Though, so far as regards the end immediately in view, Huxley is always a master of logical precision, one discovers, in reading him largely, that his ends are not always the same, and that in the total effect of his works there lies concealed an insoluble ambiguity. So it is that, though in one sense his strongest intellectual trait was, as his son

says, "an uncompromising passion for truth," yet in
the sum of his thinking he was one of the master
sophists of the age. And the tracks of his sophistry
lead straight to that confusion of positive science and
hypothetical science and philosophical science which
is, perhaps, the most characteristic mark of the last
century.

Agnosticism, according to Huxley's own definition
of the word which he invented to sum up his intellectual procedure, is neither scepticism nor dogmatism;
it "is not properly described as a 'negative' creed, nor
indeed as a creed of any kind, except in so far as it
expresses absolute faith in the validity of a principle,
which is as much ethical as intellectual, . . . that it
is wrong for a man to say that he is certain of the
objective truth of any proposition unless he can produce evidence which logically justifies that certainty."
Agnosticism, then, is merely the honest adherence to
evidence. Now no state of mind could be more exem-
plary than that of the agnostic when so defined. It
has only one weakness, that, if we could accept their
own opinion, it includes all men, and so *defines* nothing. Huxley, indeed, contrasts the procedure of the
agnostic with theology, and declares that "agnosticism
can be said to be a stage in its evolution, only as death
may be said to be the final stage in the evolution of
life." Really, the whole argument, for one so keen as
Huxley, is rather naïve. Does he suppose that Cardinal Newman, for instance, would admit that his
theological hypothesis was any less supported by evidence than the evolutionary hypothesis? As a matter
of fact Newman might retort that he had with him
the evidence of ages, whereas Huxley was depending
at bottom on the evidence of only a few decades of
time. The difference between them does not lie in
their loyalty or disloyalty to evidence *per se,* but in

the kind of evidence from which they start; nor has Huxley, so far as I know, ever shown, or even seriously tried to show, that the inner evidence which gives us the sense of moral liberty and responsibility, of sin and holiness, is less logically trustworthy than the evidence of the eye and the ear.

That is the weakness of agnosticism as defined by its inventor, but it has a compensating advantage. As actually used by him it is at once a sword of offence and a buckler of safety; permitting the most truculent dogmatism when the errors of an enemy are to be exposed and the most elusive scepticism when the enemy charges in return. Indeed, an agnostic might briefly and not unfairly be defined as a dogmatist in attack and a sceptic in defence, which is but another way of calling him a sophist. With what dexterity Huxley wielded this double weapon may be seen in his use of the great question of scientific law. More than once (*e.g., Science and Christian Tradition*, p. 134), when certain deductions from the rigid application of law are brought home to him, he takes refuge in a sceptical limitation of law to the mere formulation of objective experience in a world which is ultimately moved by forces beyond the reach of man's perceptive faculties. And against the preacher who rashly invades the scientific field he can declare that "the habitual use of the word 'law,' in the sense of an active thing, is almost a mark of pseudo-science; it characterizes the writings of those who have appropriated the forms of science without knowing anything of its substance." Yet in the same essay, when he opens the attack upon those who would retreat into a region beyond scientific law, he avows boldly "the fundamental axiom of scientific thought," "that there is not, never has been, and never will be, any disorder in nature. The admission of the occurrence of any event which was

not the logical consequence of the immediately antecedent events, according to these definite, ascertained,
or unascertained rules which we call the 'laws of nature,' would be an act of self-destruction on the part
of science." And elsewhere: "We ignore, even as a
possibility, the notion of any interference with the
order of Nature." Now when we consider that to
regard the act of the will which originates the motion
of raising the arm as a force in any way contrary to
the law of gravitation, is in Huxley's mind an un-
scientific absurdity (*Pseudo-Scientific Realism, passim*), that, in other words, life and the world are to
him a pure mechanism, and when we consider further
that he identifies the claims of science with the desire
of truth (*Universities: Actual and Ideal, passim*), it
really should not have seemed to him so grave an
error to use the word law for that force which pro-
duces the absolute uniformity defined by law. It is
Huxley himself in these moments of attack who virtually, if not literally, takes law "in the sense of an active thing," which in his moments of defence he so
vigorously repudiates.

Inevitably this ambiguity of attitude becomes even
more perplexed when he applies the notion of scientific law to the deeper problems of life. In one place,
for instance, he asserts that "there lies in the nature of
things a reason for every moral law, as cogent and as
well defined as that which underlies every physical
law." But in another place he takes what, from his
principles, must be regarded as the opposite point of
view: "The notion that the doctrine of evolution can
furnish a foundation for morals seems to me to be an
illusion"; and again he states roundly that "cosmic
nature is no school of virtue, but the headquarters of
the enemy of ethical nature." This ambiguity of his
position involves not only morals but the fundamental

question of spirituality and materialism. In his freer moments of attack he does not hesitate to fling out the most relentless dogmas of materialism. The actuality of the spiritual world, he declares in one of his prefaces, lies entirely within the province of science— that is to say, is amenable to the undeviating operation of mechanical law; "the materials of consciousness are products of cerebral activity," and are "the result of molecular forces"; "we are," by an extension of the Cartesian theory of the lower animals, "conscious automata, . . . parts of the great series of causes and effects which, in unbroken continuity, composes that which is, and has been, and shall be—the sum of existence." That should seem to be the most explicit materialism and necessitarianism; yet hear the same man on the other side! "For my part, I utterly repudiate and anathematize the intruder [this same necessitarianism]. Fact I know; and Law I know; but what is Necessity, save an empty shadow of my own mind's throwing?" In other words, when your enemy talks loosely of miracles and spiritual experiences and supernatural freedom, it is easy to crush him with this bludgeon of an unbroken law of mechanical cause and effect; but when your enemy turns on you and begins to draw disagreeable conclusions from this fatal sequence, it is the part of the skilful fencer to denounce as an empty shadow any connection between such a law and necessity! Further than that, Huxley when hard pressed, instead of abiding manfully by his premises, was ready to sink into that last sophistry of the scientific mind and deny that there is any distinction between the materialistic and the spiritualistic conception of life. "In itself," he says, "it is of little moment whether we express the phænomena of matter in terms of spirit; or the phænomena of spirit in terms of matter." This view he but-

tresses (*Science and Morals*) by calmly assuming that
St. Augustine and Calvin were at one with him in
holding to a fatal determination. Is it necessary to
say that St. Augustine and Calvin—whether rightly or
wrongly is here not the question—believed in a spiritual power apart from and undetermined by natural
law? This power might have its own determinism,
but, relatively to natural law, it was spontaneous and
incalculable. The difference to philosophy and conduct between holding a spiritual first cause and holding a mechanical determinism marks the distance
between religion and science—or, at least, between the
positions of the English bishops and of Huxley. If
there is no distinction here, why then all the pother,
and what meaning is there in Huxley's cheerful assumption that science was to be the end of the
Church and that men of science were to supplant the
bishops?

Now these inconsistencies in Huxley are not the result of a progressive change in his views, nor are they
infrequent or superficial. They lie at the very foundation of the system of which he was the most distinguished spokesman, and they are more conspicuous
in him than in others merely because at any given
moment his style is so eminently transparent. They
spring, indeed, from a false extension of the procedure
of science into a philosophy of naturalism. The fact
is simply this: When the matter is squarely faced
there can be no science, properly speaking, except in
so far as the world appears to us a strictly closed mechanical system, a "block-universe" as William James
called it, which contains its end in its beginning and
displays the whole in every part. As it has been pic-
turesquely expressed: "Were a single dust-atom destroyed, the universe would collapse." Absolute regularity is the *sine qua non* of scientific law, and the

moment any element of incalculable spontaneity is admitted into the system, that moment the possibility of scientific law is so far excluded: there is no law of the individual or the unpredictable; there is no science of the soul unless man, as Taine says, is no more than "a very simple mechanism which analysis can take to pieces like clockwork." This does not mean that any given law is final and embraces the whole content of phenomena; but it does mean that further knowledge, while it may modify a law or supplant one law by another, still leaves us within the realm of absolute mechanical regularity. Such a closed system is properly called nature; it was clearly conceived and given to philosophy by the great naturalists of the seventeenth century.

Nature, thus conceived as a block-system, is the proper field of positive science, and leads to no embarrassment so long as we do not attempt anything more than the classification of physical phenomena under laws. But there is a tendency in the human mind which draws it almost irresistibly to pass from the formulation of laws to the definition of the force or cause underlying them. This is hypothetical science. Such a procedure already involves a certain violence to scientific evidence, but it does not stop here. Suppose there exists a body of testimony, accumulated through thousands of years, to the effect that a whole world of our inner life lies outside of that block-universe of mechanical determinism: what then is the man of hypothetical science to do? He may deny the validity of any evidence apart from that which leads to scientific law, and having erected this law of mechanical regularity into an active cause governing and controlling the world, he may set it in opposition to the hypothesis of a personal God which Christians have created from the evidence of their inner experience. He may be onesided, but he will be consistent. In this sense, and with a consequence different from what he intended, Frederic Harrison was justified in saying that "agnosticism as a religious philosophy *per se* rests on an almost total ignoring of history and social evolution." But suppose further that our scholar, having naturally broad interests and sympathies, is still importuned by all that evidence in the moral and political spheres which he could not bring into conformity with his hypothesis: what will he do? In attempting to cling to an hypothesis which is based on the exclusion of half the evidence of life while at the same time he feels the appeal of the whole range of evidence, he will try to develop that hypothesis into a complete philosophy of life, and in doing so he will necessarily fall into just those inconsistencies which strike us over and over again in Huxley. He will become a victim of that huge self-contradiction which I have called philosophical science.

Now we all know how completely this sophism took possession of England and the world about the middle of the last century. In particular the magnitude of Darwin's work in the field of positive science and the superb simplicity of his explanation of the whole order of existence, including man, as the product of a mechanical law of selection, easily imposed the evolutionary hypothesis as a lawgiver upon education and morals and religion and government. And to the authority of Darwin was added the persuasiveness of Huxley's masterly skill as lecturer and writer. It seemed to the men who heard his voice as if the long obscurity that had involved human destiny was to be rolled away, as if at last the pathway of truth had been found, and the world's great age was about to be renewed. And however we may now see the inconsistencies and feel what in another man might be called the duplicity that underlay Huxley's method of attack and defence, there was enough of the stuff of positive science in his doctrine to give it a certain moral stiffness and intellectual rigour which must always claim our admiration. But with the passage of years a change has come upon philosophical science. The human mind could not long rest content with a system which was so glaringly at war with itself, and indeed there are signs that Huxley himself was not always satisfied with his position. But where lay the way of escape? These men would not willingly give up the authority which seemed to be derived from the actualities of positive science, yet they began to see that the hypothesis of a block-universe had brought them to an absolute *impasse*. The history of the intellect since the days of Darwin's supremacy, therefore, has been marked by an attempt to preserve the facts of evolution as the basis of a scientific philosophy, but to alter the evolutionary hypothesis so as to bring it into harmony with the spontaneous part of human nature. The process has widened the distance between positive science and philosophical science; it has introduced a new set of inconsistencies, not to say absurdities, into thought, but it is extremely interesting for the way in which it has finally brought together two currents of the nineteenth century that might have seemed to a superficial observer the very opposites of each other. What appeared in Huxley's time, and still more in the half-century preceding him, to be the very bulwark against those laxer principles and tendencies which may be grouped together as romantic, has gradually thrown off its hard rationalism, until now in our day philosophical science and romanticism are actually merging together and becoming almost indistinguishable. In place of Hux-

ley we have William James and Bergson. The change
is significant and worthy of analysis, for the true
meaning of a movement is known by its end. So
much we may learn from Pragmatism, even while
criticizing it.

Nor is it difficult, if we regard the material and
moral forces from which science and romanticism
respectively take their start, to see how these two
apparent enemies have come to join hands in a truce
if not in an alliance. We do not often stop to reflect
on the world of pain and horror which underlies this
surface of things on which we move so comfortably.
Only now and then some accident, some physical
rebellion as it might be called, sets loose the pent-up
dæmonic powers, and for a moment life is as it
would be if in a mad-house the phrensied patients
were to break their fetters and overcome their keepers. Each force of nature in itself seems to be
limitless in its potential activity, and in so far as it
is unchecked or unbalanced by some other force becomes the source of ruin to mankind. Manifestly
that orderly subordination which is the condition of
our physical well-being depends on some principle
of control and balance which is not inherent in the
individual forces of nature. Furthermore, if our horror at these calamities, if the physical repugnance
that lies always concealed in our breast, has any
meaning, it is in the testimony they bear to a certain
correspondence on the one hand between our sense
of moral evil and the destructive limitlessness of any
natural force in itself, and on the other hand between our sense of moral justice and the imposition
of order and subordination upon those forces. We
are thrust by our emotions into an absolute dualism.
Now the point to consider is that pure science deals
with these forces in themselves and as unlimited, and

without any thought of such human distinctions. A little spark kindles a fire, and instantly the flames sweep over a city, consuming life and property and spreading everywhere destruction and terror. Yet with this terror science has nothing to do; it is concerned with the laws of heat. Again some movement takes place within the earth; the crust on which we walk is rent and shaken, and the helpless human creatures are killed and mutilated as ruthlessly as the ants in their little mound over which we inadvertently stumble. Yet with this hideous fear science has nothing to do; it is concerned with the laws of motion. Nor is the human body itself free from these incursions of uncontrolled energy. One very close to us, one whose fragile beauty has filled us with a long apprehension of love, is seized by a loathsome disease; those lower forms of life which to our vanity we seem to have trampled down in our progress have suddenly risen up like avenging furies and laid their obscene grip on what was dearest and fairest to us. We look on in an agony of suspense, as if in this precious body the very armies of good and evil were at war. Yet all the while the physician watches with impassive, critical eye, studying symptoms, applying remedies, awaiting calmly the results: his very efficacy as a man of science depends on his freedom from those emotions which are tearing at our heartstrings; he is concerned with the laws of parasitic life.

Science is properly the servant of our emotions and of the corresponding sense of dualism, but in its method of work it not only ignores our emotions, but can perform its true service only so long as it ignores them and deals with the pure forces of nature. The error and danger arise when it disdains to be a servant and sets itself up as mistress, raising its means into an end and its procedure into a philosophy.

Moved by our importunate consciousness of order and disorder, yet bound in its hypothetical explanation of evolution to consider the forces of nature alone, without the admission of any law of control outside of them, it has come gradually to a conception of the world as an entity containing within itself some force of vitalism, some *élan vital*, which by its inherent limitlessness is the source of constant creation, making the sum of things actually greater to-day than it was yesterday and, from our human point of view, more orderly. Sheer expansiveness becomes the law of physical life. The acceptance of this hypothesis of an incalculable energy, whose action to-day can in no wise, or only imperfectly, be predicted from its action yesterday, might seem to evict the very possibility of scientific law; but there are two things to consider. In the first place this hypothesis is just an hypothesis and has little or no relation to the actual work of positive science. And in the second place it seduces the scientific mind by seeming to get rid altogether of that dualism which is ignored in scientific procedure. As a matter of fact it merely changes the character of that dualism by setting the two terms apart at the beginning and end of time instead of regarding them as existent together and independent of time.[1]

From this rather slippery hypothesis of a universe in the process of continual self-expansion it is but a step to the modern scientific philosophy of human progress as depending, not on any ideal outside

[1] The middle term between the hypothesis of a purely mechanical evolution and the hypothesis of evolution as conceived by Bergson may be found in the evolutionary monism of Haeckel, which has been beautifully analyzed and demolished by M. Émile Boutroux in his recent work, *La Science et la Religion dans la philosophie contemporaine*.

of evolution, but as—what shall I say?—as self-causative. Here precisely enters the point of connection between philosophical science and romanticism;[1] but to understand its full meaning we must look back into the sources of the second member of the alliance.

Now, in attempting to characterize the historic romanticism of the nineteenth century, the first trait that is forced upon our attention is the note of rebellion from the classics. That hostility between romanticism and classicism is fundamental: we cannot escape it. Greek philosophy, as it touches upon human conduct and as it was handed down to the modern world, was summed up in the *Nicomachean Ethics,* at the very heart of which lies the classical distinction between the infinite, as the absolute, and the limitless. According to Aristotle the active nature of man is made up of desires, or impulses ($\dot{\epsilon}\pi\iota\theta\upsilon\mu\dot{\iota}\alpha\iota$), which in themselves are incapable of self-restraint and therefore limitless ($\ddot{\alpha}\pi\epsilon\iota\rho\sigma\varsigma$ $\gamma\grave{\alpha}\rho$ $\dot{\eta}$ $\tau\hat{\eta}\varsigma$ $\dot{\epsilon}\pi\iota\theta\upsilon\mu\dot{\iota}\alpha\varsigma$ $\phi\dot{\upsilon}\sigma\iota\varsigma$, *Pol.,* 11,7; the translation of $\ddot{\alpha}\pi\epsilon\iota\rho\sigma\varsigma$ in Greek generally as "infinite" instead of "limitless" has been the source of endless confusion of ideas). Furthermore this limitlessness is of the very essence of evil, whereas good in itself may be defined as a limit ($\tau\grave{\sigma}$ $\gamma\grave{\alpha}\rho$ $\kappa\alpha\kappa\grave{\sigma}\nu$ $\tau\sigma\hat{\upsilon}$ $\dot{\alpha}\pi\epsilon\dot{\iota}\rho\sigma\upsilon$ $\tau\grave{\sigma}$ δ' $\dot{\alpha}\gamma\alpha\theta\grave{\sigma}\nu$ $\tau\sigma\hat{\upsilon}$

---

[1] This union was clearly foreshadowed in Diderot; it was developed by Comte; but its great authority could not come until after the work of Darwin. In one of his essays Huxley speaks with scorn of Mr. Frederic Harrison's Positivism, and asks: "What has Comtism to do with the 'New Philosophy' [*i.e.,* the philosophy of science]?" Mr. Harrison might easily have retorted. In fact when Huxley boasted that the bishops were to be replaced by the "new school of the prophets [*i.e.,* men of science]" as "the only one that can work miracles," and when he acknowledged that "the interests of science and industry are identical," he was merely repeating Comte's early theory of the supplanting of the priest and the soldier by the man of science and the man of business.

πεπερασμένου), and the aim of conduct is to acquire that golden mean which is nothing other than a certain bound set to the inherent limitlessness of our impulsive or desiring nature. The determination of this bound in each case is the function of reason, which embraces the whole existence of man as an organism in his environment and says to each impulse as it arises, thus far shalt thou go and no further. But as the material of practical life is the limitless sway of unrelated impulses, reason, to establish its balance and measure, to find, that is, its norm of unity, must look ultimately to some point quite outside of the realm of impulse and nature. Hence the imposition of the theoretical life, as Aristotle calls it, upon the practical—the contemplation of that absolute unity which is unmoved amid all that moves. This unity not of nature is the infinite; it is the very opposite of that limitlessness which is the attribute of nature itself; it is not a state of endless, indefinite expansion, but is on the contrary that state of centralization which has its goal in itself (παρ' αὑτὴν οὐδενὸς ἐφίεσθαι τέλους).

The revolt from this essential dualism of classical philosophy began in the seventeenth century. That age was notably a time of confused thinking and of reaching out in many directions. But at its beginning, and always in the background, lay a certain mode of regarding life, the orthodox mode of supernaturalism. On the one side was the great flux of nature, embracing in its endless activity the heart of man and the phenomenal world. "The sea itself," says Bossuet, "has not more waves when it is agitated by the winds than are the diverse thoughts that rise from this abyss without bottom, from this impenetrable mystery of the heart of man." Within this chaos of the human breast sat reason as a kind of king or arbiter, by its command bringing order out of disorder. But reason itself, as understood by the characteristic minds of the age, belonged to nature, and was a sufficient guide only so long as it listened to the voice of a restraining power above and outside of nature. The true division was not between reason and instinct or desire, but between all these together, as forces of nature, and superrational insight. That is to say, the orthodox view of the seventeenth century was the classical dualism which had become involved and obscured in a vast system of Christian mythology and theology. The irremediable fault, default one might say, of the age was that it never attained to a clear and untrammelled definition of the superrational insight upon which its faith was based. Pascal, indeed, approached such a definition when he set the heart over against reason and concupiscence, meaning by heart not so much the desires and emotions, as the contrast with concupiscence plainly shows, but that faculty by which we intuitively apprehend the infinite and eternal. Yet even in Pascal this faculty of intuition was never freed from the bondage of revelation and questionable authority, while in most of his religious contemporaries it was inextricably confused with some external voice of the Bible or the Church. Not many men to-day have the patience to read far in the endless theological literature of that age; and with reason. It is the curse of the Reformation that the search for truth was largely diverted by it into a monstrous and deadening discussion over the particular instrument or institution to which the truth was supposed to be once and for all imparted as a sacred deposit. He who is willing and strong to read those mighty books may be fortified in his own soul by feeling that the tremendous earnestness of this war over authority must have implied, beneath all the battle of words, an equal earnestness over the truth for which the debated authority was supposed to stand. But the actual result of that debate was to weary and bewilder the mind of contemporary men. Gradually the whole question of traditional authority, and with it the higher intuition which had been so obstinately identified with this authority, begins to lose its hold, and in its place comes the new reign of naturalism.

Now nauralism is precisely the denial of any revealed authority or supernatural intuition whatsoever. For the government of the fluctuating element of nature it looks to reason alone, which it recognizes as but another, if higher, aspect of the same nature. Hence the dominant philosophy of the eighteenth century was a rationalism, which in religion denied, or at least minimized, all that is mysterious and escapes the net of logic, and in science regarded the world as a vast machine which can be perfectly expressed in a mathematical equation. Literature followed the lead and became rational and pseudo-classic. I would not exaggerate the regularity of this development, for, after all, the human mind remains always essentially the same and varies only as one or another element comes uppermost. And in particular any comment on the pseudo-classic literature (which in itself has many comfortable excellences) should not fail to distinguish the truly Augustan circle of Butler and Johnson and Reynolds and Goldsmith and Burke, whose humanism, like that of Horace, contained, not so much explicitly as in solution, the higher insight which the philosophy of their age was so busily hiding away. They contained, that is to say, some marks of true classicism as contrasted with pseudo-classicism. Nevertheless the main current of the times was evident enough, and on its surface carried religion and science and literature in a compliant brotherhood.

Johnson and his school belonged essentially to the main rationalistic stream of the age, though in some respects they surpassed it. But by their side there was springing up another school, equally a child of naturalism, but hostile to what may be called the official philosophy. Naturalism acknowledged both the reason and the instincts or emotions as belonging to the nature of man, and thus manifestly left the door open to a revolt against the tyranny of one element of nature over the other. Accordingly, almost with the beginning of rationalism we see springing up, timidly and uncertainly at first, various forms of appeal to pure instinct and unrestrained emotion. This voice of insubordination first became clear and defiant and fully self-conscious in Blake; and the message of Blake, repeated in a hundred various notes, now tender and piercingly sweet, now blurred by strange rumblings of thunderous madness, is everywhere a summons to the perfect freedom of instinct and primitive emotion and a denunciation of the control demanded by reason or by authority of any sort:

Those who restrain desire, do so because theirs is weak enough to be restrained; and the restrainer or reason usurps its place and governs the unwilling.

The road of excess leads to the palace of wisdom.

He who desires but acts not, breeds pestilence.

These epigrams are from *The Marriage of Heaven and Hell,* a book which Swinburne was to rank "as about the greatest produced by the eighteenth century in the line of high poetry and *spiritual specula-*

tion," and which to Mr. Arthur Symons was an anticipation of Nietzsche: "No one can think and escape Nietzsche; but Nietzsche has come after Blake, and will pass before Blake passes." Now Swinburne and Mr. Symons were indubitably right in seeing in such passages as these the very bible of romanticism, and Blake's place as an expositor of that movement, for England at least, is coming to be generally admitted. But in holding up Blake's revolt against reason as *spiritual speculation* they, and others, have fallen into the error which, as it seems to me, has made of romanticism the source of endless illusions.

In the field of the imagination the school of Blake at the last carried victory with a high hand over the pseudo-classic and humanistic writers, and the nineteenth century opens upon a world pretty well divided between the quarrelsome twins of rational science and irrational romanticism. In so far as the romantic imagination yields to the self-sufficiency of instinct and emotion it implies a real revolt from rationalism; it is in a way even more hostile to rationalism than the classic use of the imagination, for classicism never involved a rejection of the reason, though it differed from pseudo-classicism by leaving the door open to an intuition above reason. But the peculiar tone of romantic writing comes not so much from the mere revolt against pseudo-classicism as from *the illusion that this revolt is a return to spiritual insight.* Here I am treading on slippery ground, and it behooves me to walk warily. That all the spiritual aspirations of the nineteenth century were of a bastard birth, only a very ignorant or wilful man would assert. Humanity is larger than any formula, and no age can be limited by a label. In the romantic literature that unfolds from Blake there is much that is simply true, much that is beautiful and magnificent, and there are moments that express the divine awe which belongs to the sudden inflooding of the veritable other-world; but in the most characteristic moods of that literature, when it expresses most perfectly the main current of the age, there will be found, I believe, a deep confusion of ideas which results from assimilating the rebellion of the lower element of our nature with the control that comes from above nature. For the infinite spirit which makes itself known as a restraining check and a law of concentration within the flux of nature, this new aspiration of liberty would substitute the mere endless expansion which ensues upon the denial of any restraint whatsoever; in place of the higher intuition which is above reason it would commit mankind to the lower intuition which is beneath reason. This illusion of the senses has dazzled the human mind in other ages as well as in the present. It shows itself here and there in the classics of antiquity. It developed a special form in the Alexandrian union of Oriental religion and Occidental philosophy, and was thus passed on to the Middle Ages. It can be found in the seventeenth century beside the true insight. It assumes many disguises and is often extremely difficult to distinguish from the supreme disillusion. The very fact that the same word, romantic, is used to designate the wonder of the infinite and the wonder of the limitless shows how easily we merge together these extreme opposites. But the historic romanticism of the nineteenth century, when it strikes its central note, whether it be the morbid egotism of a Beckford, or the religious defalcation of a Newman, or the æstheticism of a Pater, or the dregs of naturalistic pantheism seen in a Fiona Macleod, or the impotent revolt from humanitarian sympathy of a Nietzsche—this romanticism is in its essence a denial of classical dualism and an illusory substitution

of the mere limitless expansion of our impulsive
nature for that true infinite within the heart of man,
which is not of nature and whose voice is heard as
the inner check, restraining, centralizing, and forming.

If romanticism is thus rightly defined, its point of
contact with science is easily marked. Those limitless
forces which were raised into the scientific hypothesis
of a self-evolving, or rather self-creating, universe are
the exact counterpart in outer nature of these limitless
desires or impulses in the heart which are the substance of the romantic illusion. They find their union
in that very modern philosophy of life which may be
called indifferently scientific or romantic. As it is
concerned with conduct and the inner life rather than
with material phenomena, it may be regarded as the
offspring of romanticism; as it enjoys its great authority from a supposed connection with the actual discoveries of physical law, and has obtained its precise
character from the evolutionary hypothesis, it may
with equal propriety be regarded as the bastard offspring of science—as, in a word, the latest form of
philosophical science. The keynote of this new philosophy, whether it take one of the many forms of
Pragmatism or express itself in the evolutionary language of M. Bergson or conceal itself in the sardonic
indifference of the man in the street, is a kind of
laisser-faire, a belief that, as the physical world has
unrolled itself by its own expansive forces, so human
society progresses by some universal instinct, needing
no rational and selective guidance, no imposition of
moral restraint, no conscious insight.

And mark well, we are here concerned not with
an idle question of the schools, but with a very real
outcome in conduct. You will find the trace of this
philosophy in every department of life. It has re-

moulded our whole practice of education; and this perhaps is the point where its influence is clearest and where attack may be most successfully directed. Perhaps we do not often stop to consider the relation between the usurpation of purely scientific studies in our college curriculum with the Rousselian notion that education must place no restraint upon the child, but must merely help him to expand in the direction of his emotional instincts; yet in reality that relation is to-day the main factor in shaping our pedagogical theories. Positive science is a noble vocation, but just so sure as it is made in considerable part the basis of education, instead of being treated as a profession, like law or medicine, to be taken up after a general education, just so surely the confusions of philosophical science will follow and claim authority in our schools. The unhampered elective system, which is merely the pedagogical form of the new philosophy of *laisser-faire,* is in a way anything and everything; but one characteristic and one result of it are omnipresent. It is characterized by a revolt from Greek and Latin, due in part no doubt to such subsidiary causes as the pedantry which laid its paralyzing hand on classical instruction, but due more essentially to the hostility between the classical way of viewing life and the new juncture of romantic and scientific philosophy. The result of the modern system is a laxity of mind in those who have drifted through our institutions from kindergarten to university, a repugnance for good reading, in a word, that lack of real education which is more and more deplored by instructors in school and college.

In politics the spirit of *laisser-faire* shows itself in the feeling that to be right we need only follow unhesitatingly the clamour of the day; whereas any suppression of a self-assertive movement in favour of a saner ideal already established is denounced as reaction and death. Take, for instance, our attitude towards socialism. Perhaps no comment is more frequently on the lips of the man in the street—that mysterious arbiter of civilization—than the words: It is bound to come, why strive against it? As a matter of fact socialism, in some very imperfect form, may indeed come, but is by no means bound to come. To say that the whole teaching of history proves its necessity is to forget most of the chapters of that book, and is to fall into the common error of the half-educated who extend their knowledge of one age over all ages. I cannot see much difference between those who accept some form of socialism because by the very definition of Karl Marx it is a "fatal necessity," and those who accepted the old scholastic notion of God, with all its consequences, because by their own definition of God he must exist. The question here, however, is not the goodness or evil of socialism in itself, but the perilous state of any society which for some blind law of evolution surrenders its right to criticize and to determine its own course rationally. "Man," says M. Georges Sorel, the philosopher and for a time one of the leaders of the "syndicalist" branch of socialism in France—"man has genius only in the measure that he does not reflect." And when asked what new form of government should be erected on the ruins of society brought about by the general strike, M. Sorel replied that with such constructive thought for the future we had nothing to do; we had learned from Bergson to trust ourselves implicitly to the blind instinctive forces of nature.

In like manner in regard to female suffrage: we deceive ourselves if we suppose that its admission or rejection will be the result of argument and rational conviction. The power that is bringing it into practical life is the sentiment heard from the mouth of every other man you meet: If the women want it, why, let them have it. And this sentiment finds support in the weary fatalism of the day: It is bound to come whether you like it or not; why resist the irresistible? Again, the question is not whether female suffrage is a good or an evil thing in itself, but the ignoble abdication of judgment in accepting any present tendency as a fatal force which it is useless, if not wrong, to curb.

And so, to pass to quite another field, the *laisserfaire* of philosophical science is beginning to modify our whole treatment of crime. We no longer punish the criminal as a being responsible for his acts, under the belief that there is in man a voluntary power to shape his own character, but when we punish him at all, we do so apologetically, as if society and not he were the guilty party, and as if his crime were merely one of the products of evolution, like any disease to be cured by fresh air and flattery. I have no desire to enter into the intricacies of the new penology. But I have been impressed by two opinions from very diverse sources. I recall reading in one of the books of that connoisseur of the underworld, the late Josiah Flynt, the remark of a professional burglar to the effect that the only prevention against crime was sure and sharp punishment. And I connect with this observation the recent statement of the Police Commissioner of New York, to the effect that the excess of violence and lawlessness in this city is due to the number of suspended sentences and the general feeling among those criminally disposed that the courts will not convict. Mr. Waldo may have had various reasons for offering such an apology for his department, but it is significant to compare certain statistics of New York with those of London where the older habits of swift and relentless judgment still prevail. In our American city the average annual number of murders for the years 1908-10 was one hundred and seventeen, while the average number of convictions was only twenty-five. In London, with its population of seven million, the average for those years was twenty murders, for which fifteen persons either committed suicide before police action or were convicted.[1] Among the causes for this alarming disproportion our evolutionary attitude towards crime is certainly not

[1] The following statistics from a leading article in the London *Nation* of March 30, 1912, entitled *The Breakdown of American Justice,* give a wider range to the question: "Since 1885 there have been some 177,000 murders and homicides in the United States, but under 3000 executions. In 1885 the number of murders was 1808; in 1895 it had risen to 10,500; in 1910 it stood at 8975. In 1885 the number of executions was 108; in 1895 it was 132; in 1910 it was 104. Roughly speaking, Americans are now killing one another at the rate of over 9000 a year. Looking over the statistics of the past seven-and-twenty years, one finds that, while executions have remained virtually stationary, murders and homicides have multiplied five-fold. In 1885 for every murderer executed seventeen murders were committed; in 1895 the proportion was one to seventy-nine; in 1910 it was one to eighty-six. There are, indeed, few crimes of which an American can more safely be guilty. If he commits a murder the odds are more than three to one against his ever being brought to trial; they are more than ten to one against his being sentenced to imprisonment; and, as has been said, they are more than eighty to one against his suffering the extreme penalty of the law. Those are the chances officially ascertained from official statistics, and they apply to the country as a whole and to all its people. But it need hardly be said that if the murderer is a white man the odds in his favour are very much above the statistical average, and very much below them if he is a negro. Only one country in the world, Mexico, exceeds the American record of murders, a record that is proportionately five times as great in the United States as in Australia, more than fourteen times as great as in England and Wales, eight times as great as in Japan, ten times as great as in Canada, and about twenty-five times as great as in Germany."

the least effective. In the end this whole philosophy of naturalism, which bids us follow the lead of some blind self-developing instinct, is subject to the rebuke uttered by Bishop Butler long ago: "A late author [Wollaston] of great and deserved reputation says, that to place virtue in following nature, is at best a loose way of talk. And he has reason to say this, if what I think he intends to express, though with great decency, be true, that scarce any other sense can be put upon those words, but acting as any of the several parts, without distinction, of a man's nature happened most to incline him."

In these practical and, perhaps, debatable applications we may seem to have got far away from the man whom I upheld as the typical spokesman of philosophical science. In fact the rational hypothesis of evolution as proclaimed by Huxley was, superficially considered, the very opposite of the confessedly anti-rational hypothesis that lends authority to the doctrine of moral *laisser-faire*. Nevertheless their parentage is certain, and even in Huxley hints of the derived philosophy are not infrequent.

In education, though Huxley's interests were too broad and in some respects too literary to permit a harsh condemnation of the humanities, yet all his energy was devoted to introducing science into the curriculum of the universities and schools. No doubt his action was justifiable to a certain extent and redounded to the genuine profit of pure science; but it had also the negative result at least of starting that transformation which has made of our classrooms a nursery for the sophisms of philosophical science. He was convinced that the sciences in themselves are sufficient for a liberal education, and on occasion he was ready to commend a foundation which made "no provision for 'mere literary instruction and education,'" meaning by this "the ordinary classical course of our schools and universities." Biology, he thought, included really the whole philosophy of life; and education he limited to "instruction of the intellect in the laws of nature." If there was apparent liberality in his extension of these laws of nature to include "not merely things and their forces, but men and their ways," there was also in it the germ of a mischievous ambiguity.

In matters political Huxley's practical sense of affairs kept his judgment clearer, and I do not know that there is anything in his writings which contradicts his expressed fear and dislike of *"regimentation* and *individualism*—enforced Socialism and Anarchy." He has ringing words of rebuke for the whole policy of drifting (see, for instance, his letter of March 21, 1886, to a Member of Parliament). Yet the real tendency of his ideas comes out plainly enough in his attitude towards female suffrage. He was himself strongly opposed to the admission of women into politics, holding for biological reasons a sharp distinction between the spheres of the two sexes. Nevertheless, when he came to deal directly with the emancipation of women his method was that of the man in the street. "Let them have a fair field," he said, "but let them understand, as the necessary correlative, that they are to have no favour. Let nature alone sit high above the lists, 'rain influence and judge the prize.'"

The new romantic philosophy of evolution as a continuous process of self-creation had scarcely arisen to perturb the rationalism of Huxley, and he was too stalwartly intellectual to have succumbed to it even if it had been in the air; yet the outcome of his teaching was that exaltation of science which laid the minds of the next generation open to its alluring seduction. The final influence of his words, if not always his avowed intention, was to establish the new law of progress: *Let nature sit high above the lists;* which may be interpreted by his own remark on another occasion: "The best way of getting disorder into order [is] to let it alone." Not many lives in the Victorian era were more unselfish than his, not many men pursued truth with a nobler devotion, not many had broader and finer interests; nevertheless, in the end it must be said, sadly and reverently, that his legacy to mankind was confusion of ideas and relaxation of judgment.

We have seen the triumphs of Huxley at Oxford, the seat of his enemies. Let us take leave of this somewhat ungrateful theme by calling up another scene at the same university. In 1864, there was a Diocesan Conference at Oxford. There chanced at this time to be in the neighbourhood a man who was neither priest nor scientist, a man given to absurd freaks of intellectual charlatanry, yet showing at times also such marvellous and sudden penetration into the heart of things as comes only to genius. It was Disraeli. "He lounged into the assembly," so the scene is described by Froude, "in a black velvet shooting-coat and a wide-awake hat, as if he had been accidentally passing through the town. . . He began in his usual affected manner, slowly and rather pompously, as if he had nothing to say beyond perfunctory platitudes." And then, turning to the presiding officer, the same Bishop Wilberforce whom four years earlier Huxley had so crushingly rebuked, he uttered one of his enigmatic and unforgettable epigrams: "What is the question now placed before society with a glibness the most astounding? The question is this: Is man an ape or an angel? I, my lord, am on the side of the angels." The audience, not kindly disposed to the speaker, applauded the words as a jest; they were carried the next day over the whole land by the newspapers; they have often been repeated as an example of Disraeli's brilliant but empty wit. I suspect that beneath their surface glitter, and hidden within their metaphor pointed to suit an Oriental taste, these words contain a truth that shall some day break to pieces the new philosophy which Huxley spent his life so devotedly to establish.

JONATHAN EDWARDS

JONATHAN EDWARDS was born at Windsor, Connecticut, in 1703. He belonged, unlike his great contemporary Franklin in this, to the "Brahmin families" of America, his father being a distinguished graduate of Harvard and a minister of high standing, his mother being the daughter of Solomon Stoddard, the revered pastor of Northampton, Massachusetts, and a religious author of repute. Jonathan, one of eleven children, showed extraordinary precocity. There is preserved a letter of his, written apparently in his twelfth year, in which he retorts upon the materialistic opinions of his correspondent with an easiness of banter not common to a boy; and another document, from about the same period, an elaborate account of the habits of spiders, displays a keenness of observation and a vividness of style uncommon at any age. He who could write such a sentence as the following was already a master in his own right: "In very calm and serene days in the forementioned time of year, standing at some distance behind the end of an house or some other opaque body, so as just to hide the disk of the sun and keep off his dazzling rays, and looking along close by the side of it, I have seen a vast multitude of little shining webs, and glistening strings, brightly reflecting the sunbeams, and some of them of great length, and of such a height that one would think they were tacked to the vault of the heavens, and would be burnt like tow in the sun."

He studied at Yale, receiving his bachelor's degree in 1720, before his seventeenth birthday. While at college he continued his interest in scientific observations, but his main concern was naturally with theology and moral philosophy. As a sophomore he read Locke *On the Human Understanding,* with the delight of a "greedy miser" in "some newly discovered treasure." Some time after reading Locke and before graduation he wrote down a series of reflections, preparatory to a great metaphysical treatise of his own, which can only be compared with the *Commonplace Book* kept by Berkeley a few years earlier for the same purpose. In the section of *Notes on the Mind* this entry is found: "Our perceptions or ideas, that we passively receive by our bodies, are communicated to us immediately by God." Now Berkeley's *Principles* and his *Hylas and Philonous* appeared in 1710 and 1713 respectively, and the question has been raised, and not answered, whether this Berkeleian sentiment was borrowed from one of these books or was original with Edwards. Possibly the youthful philosopher was following a line of thought suggested by the English disciples of Malebranche, possibly he reached his point of view directly from Locke; in any case his life work was to carry on the Lockian philosophy from the point where the Berkeleian idealism left off.

After graduation Edwards remained for two years at Yale, preparing for the ministry. In 1722 he was called to a Presbyterian church in New York. Here he preached acceptably for eight months, returning then to his father's house, and later to New Haven, where he held the position of tutor in the college. In 1727 he went to Northampton as colleague, becoming in due time successor, to his grandfather. Almost immediately after ordination he married Sarah Pierrepont, like himself of the Brahmin caste, whom he had known as a young girl, and whose beauty of body and soul he had described in a passage of ecstatic wonder. "They say," he began, being himself then twenty and the object of his adoration thirteen, "there is a young lady in New Haven who is beloved of that great Being who made and rules the world, and that there are certain seasons in which this great Being, in some way or other invisible, comes to her and fills her mind with exceeding sweet delight." The marriage, notwithstanding this romantic rapture, proved eminently wise. Lying on his deathbed at Princeton, while his wife was far away in Northampton, he could, after a life not without sore trials and difficulties, send her this message: "Tell her that the uncommon union which has so long subsisted between us, has been of such a nature as I trust is spiritual, and therefore will continue forever." They had eleven children, one of whom married the Reverend Aaron Burr, president of Nassau Hall (now Princeton University), and was the mother of a more famous son of the same name.

Like a good many other men of his age Edwards lived his inner life, so to speak, on paper—a custom which may seem morbid to a generation taught to believe that it is better to look out than to look in, but which has the advantage of counteracting the disruptive work of time and of linking the periods of life together into one conscious whole. There is therefore nothing peculiar or priggish in the fact that at the beginning of his religious career he should have written out a set of formal resolutions, which he vowed to read over, and did read over, at stated intervals in order to keep watch on his spiritual progress. A number of these resolutions have been printed, as has also a part of the diary kept at about the same time. Neither of these documents, the time of their writing considered, contains anything remarkable, unless our knowledge of the author's life justifies us in attaching unusual significance to such words as the following, which in themselves might have been set down by a thousand other young men of the age: "I have been to God this morning, and told him that I gave myself *wholly* to him."

But it is quite otherwise with the private reflections which he wrote out some twenty years later (about 1743) at Northampton, apparently on some occasion of reading over his youthful diary. In this we have an autobiographical fragment that, for intensity of absorption in the idea of God and for convincing power of utterance, can be likened to the *Confessions* of St. Augustine, while it unites to this religious fervour a romantic feeling for nature foreign to the Bishop of Hippo's mind and prophetic of a movement that was to sweep over the world many years after Edwards' death. A few extracts from this document (not so well known as it would have been if not printed with the works of a thorny metaphysician) must be given for their biographical and literary interest:

From my childhood up, my mind had been full of objections against the doctrine of God's sovereignty, in choosing whom he would to eternal life, and rejecting whom he pleased; leaving them eternally to perish, and be everlastingly tormented in hell. It used to appear like a horrible doctrine to me. But I remember the time very well, when I seemed to be convinced, and fully satisfied, as to this sovereignty of God. . . . I have often, since that first conviction, had quite another kind of sense of God's sovereignty than I had then. I have often since had not only a conviction, but a delighted conviction. The doctrine has very often appeared exceedingly pleasant, bright, and sweet. Absolute sovereignty is what I love to ascribe to God. But my first conviction was not so.

The first instance that I remember of that sort of inward, sweet delight in God and divine things that I have lived much in since, was on reading those words, *Now unto the King eternal, immortal, invisible, the only wise God, be honour and glory for ever and ever, Amen.* As I read the words, there came into my soul, and was as it were diffused through it, a sense of the glory of the Divine Being.

Not long after I first began to experience these things, I gave an account to my father of some things that had passed in my mind. I was pretty much affected by the discourse we had together; and when the discourse was ended, I walked abroad alone, in a solitary place in my father's pasture, for contemplation. And as I was walking there, and looking up on the sky and clouds, there came into my mind so sweet a sense of the glorious *majesty* and *grace* of God, that I know not how to express. I seemed to see them both in a sweet conjunction; majesty and meekness joined together; it was a sweet and gentle, and holy majesty; and also a majestic meekness; an awful sweetness; a high, and great, and holy gentleness.

God's excellency, his wisdom, his purity and love, seemed to appear in everything; in the sun, and moon, and stars; in the clouds and blue sky; in the grass, flowers, trees; in the water, and all nature; which used greatly to fix my mind. I often used to sit and view the moon for continuance; and in the day spent much time in viewing the clouds and sky, to behold the sweet glory of God in these things; in the mean time, singing forth, with a low voice, my contemplations of the Creator and Redeemer.

I spent most of my time in thinking of divine things, year after year; often walking alone in the woods, and solitary places, for meditation, soliloquy, and prayer, and converse with God.

Holiness, as I then wrote down some of my contemplations on it, appeared to me to be of a sweet, pleasant, charming, serene, calm nature; which brought an inexpressible purity, brightness, peacefulness and ravishment to the soul. In other words, that it made the soul like a field or garden of God, with all manner of pleasant flowers; all pleasant, delightful, and undisturbed; enjoying a sweet calm, and the gentle, vivifying beams of the sun. The soul of a true Christian, as I then wrote my meditations, appeared like such a little white flower as we see in the spring of the year; low and humble on the ground, opening its bosom to receive the pleasant beams of the sun's glory; rejoicing as it were in a calm rapture; diffusing around a sweet fragrancy; standing peacefully and lovingly, in the midst of other flowers round about.

This is not the Edwards that is commonly known, and indeed he put little of this personal rapture of holiness into his published works, which were almost exclusively polemical in design. Only once, perhaps, did he adequately display this aspect of his thought to the public; and that was in the *Dissertation on the Nature of Virtue,* wherein, starting from the definition of virtue as "the beauty of the qualities and exercises of the heart," he proceeds to combine ethics and æsthetics in an argument as subtle in reasoning as it is, in places, victorious in expression. One cannot avoid the feeling when his writings are surveyed as a whole, despite the laxness of his style, that in his service to a particular dogma of religion Edwards deliberately threw away the opportunity of making for himself one of the very great names in literature.

It should seem also that he not only suppressed his personal ecstasy in his works for the press, but waived it largely in his more direct intercourse with men. He who himself, like an earlier and perhaps greater Emerson, was enjoying the sweetness of walking with God in the garden of earth, was much addicted to holding up before his people the "pleasant, bright, and sweet" doctrine of damnation. Nor can it be denied that he had startling ways of impressing this sweetness on others. It is a misfortune, but one for which he is himself responsible, that his memory in the popular mind to-day is almost exclusively associated with certain brimstone sermons and their terrific effect. Best known of these is the discourse on *Sinners in the Hands of an Angry God,* delivered at Enfield, Connecticut, in the year 1741. His text was taken from Deuteronomy: "Their foot

shall slide in due time"; and from these words he
proceeded to prove, and "improve," the truth that
"there is nothing that keeps wicked men at any
moment out of hell, but the mere pleasure of God."
He is said to have had none of the common qualities
of the orator. His regular manner of preaching, at
least in his earlier years, was to hold his "manuscript
volume in his left hand, the elbow resting on the
cushion or the Bible, his right hand rarely raised but
to turn the leaves, and his person almost motionless";
but there needed no gesticulation and no modulation
of voice to convey the force of his terrible conviction,
when, to an audience already disposed to accept the
dogma, he presented that dogma in a series of pictures
beside which the Inferno of Dante seems like the
naïveté of a child:

How awful are those words, Isaiah lxiii, 3, which are the
words of the great God: "I will tread them in mine anger, and
trample them in my fury, and their blood shall be sprinkled
upon my garments, and I will stain all my raiment." It is
perhaps impossible to conceive of words that carry in them
greater manifestations of these three things, viz., contempt and
hatred, and fierceness of indignation. If you cry to God to
pity you, he will be so far from pitying you in your doleful
case, or showing you the least regard or favour, that instead of
that he will only tread you under foot: and though he will
know that you cannot bear the weight of omnipotence treading
upon you, yet he will not regard that, but he will crush you
under his feet without mercy; he will crush out your blood,
and make it fly, and it shall be sprinkled on his garments, so
as to stain all his raiment. He will not only hate you, but
he will have you in the utmost contempt; no place shall be
thought fit for you but under his feet, to be trodden down as
the mire in the streets.

There is reason to think, that there are many in this congregation now hearing this discourse, that will actually be the
subjects of this very misery to all eternity. We know not who

they are, or in what seats they sit, or what thoughts they now have. It may be they are now at ease, and hear all these things without much disturbance, and are now flattering themselves that they are not the persons; promising themselves that they will escape. If we knew that there was one person, and but one, in the whole congregation, that was to be the subject of this misery, what an awful thing it would be to think of! If we knew who it was, what an awful sight it would be to see such a person! How might the rest of the congregation lift up a lamentable and bitter cry over him! But alas! Instead of one, how many is it likely will remember this discourse in hell! And it would be a wonder, if some that are now present should not be in hell in a very short time, before this year is out. And it would be no wonder if some persons, that now sit here in some seats of this meeting-house in health, and quiet and secure, should be there before to-morrow morning.

The congregation of Enfield, we are told, was moved almost to despair; "there was such a breathing of distress and weeping" that the speaker was interrupted and had to plead for silence. Sincerity of vision may amount to cruelty, and something is due to the weakness of human nature. Dr. Allen, the biographer of Edwards, is right in saying that "he was almost too great a man to let loose upon other men in their ordinary condition. He was like some organ of vast capacity whose strongest stops or combinations should never have been drawn."

The result was inevitable. Life is made up of ordinary men in their ordinary condition. The people of Northampton listened to Edwards for a time; were rapt out of themselves; suffered the relapse of natural indolence; grew resentful under the efforts to keep them in a state of exaltation; and freed themselves of the burden when it became intolerable. That, in brief, is the explanation of the difference between Edwards and the people of his parish, ending in his dismissal from Northampton. So at least it would be if we judged from the contemporary point of view; from another point of view it may be described as the certain outcome of a combat between inhuman logic and common sense.

At first all went well. Mr. Stoddard, in whose declining years the discipline of the church had been somewhat relaxed, died in 1729, and the fervour of his successor soon began to tell on the people. In 1733, as Edwards notes in his *Narrative of Surprising Conversions,* there was a stirring in the conscience of the young, who had hitherto been prone to the awful sin of "frolicking." The next year the sudden conversion of a young woman, "who had been one of the greatest company keepers in the whole town," came upon the community "like a flash of lightning"; the Great Awakening was started, which was to run over New England like a burning fire, with consequences not yet obliterated. The usual accompaniments of moral exaltation and physical convulsions showed themselves. Edwards relates with entire approbation the morbid conversion of a child of four. The poor little thing was overheard by her mother in her closet wrestling with God in prayer, from which she came out crying aloud and "wreathing her body to and fro like one in anguish of spirit." She was afraid she was going to hell! And so, "she continued thus earnestly crying and taking on for some time, till at length she suddenly ceased crying and began to smile, and presently said with a smiling countenance—Mother, the kingdom of heaven is come to me!" This was the beginning of "a very remarkable abiding change in the child"; thereafter she loved "to hear Mr. Edwards preach," delighted in religious conversations, and had "a great concern for the good of other souls." Like saints of an older age she could not always distinguish between rapture and despair:

> At some time about the middle of winter, very late in the night, when all were in bed, her mother perceived that she was awake, and heard her as though she was weeping. She called to her, and asked her what was the matter. She answered with a low voice, so that her mother could not hear what she said; but thinking it might be occasioned by some spiritual affection, said no more to her; but perceived her to lie awake, and to continue in the same frame for a considerable time. The next morning she asked her whether she did not cry the last night: the child answered yes, I did cry a little, for I was thinking about God and Christ, and they loved me. Her mother asked her, whether to think of God and Christ's loving made her cry: she answered yes, it does sometimes.

It was inevitable that such a wave of superheated emotion should subside in a short time. In fact the enthusiasm had scarcely reached its height when it began to show signs of indubitable perversion, and decay. Immediately after the story of the young convert Edwards notes that "the Spirit of God was gradually withdrawing" and "Satan seemed to be let loose and raged in a dreadful manner." An epidemic of melancholy and suicidal mania swept over the community, and multitudes seemed to hear a voice saying to them: "Cut your own throat, now is a good opportunity." Strange delusions arose and spread, until common sense once more got the upper hand.

It was an old tale, told in New England with peculiar fury. The saddest thing in the whole affair is the part played by Edwards. Other leaders saw the danger from the first, or were soon aroused to it; but Edwards never, either at this time or later, wavered in his belief that the Awakening, though marred by the devil, was in itself the work of the Divine Spirit. His *Thoughts on the Survival of Religion* and his *Marks of a Work of the True Spirit* are both a thoroughgoing apology for the movement, as they are also an important document in his own psychology. The jangling and confusion he admits; he recognizes the elements of hysteria that were almost inextricably mixed up with the moral exaltation of conversion; but his defence is based frankly on the avowal that these things are the universal accompaniments of inspiration—they attended the founding of the church in the Apostolic age, they were to be expected at the reinstauration of religion. Often the reader of these treatises is struck by a curious, and by no means accidental, resemblance between the position of Edwards and the position of the apologists of the romantic movement in literature. There is the same directness of appeal to the emotions; the same laudation of expansiveness, at the cost, if need be, of judgment or measure or any other restraint. Prudence and regularity may be desirable in the service of God, yet it is still true that "the cry of irregularity and imprudence" has been chiefly in the mouths of those who are enemies to the main work of redemption. Perturbation, in truth, is not properly so called when it is the means of rousing the cold and indifferent from their lethargy; we are bound to suppose that not even the man "of the strongest reason and greatest learning" can remain master of himself if "strongly impressed with a sense of divine and eternal things." And thus the religious apologist rises into the equivalent of "Titanism": "When God is about to bring to pass something great and glorious in the world, nature is in a ferment and struggle, and the world as it were in travail." It comes in the end to this, that, notwithstanding his verbal reservations, Edwards had no critical canon to distinguish between the order and harmony governed by a power higher than the tumultuous sway of the emotions and the order and harmony that are merely stagnation.

One factor in his confidence was a belief that the discovery of America, coinciding as it did with the beginning of the Reformation, came by Providence for "the glorious renovation of the world"; nay more, that the humble town in which he was preaching might be the cradle of the new dispensation, from whence it should spread over the whole earth. His language may even seem to betray a touch of spiritual pride over the part he himself should be called upon to play as the instrument of Grace in this marvellous regeneration. That vice of the saints was indeed a subject much in his meditations, and one of the finest pieces of religious psychology in his works is the passage of the *Revival* in which he tracks it through the labyrinthine deceits of the human heart. Pride no doubt was a sin against which he had to keep particular ward in these years, but we should not say that he ever, in any proper sense of the word, lapsed from the virtue of Christian humility. If he seemed to set himself above other men as an exigent judge, this was rather due to a faulty sympathy, an inability to measure others except by the standard of his own great faculties. Thus, for all his emotionalism, he lived under the control of an iron will, and he could not comprehend how the over-stimulation of terror and joy in a weaker disposition would work moral havoc. Nor from his own constant height could he understand how brief and fitful any mood of exaltation must be among ordinary men in their ordinary condition. Hence he not only failed to see the gravity of the actual evils at the time of the Awakening, but failed also, with more grievous results for himself, to recognize the impossibility of flogging the dead emotion into new life.

The issue came on a point of church discipline. Edwards believed that religion was essentially a matter of the emotions, or affections. A man might have perfect knowledge of divine things, as indeed the devil had, but unless the love of God was implanted in his heart by the free act of Grace he had no lot with the faithful. To develop this theme he wrote his great *Treatise Concerning Religious Affections,* a work which without exaggeration may be said to go as far as the human intellect can go in the perilous path of discriminating between the purely spiritual life and the life of worldly morality. The hard kernel of the argument is stated thus:

From these things it is evident, that those gracious influences which the saints are subjects of, and the affects of God's Spirit which they experience, are entirely above nature, altogether of a different kind from any thing that men find within themselves by nature, or only in the exercise of natural principles; and are things which no improvement of those qualifications, or principles that are natural, no advancing or exalting them to higher degrees, and no kind of composition of them, will ever bring men to; because they not only differ from what is natural, and from every thing that natural men experience, in degree and circumstances but also in kind; and are of a nature vastly more excellent. And this is what I mean, by supernatural, when I say that gracious affections are from those influences that are supernatural.

From hence it follows, that in those gracious exercises and affections which are wrought in the minds of the saints, through the saving influences of the Spirit of God, there is a new inward perception or sensation of their minds, entirely different in its nature and kind. . .

. . . And even in those things that seem to be common, there is something peculiar; both spiritual and natural love cause desires after the object beloved; but they be not the same sort of desires: there is a sensation of soul in the spiritual desires of one that loves God, which is entirely different from all natural desires: both spiritual love and natural love are attended with delight in the object beloved; but the sensations of delight are not the same, but entirely and exceedingly diverse. Natural men may have conceptions of many things about spiritual affections; but there is something in them which is as it were the nucleus, or kernel of them, that they have no more conception of, than one born blind, has of colours.

Now even this simple statement of the difference between the condition of Grace and the condition of nature is hard for the natural man to follow; but when Edwards, with the acumen of a genius and the doggedness of a scholar, imposed his distinction on all the intricate feelings of life, the natural man was dazed; and when he attempted to make it the criterion of admission to the Lord's Table, the natural man who called himself a Christian rebelled. Stoddard had thought it right to admit to communion all those who desired honestly to unite themselves with the church. Edwards protested that only those who had undergone a radical conversion and knew the affections of supernatural love should enjoy this high privilege. His congregation sided with their old guide against him.

The quarrel was further embittered by another issue. It came to light that certain young folk of the church were reading profane books which led to lewd conversation. Edwards called for public discipline of the sinners; the congregation supported him until investigation showed that the evil was widespread and would bring discredit on most of the better families of the town, and then they blocked further proceedings. If tradition is correct in naming *Pamela* as one of the guilty books, we may admire the literary taste of youthful Northampton, yet think that their pastor was justified in condemning such reading as incendiary. However that may be, when, on the 22nd of June, 1750, a public vote was taken whether Mr. Edwards should be dismissed from his pastorate, a large majority was counted against him. Northampton has the distinction of having rejected the greatest theologian and philosopher yet produced in this country. As Socrates taunted the ancient politicians for the injuries they suffered at the hands of those they were supposed to have trained in civic virtue, so perhaps the townsmen of Edwards might retort upon any accuser that, if they failed in religious duty, it was the business of their pastor to have instructed them more effectively.

The behaviour of Edwards when the crisis actually came was simple, dignified, and even noble. His *Farewell Sermon,* with its dispassionate and submissive appeal from the tribunal of men to that final judgment which shall be given in knowledge and righteousness, cannot be read to-day without a deep stirring of the heart: "And let us all remember, and never forget our future solemn meeting on that great day of the Lord; the day of infallible decision, and of the everlasting and unalterable sentence. Amen."

At the age of forty-six Edwards was thrust upon the world, discredited, in broken health, with a large family to support, undaunted. Then befell a strange thing. This philosopher, whose thoughts and emotions ranged beyond the ken of most educated men, was sent to the frontier town of Stockbridge as a missionary to the Indians. There for six years he laboured faithfully and, at least in the practical management of affairs, successfully. It must have been one of the memorable sights of the world to have seen him returning on horseback from a solitary ride into the forest, while there fluttered about him, pinned to his coat, the strips of paper on which he had scribbled the results of his meditations. His days were little troubled, and not overburdened with work, peaceful it is thought; and now it was he wrote the treatise on the *Freedom of the Will* upon which his fame chiefly depends.

In 1757 his son-in-law died, and Edwards was chosen by the Trustees of the College of New Jersey to succeed him as president. Edwards hesitated, stating frankly to the Trustees his disabilities of health and learning; but finally accepted the offer. He left his family to follow him later, and arrived in Princeton in January of 1758. Small-pox was in the town and the new president was soon infected. His death took place on the 22nd of March, in the fifty-fourth year of his age. His last recorded words were: "Trust in God and ye need not fear."

The child was indeed father of the man, and it was peculiarly fitting that he who from youth upward had been absorbed in the idea of God should have died with the sacred word on his lips. But what shall be said of the fearlessness of one who had made terror the chief instrument of appeal to men and had spent his life in fighting for a dogma which the genial author of *The One-Hoss Shay* thought no decent man could hold without going crazy?

Now the Edwardian theology was a part of the great deistic debate which took its root in the everlasting question of the origin of evil in the world. It was a three-cornered contest. The Calvinists and the infidels both believed in a kind of determinism, but differed over the nature of the determining cause. The Calvinists found this cause in a personal Creator, omnipotent and omniscient, to whom they did not scruple to carry up all the evil as well as the good of the universe—"c'est que Dieu," as Calvin himself states categorically, "non seulement a preveu la cheute du premier homme, et en icelle la ruine de toute sa posterité, mais qu'il l'a ainsi voulu." The Deists, who at this time formed the fighting line of the infidels, while verbally acknowledging the existence of God and theorizing on the nature of evil, virtually regarded the universe as a perfectly working machine in which there was no room for a personal governor or for real sin. To the Arminians, including the bulk of the orthodox Churchmen, the alliance between Calvinism and Deism seemed altogether to outweigh the differences. As Daniel Whitby declares in the preface to his discourses *On the Five Points of Calvinism,* to hold God responsible for evil is to play directly into the hands of the atheists. And so the age-old dispute between Augustinian and Pelagian, and between Calvinist and Arminian, took on a new life from the deistic controversy, and there sprang up a literature which undertook to preserve the idea of an omnipotent personal Creator and at the same time to save His face, if the expression may be tolerated, by attributing to man complete free will and accountability for his actions. Dr. Whitby, whose discourses appeared in 1710 (reprinted in America), was a man of considerable learning but of no great metaphysical acumen, and a writer, as one of his critics said, of "disgusting tautology." His argument consists mainly in heaping up quotations from the philosophers and early Fathers, typical of which are these two, chosen with cunning application to his opponents from St. Augustine himself: "It is the height of madness and injustice to hold any person guilty because he did not that which he could not do," and "Who will not pronounce it folly to command him who is not free to do what is commanded?" The clear moral inference follows: God does punish men, therefore they have in themselves the power to live righteously; and God does command and exhort men, therefore their will is free to obey or disobey.

It was in answer to Whitby's book and one or two others of the kind that Edwards composed his *Freedom of the Will*. His argument has a psychological basis. In the *Treatise Concerning Religious Affections* he had divided the soul into two faculties: one the understanding, by which it discerns, views, and judges things; the other called the heart or will, being nothing else but the inclination of the soul towards, or the disinclination from, what is discerned and judged by the understanding. In the *Freedom of the Will* he starts with Locke's statement that "the Will is perfectly distinguished from Desire, which in the very same action may have a quite contrary tendency from that which our Wills set us upon." This theory Edwards analyses and rejects, and then proceeds to show that a man's desire and will are virtually the same faculty of the soul. It follows from this that the will at any moment is determined by the strongest motive acting upon the soul; we are free in so far as no obstacle is presented to our willing in accordance with our inclination, but our inclination is determined by what at any moment seems to us good. In his attack on the common arguments for the freedom of the will Edwards is magnificently victorious. If the psychology by which the Arminians sought to relieve God of the burden of evil in human life is pushed into a corner, it shows itself as nothing more than this: Man's will is a faculty absolutely indeterminate in itself and entirely independent of his inclinations. When, therefore, a man errs, it is because, the choice between evil with its attendant suffering and good with its attendant happiness being presented to him, the man, having full knowledge of the conse-

quences and being impelled by no momentary pre-
ponderance of the one or the other from his innate
disposition, deliberately and freely chooses what is
evil and painful. Such an account of human action
is monstrous, inconceivable; it offered an easy mark
for so sharp a logician as Edwards.

But whence arise the conditions by which a man's
inclination is swayed in one direction or the other?
Edwards carries these unflinchingly up to the first
cause, that is, as a Christian, to God. Berkeley had
made the world to consist of ideas evoked in the mind
of man by the mind of God; Edwards accepts the
logical conclusion, and holds God responsible for the
inclination of the human will which depends on these
ideas. To the charge that such a theory makes God
the author of evil he replies in these terms:

> If, by *the author of sin,* is meant the permitter, or not a
> hinderer of sin; and, at the same time, a disposer of the state
> of events, in such a manner, for wise, holy, and most excellent
> ends and purposes, that sin, if it be permitted or not hindered,
> will most certainly and infallibly follow: I say, if this be all
> that is meant, by being the author of sin, I do not deny that
> God is the author of sin (though I dislike and reject the
> phrase, as that which by use and custom is apt to carry an-
> other sense). . . . This is not to be the *actor of sin,* but, on
> the contrary, of holiness.

Calvin, as we have seen, did not hesitate to attribute
the source of evil to God's will in franker words than
these, but at the same time he warned men against
intruding with their finite reason into this "sanctuary
of the divine wisdom." The mind of Edwards could
not rest while any problem seemed to him unsolved.
Confronted with the mystery of the divine will, he
undertakes to solve it by applying his psychology of
man to the nature of God. (He himself would put

it the other way about: "Herein does very much consist that image of God wherein He made man.") The passage in which he most explicitly develops this thesis, though generally overlooked by his critics, is of the first importance:

We must conceive of Him as influenced in the highest degree, by that which, above all others, is properly a moral inducement, viz., the moral good which He sees in such and such things: and therefore He is, in the most proper sense, a moral Agent, the source of all moral ability and Agency, the fountain and rule of all virtue and moral good; though by reason of his being supreme over all, it is not possible He should be under the influence of law or command, promises or threatenings, rewards or punishments, counsels or warnings. The essential qualities of a moral Agent are in God, in the greatest possible perfection; such as understanding, to perceive the difference between moral good and evil; a capacity of discerning that moral worthiness and demerit, by which some things are praiseworthy, others deserving of blame and punishment; and also a capacity of choice, and choice guided by understanding, and a power of acting according to his choice or pleasure, and being capable of doing those things which are in the highest sense praiseworthy.

In other words, the will of God is precisely like the will of man; it is merely the inclination, or *moral inducement,* to act as He is *influenced* by an external power. The fatal mystery of good and evil, the true cause, lies somewhere above and beyond Him; He is, like ourselves, a channel, not the source. The only difference is that God has complete knowledge of the possibilities of being, and therefore is not moved by threats and blind commands, but immediately, by what Edwards elsewhere calls the "moral necessity" of governing in accordance with the best of the "different objects of choice that are proposed to the Divine Understanding." By such a scheme God is really placed in about such a position as in the Leibnizian continuation of Laurentius Valla's *Dialogue on Free Will and Providence,* where He is naïvely portrayed as looking upon an infinite variety of worlds piled up, like cannon balls, in pyramidal form before Him, and selecting for creation that one which combines the greatest possible amount of good with the least possible admixture of evil.

From this pretty sport of the imagination Edwards would no doubt have drawn back in contempt, and, indeed, in his ordinary language God is merely the supreme Cause, without further speculation. One of the Leibnizian inferences, moreover, is utterly excluded from his philosophy. He was no optimist; was in fact the last man to infer that, because this world is the best possible conceivable, evil is therefore a small and virtually negligible part of existence. On the contrary the whole animus of his teachings springs from a deep and immediate hatred of evil in itself and apart from any consideration of its cause. "The thing," he says, "which makes sin hateful, is that by which it deserves punishment; which is but the expression of hatred. . . Thus, for instance, ingratitude is hateful and worthy of dispraise, according to common sense; not because something as bad, or worse than ingratitude, was the cause that produced it; but because it is hateful in itself, by its own inherent deformity."

To the charge of the Arminians that the doctrine of predestination leaves no place for the punishment of sin, this is an adequate reply; but the consequences are, in another way, disastrous to the Edwardian theology. If we are right, as we indubitably are right, in detesting evil in itself and wherever seen, and if we hold with Edwards that the will of God, like the will of man, is merely the inclination towards the best object presented to its choice, and there is no power either in God or in man above the will, in what essential way, then, does the act of God in creating a world mixed with evil differ from the act of Judas in betraying God, and how are we relieved from hating God for the evil of His work with the same sort of hatred as that which we feel for Judas? Edwards had terrified the people of Enfield with a picture of God treading down sinners till their blood sprinkled His raiment, and exulting in His wrath. The retort is obvious, and unspeakable. Nor can he, or any other Predestinarian, escape the odium of such a retort by hiding behind the necessity of things which all men must, in one way or another, admit. There is a war between the nations, he will say, and suddenly a bomb, dropping upon a group of soldiers, themselves innocent of any crime, horribly rends and mangles them. Here is a hideous thing, and by no twisting of the reason can you or I avoid carrying the responsibility for this evil back to the first great cause of all. Shall I be held impious for saying metaphorically that the blood of these soldiers is sprinkled on the raiment of that Cause?—Aye, but the difference to us morally if we leave that cause in its own vast obscurity, unapproached by our reason, untouched by our pride; or if we make it into an image of ourselves, composed only of understanding and inclination like our own, and subject to our reprobation as surely as to our love!

Edwards had riddled and forever destroyed the arguments for free will commonly employed by the Arminians; is there no alternative for the human reason save submission to his theological determinism or to fatalistic atheism?

One way of escape from that dilemma is obvious and well known. It is that which Dr. Johnson, with

his superb faculty of common sense, seized upon when
the Edwardian doctrine came up in conversation before him. "The only relief I had was to forget it,"
said Boswell, who had read the book; and Johnson
closed the discussion with his epigram: "All theory is
against the freedom of the will, all experience for it."
That is sufficient, no doubt, for the conduct of life;
yet there is perhaps another way of escape, which,
if it does not entirely silence the metaphysical difficulties, at least gives them a new ethical turn. Twice
in the course of his argument Edwards refers to an
unnamed Arminian[1] who placed the liberty of the
soul not in the will itself, but in some power of sus-
pending volition until due time had elapsed for judg-
ing properly the various motives to action. Edwards'
reply is that this suspension of activity, being itself
an act of volition, merely throws back, without an-
nulling, the difficulty; and as the argument came to
him, this refutation is fairly complete. But a fuller
consideration of the point at issue might possibly
indicate a way out of the dilemma of free will and
determinism into a morally satisfying form of dualism
within the soul of man himself.[2] At least it can be
said that the looseness of the Arminian reasoning
leaves an easier loophole of escape into a human
philosophy than does the rigid logic of the Predesti-
narians.

Yet for all that, though we may follow Edwards'
logical system to the breaking point, as we can follow

---

[1] Edwards, it should seem, had immediately in mind the
Essay on the Freedom of Will in God and the Creature of
Isaac Watts; but the notion had been discussed at length by
Locke (*Essay* II, xxi), and at an earlier date had been touched
on with great acumen by John Norris in his correspondence
with Henry More.

[2] This argument is developed in my *Platonism*, 127 ff.

every metaphysical system, and though we may feel that, in his revulsion from the optimism of the Deists, he distorted the actual evil of existence into a nightmare of the imagination,—yet for all that, he remains one of the giants of the intellect and one of the enduring masters of religious emotion. He had not the legal and executive brain of Calvin, upon whose *Institutes* his scheme of theology is manifestly based, but in subtle resourcefulness of reasoning and still more in the scope of his spiritual insight he stands, I think, above his predecessor. Few men have studied Edwards without recognizing the force and honesty of his genius. To Hazlitt he ranked with Hobbes, Berkeley, Butler, Hartley, Hume, and Leibniz as a metaphysician. To Crabb Robinson the reading of his book on *Original Sin,* in early youth, was "an irreparable mischief." Let us take our leave of him with one of his more gracious meditations impressed on our memory:

All the truly great and good, all the pure and holy and excellent from this world, and it may be from every part of the universe, are constantly tending toward heaven. As the streams tend to the ocean, so all these are tending to the great ocean of infinite purity and bliss.

VISCOUNT MORLEY

"THE world," says Lord Morley in the introduction to his *Recollections,* "is travelling under formidable omens into a new era, very unlike the times in which my lot was cast." And, indeed, those of us who had our beginnings in the Victorian age seem, as we read his pages, to hear a voice out of our own youth, speaking to us almost as strangers—so hard is it for a man in the season of harvest to recall the days of his sowing. That is the deeper meaning of the book. Of the ordinary intimacies of biography it contains small measure. Save for a few sentences about his parents in the first chapter, and the casual mention of "my wife," the writer might be regarded as a modern Melchisedec, "without father, without mother, without descent." Nor has he much to say of his own more private emotions, of the sweet and bitter currents of self-approval and self-distrust that flow through the heart when the world is shut out. In that respect we may call his taste impeccable or his intellect cold, as our judgment inclines. But of the other ingredients of good biography there is abundance. Everywhere there is felt the charm of a writer who has borne a great rôle among great men, and who knows how to wield all the necromantic devices of literary art.

No small part of the record is purely bookish, the reflections of a man who began life as an author and through all the distractions of a public career never forgot the seclusions of his library. There was in Morley the making, perhaps the actuality, of a first-rate critic, in the narrower sense of the word, and the interest of these critical comments is enhanced by the fact that much of it relates to writers whom he

knew personally, often intimately. No finer tribute
to the overflowing courage of Meredith, "his spacious-
ness of mind and outlook," will be found anywhere
than in these pages. What, for instance, could be
more significant than this extract from a letter of
Meredith's written after Morley had called his attention to Goethe's psalm of life, *Das Göttliche?*—
"Anything grander than the days and nights at my
porch, you will not find away from the Alps, for the
dark line of my hill runs up to the stars, the valley
below is a soundless gulf. There I pace like a ship-
man before turning in. In the day, with a S.W.
blowing, I have a brilliant universe rolling up to me;
after midnight I sat and thought of Goethe, and of the
sage in him and the youth." That, as Morley adds,
is Meredith as he lived, and at his best. Yet, as a
critic, Morley was not blind to the strain of contortion
in Meredith's genius, and to what such contortion
means. "It is of no avail," he says, "for any writer
to contend that he is not obscure. . . The truth is
that Meredith often missed ease. Yet ease in words
and artistic form has been a mark of more than one
of his contemporaries, who amid the world's riddles
saw deepest and felt warmest. Even into his best
talks there came now and again a sense of strain; if
a new-comer joined the little circle of intimates, he
was transformed, forcing himself without provocation
into a wrestle for violent effects." It would be well
if the implication of these words were remembered
not only by the over-zealous partisans of Meredith,
particularly of Meredith the poet, but by all those
would-be "intellectuals" who measure the wisdom of
an author by his difficulty.

Space would fail if I undertook to recall the judgments of like clarity passed on R. L. Stevenson and
Matthew Arnold and Leslie Stephen and Browning

and other lights of the Victorian age. Only one of the greater names is conspicuous by its absence; Thackeray is nowhere even named. I have inquired whether there was any personal reason for this strange silence, but no one has been able to explain it on such grounds. And so I can only fall back on the suggestion of a very wise friend, that Morley may have been repelled by the novelist's insight into the vanities of the human heart, and made uneasy by the realism of the social ideas expressed in the conversation between Pendennis and Warrington. That is mere conjecture, but there are, in fact, sentences in the talk of those observers of the Upper Temple which might strike as a chilling wind on the illusions of a sentimental Liberal.

But the literature of the *Recollections* is not confined to contemporary writers. To the end, Morley carries on the love of the Classics which came to him, we may suppose, by right of his Oxford training. Late in life, when released for a while from business, he finds more refreshment from a treatise of Cicero than from the daily press. And one of the best of his chapters is really an independent essay in little on Lucretius, to whom, as to the greatest of those who have "denied divinely the divine," he was peculiarly drawn. It is even characteristic of his reserve that nowhere else do we seem to get so near a glimpse into his own more intimate thoughts as in his lingering reflections on the lines of the *De Rerum Natura* which describe the inroad of death upon the pleasant customs of life:

It was impossible that our own glorious literature should not contain, in prose and verse alike, a thousand things of superlative beauty about this universal theme, from Raleigh's *"O eloquent, just, and mighty death,"* or the thrilling dialogues in Claudio's prison, down to the most melting and melodious single verse in all the exercises of our English tongue, *"After life's fitful fever he sleeps well,"* the tender summary of it all. Still, the famous passage of Lucretius at the close of his third book is of such quality that I hardly find in my heart to quarrel with the accomplished critic of to-day who suggests that "its lofty passion, its piercing tenderness, the stately roll of its cadences, is perhaps unmatched in human speech."

Death is the tritest of events save only birth, and the world, it should seem, has agreed to debar it from further exploitation in literature, as a theme long ago exhausted. Yet in this same chapter—the record of an Easter holiday spent in turning over a volume of collectanea on *les grands hommes qui sont morts en plaisantant*—Lord Morley has prefaced his criticism of Lucretius with a sheaf of quotations from English sources which might make the act of dying appear as a new experience to each of us. I will not apologize for writing out two of these extracts; for the more personal flavour of Lord Morley's book is in these things, and still, despite our modern convention of silence, death is closer to our minds than any man.

QUEEN ELIZABETH. (*Philosophy of the man of action.*)—As for me, I see no such great reason why I should either be proud to live, or fear to die. I have had good experience of this world. I have known what it is to be a subject, and I now know what it is to be a sovereign. Good neighbours I have had, and I have met with bad; and in trust, I have found treason. I have bestowed benefits on ill deservers; and where I have done well, I have been ill reputed and spoken of. When I call to mind things past, behold things present, and look forward to things to come, *I count them happiest that go hence soonest.* Nevertheless . . . I am armed with better courage than is common in my sex, so that whatsoever befalls me, death shall never find me unprepared.

LEIGHTON. (*The Scotch divine of the time of the Restoration, indifferently episcopal and presbyterian, the friend of Bishop Burnet who reports this of him.*)—There were two remarkable circumstances in his death. He used often to say that if he were to choose a place to die in, it should be an inn, it looking like a pilgrim's going home, to whom this world was all an inn, and who was weary of the noise and confusion of it. He added that the officious tenderness of his friends was an entanglement to a dying man, and that the unconcerned attendance of those that could be procured in such a place would give less disturbance. He had his wish.

In comparison with the point and variety of the literary comments the narrative of Lord Morley's political career is, it must be admitted, rather monotonous. I do not mean that these chapters are wholly without interest. Here and there they are enlivened by sprightly anecdote, as when he tells the story of the Irish peasant in the dock for a violent assault.— *Prisoner,* puzzled by the legal jargon of the indictment: "What's all that he says?" *Warder:* "He says ye hit Pat Curry with yer spade on the side of his head." *Prisoner:* "Bedad, an' I did." *Warder:* "Then plade not guilty." All this aloud and in full hearing of the court.—We may be grateful to an Irish Secretary for assuring us that one of the ancient phantoms of Hibernian humour was a real creature of flesh and blood; it is in a small way a footnote to the veracity of history. There are also in these political chapters several set character sketches of statesmen—notably of Harcourt, Rosebery, Chamberlain, and Lord Spencer —which are scarcely less elaborately drawn than the literary portraits. Nevertheless, the main narrative, when it gets caught in the backwash of Home Rule and Indian administration, moves with a provokingly sluggish tide. Here Lord Morley contrives to be almost as dull about himself as he was about Gladstone in that biography of which he has been heard to say that no one ever read it through.

Yet, withal, it is true that the main, or at least the

final, interest of the *Recollections* is drawn from this political background. In telling his story Lord Morley makes rather a sharp division between his hours in Parliament and the hours spent among his books. Such an arrangement would suggest rather an incompatibility between the two parts of his life than their harmony. And so, in fact, after relating his election to Parliament, he pauses a moment to reckon up the difficulties that have beset the literary man in politics, beginning with Cicero, who came to a bloodstained end on the Italian seashore, and closing with Thiers, who used to say that "he would willingly give the writing of ten successful histories for a single happy session in the Assembly or a single fortunate campaign in arms." But certainly the reader of Lord Morley's life feels no such difficulties; on the contrary, he is charmed by the apparently easy blending of fine culture with practical success. Perhaps we are the more sensitive to the beauty of this delicate adjustment for the reason that in its perfection it is not likely soon to appear again. We shall, no doubt, continue to see literary men engaged in politics, but scarcely of Lord Morley's type; and even if such appear, their literature will be a thing rather held apart, easily forgotten when they stand in Parliament before the representatives of the people, or when they are talking business in private with their colleagues. At least the habit of the Classics, linking the senate with the schoolroom and associating the problems of to-day with the long tradition of experience, is passing, or has passed, away.

Somewhere Lord Morley tells of a conversation with Harcourt when it was a question of letting Home Rule fall into the limbo of pious opinions or of pressing it to a quick and perhaps hazardous issue. Harcourt was for postponement, and one of the strongest incentives Morley could bring for action was the appeal of three lines of Virgil. "Harcourt," he observes, "could be trusted in passing to forgive desperate politics for the sake of a classic quotation." In another place he imagines a debate between Harcourt and Fox, in which the elder statesman expounds his well-known theory that if a man's aim is public speaking, Euripides ought to be his constant study, scarcely less than Homer himself. (Ah, if one could have been present at such a meeting, and could have been allowed to put in a word for Thucydides as the master statesmen of them all!) And the reply is that Homer and Euripides alike have long followed the power of the Crown. "Never again," adds the recorder of the imaginary scene—"never again will either House hear a Minister declaim the solemn hexameters of Lucretius, among the noblest in all poetry; or the verses where Virgil describes the husbandman turning up with rake and plow the rusty javelins, empty helms, and mighty bones of a forgotten battle-field of long ago; or like Pitt in his glorious speech against the Slave Trade, inspired by the shooting of a beam of the rising sun through the windows of the House to the most beautiful and apt of recorded parliamentary impromptus in the two Latin lines:

> Nos . . . primus equis Oriens afflavit anhelis,
> Illic sera rubens accendit lumina Vesper."

These are but pretty customs, the practical man may say, the frippery and baubles of political life, which only the dilettante will regret much to see stripped off. Does human welfare depend on the memory of a few scraps of Latin? The matter is not so simple as that. The disappearance of the ancient habit, as Lord Morley himself acknowledges, is "significant of a great many more important things than a casual change in literary taste"; it means a new kind of men in the seats of authority, a new sort of life as the aim of government, a new standard of morality, other hopes and other prizes, a world set free from its moorings. The change began with the Reform Bill of 1832; it was a revolution by the time the century closed; its fruits, whether bitter or sweet, our children shall eat. Lord Morley speaks of Harcourt as the last of the line of orators and lawmakers, great from Somers and Sir Robert Walpole onwards, who, one might add, like the riders seen by Socrates in the Piræus, carried lighted torches which they passed from one to another as they raced through the night. The reader of these memoirs will probably think of Lord Morley himself as the last of the bearers of the torch. When that light has flickered out, will the dawn have come, or will it be only darkness?

Of this revolution which has been going on under our eyes Lord Morley was sufficiently aware, as may be known from the sentence of his Introduction already quoted in this essay. But it is not clear—and this is the question that has constantly perplexed us while reading the *Recollections*—whether he really ever stopped to reflect on his own ambiguous position in the movement. That absorption in the great literary tradition, especially the vivid reality of the Classics which has formed so large a part of the consolation and dignity of his life, and has made him a citizen of the world of Ideas whilst engaged in the pursuits of time—what is this but the fine flower of his Oxford training? And it is incontrovertible that Oxford, whatever the disadvantages or virtues of its discipline, is, or at least certainly still was when Morley went up, a creation of the Church. Take away the influence of those priests, whose semi-seclusion from present affairs threw them back upon the past, and whose study of the Christian Fathers was curiously blended with reverence for the earlier antiquity of paganism, and you have taken away the very spirit of the place. I am not unaware of the paradox inherent in the age-long coördination of Aristotle with Saint Paul, nor do I believe that a truly classical education is necessarily dependent on the maintenance of such a paradox; but it is a fact nevertheless that the culture of Oxford was of this sort, a working compromise between the authority of the Church and the liberty of ancient literature; to discredit the one has been to weaken the other. Now if Morley had seen the intricacy of this compromise and had sought to justify it or with tender touch to readjust its members, or if he had cast away both elements together as rubbish, one could understand his motives, whether one approved or disapproved. But he nowhere hints that he was even conscious of such a problem, and one is left to feel in his attitude towards his intellectual nurse something that smacks of mere disloyalty. The few paragraphs on his undergraduate days are the shabbiest thing in the book. He does not deny the spell of "antique halls and gray timeworn towers"—his whole autobiography would prove his sensitiveness to such a spell, had he not expressly acknowledged it—but at the close of his career, as he looks back on those days, it seems as if the only intellectual matter that seriously concerned him then was the spread of Liberal principles as they percolated into the university from the writings of John Stuart Mill. His scant gratitude to the real *genius loci* has not even the dignity of Gibbon's outspoken contempt. And after that, if one stops to think, there is something disquieting in the cold and calculating purpose of his life to undermine the religious faith of Oxford while continuing to indulge

himself in the glamour of her hoarded literary faith.
It were better to feel the power of Lucretius and still
to believe in God, as the Oxford priests had been
content to do, than to be blind, as Morley seems to be,
to the subtle complexity of the forces that moulded
his taste. A positivist who loves Plato, after the
manner of Mill and Morley, is a harsher paradox than
ever held the heart of the charmed city by the Isis.

And Morley's acceptance of the finer pleasures of
society is of a piece with his ingratitude towards the
source of his culture. It would be hard to name a
recent book that brings us into higher company than
do these *Recollections*. Considering the humbleness
of the author's origin—he was the son of an insignificant Lancashire surgeon—one might be tempted
to regard his relish of noble names as a sign of snob-
bishness. But it is nothing of the sort. He moved
among the best of the land because by taste and character and achievement he was one of them. His easy
familiarity with men born into the ruling caste, if any
criticism is to be pronounced, is rather an apology
for the existence of such a caste than an indication of
subservience on his part. But that is a question beside the point. We are only concerned with his un-
concealed delight in the inherited manners of great
families and in the decorum of great houses. No
Tory of them all could show a franker appreciation of
the political advantages coming by natural right to
a man like Lord Houghton, now Lord Crewe, from
a father "of singular literary and social mark." With
such a colleague he admits that he found it easy to
work harmoniously. And he is equally sensitive to
the grace of noble surroundings. He was never, we
may suppose, much attracted to Disraeli's tinselled
splendours, but there is no note of disapprobation
when to the account of an evening in the magnificent

library of Althorpe he adds: "Like a scene from one of Dizzy's novels, and all the actors men with parts to play." Still more characteristic perhaps is his record of two visits to Lord Rosebery. "Meanwhile," he says of one of these, "the upshot of our various talks as we drove, or strolled about Epsom Downs, or chatted in the library, was something of this kind:— The triple alliance (Harcourt, himself, and me)—so much more really important, as I said, laughing, than that of the Central Powers—to remain on its proposed footing." From the account of the second visit I may quote at greater length:

Later and after tea we had an hour's drive, and then at 8:30 we had dinner served under a verandah in the garden. Reminded me of a dinner I once had at Berchtesgaden with Chamberlain years ago. Only we had now a perfect service, instead of two German waiters attending on twenty miscellaneous people, screaming and being screamed at by an overdriven cook. After dinner we walked for an hour in the woods, the silver moon gleaming through the branches. R. a charming companion. Before going to bed, he showed me a truly deep and beautiful page in one of Newman's Sermons. When I can get the proper volume, I shall like to transcribe it. [Would that he had transcribed it in this book!] Among other things, he wondered how it was that members of Parliament came to see me so much, and to talk so freely to me. "They never come to me," he said. *J. M.* "You're too big a man for one thing, and for another you are uncertain—not always to be found. I am always there, you see." *R.* "Oh, that's not it. When I was in every morning at Lansdowne House, 't was just the same. No, you are sympathetic." This comparison paid me an undeserved compliment, for nobody surpassed him in that inner humanity which is the root of good manners and good feeling and other things lying at the core of character.

A triple alliance in Parliament, a sermon of Newman's, perfect service and the glamour of moonlight, sympathy and the core of character—it was of such strands as these that the cord of politics and society was twisted; and all the while he who helps in the spinning is standing with the fatal shears ready, if he may, to cut the thin-spun thread. Liberalism may bring with it the promise of many blessings to mankind, it may even be preparing the world for a society intrinsically finer than the old—I do not know—but for the privileged graces of aristocracy it certainly has little heed; and Morley was the very type of the Liberal who relishes all the pleasures of privilege while advocating every measure of reform which would make them no longer possible. It is of the essence of his whole life that, having at the close of his active career accepted, or rather chosen for himself, a seat in the House of Lords, he immediately set himself to carry through a bill which should deprive that body of its power and prerogative. Say what one will and making allowance for any necessity of the move, there is a taint of ingratitude, of unconscious duplicity one might say, in such a procedure. There is this paradox, if you will call it so, in Morley's attitude towards society, comparable to that of his attitude towards Oxford.

Perhaps thoughtlessness is a more appropriate word than ingratitude, unless, indeed, the two epithets come in the end to the same thing. The fact is that Morley, save in matters of taste, is not a man of originality, not even of steady reflection; he never quite came to terms with himself in regard to the ideas which he took over from his teachers. In religion and politics he was a professed follower of John Stuart Mill, a utilitarian agnostic and Liberal; yet one cannot read together the biographical works of Mill and the *Recollections* of Morley without feeling the profound difference between the mind of the master, who, to

some degree at least, felt the deeper complexities of
life beneath the system he was creating, and the mind
of the pupil, who took the system as a finished
formula and carried it on ruthlessly. Read Morley's
three essays on Mill. There is something almost
amusing in the change of tone from the first two, in
which he celebrates his master as "one of those high
and most worthy spirits" who never falter or compromise in their pursuit of pure truth, to the third
essay, written as a reply to Mill's posthumous volume
on religion. Lord Morley tells us in his *Recollections*
with what consternation he learned that the thinker
and complete agnostic of his reverence had fallen back
at the last upon the belief, shadowy indeed yet almost
orthodox, in a wise and beneficent Creator and upon
the hope of immortality. Let us admit a strain of
inconsistency in Mill's mental make-up. I have said
elsewhere that he is the example *par excellence* of a
philosopher who combines the most lucid powers of
exposition with an incapacity of clear thinking, and
I believe this could be demonstrated not only from
the incompatibility between his earlier positivism and
his later sentimentalism (or intuition, if you prefer),
but from his position at any given moment of his life.
Yet, after all, if inconsistency must be reckoned lower
than the consistency of clear insight, it still has its virtue when compared with a consistency bought at the
price of spiritual blindness. And in Mill the confession that seemed to his disciple only a weak retrac-
tion was really the final utterance of a deep uneasiness with his own rational theories, which at a moment in his youth had thrown him into a mood of
dark despair like Coleridge's *Dejection,* and which,
though generally concealed, continued always to lie
beneath his heart. There were in Mill stirrings of
doubt, of wise scepticism, which the Oxford scholar,

in his consistent hostility to the spirit of Oxford, never fathomed. His only substitute for these would appear to be the art of commenting prettily on the universality of death.

Nor does Morley give any sign that he ever in his active years felt Mill's hesitations in regard to the ulterior consequences of social reform. There is a problem that has lain heavily upon the conscience of the more philosophic Radicals, a problem that Mill faced honestly in his treatise on *Liberty*—the natural antagonism between the equality to which progress looks as its practical end and that freedom of the individual the benefit and necessity of which might seem to be recognized in the very name of Liberalism. Were it not for a habit of obstinate forgetfulness in human nature we should think it needless to recall the great passages wherein Morley's acknowledged teacher dilates on "the tyranny of opinion" almost inevitable in a State governed by the immediate will of the majority—a tyranny more far-reaching in its grasp than the arbitrary despotism of any single man or group of men. And Mill, the progressive Radical, was not blind to the peculiar tendency of this tyranny to produce a condition of dead mediocrity. "All the political changes of the age," he declares, "promote it [this level of mediocrity], since they all tend to raise the low and to lower the high. Every extension of education promotes it, because education brings people under common influences, and gives them access to the general stock of facts and sentiments. Improvement in the means of communication promotes it, by bringing the inhabitants of distant places into personal contact, and keeping up a rapid flow of changes of residence between one place and another. The increase of commerce and manufactures promotes it, by diffusing more widely the advantages of easy circumstances, and opening all objects of ambition, even the highest, to the general competition, whereby the desire of rising becomes no longer the character of a particular class, but of all classes. A more powerful agency than even all these, in bringing about a general similarity among mankind, is the complete establishment, in this and other free countries, of the ascendency of public opinion in the State. As the various social eminences which enabled persons entrenched on them to disregard the opinion of the multitude gradually become leveled; as the very idea of resisting the will of the public, when it is positively known that they have a will, disappears more and more from the minds of practical politicians; there ceases to be any social support for non-conformity—any substantive power in society, which, itself opposed to the ascendency of numbers, is interested in taking under its protection opinions and tendencies at variance with those of the public."

And so we have, as Mill would say, this clamorous paradox: an equalitarian Liberalism is based on and justified by the doctrine of progress, yet by its own weight tends to depress that variety of situations and that liberty of the individual which are the efficient causes of progress. Mill's own solution of this difficulty depends on the feasibility of training the better endowed few to a consciousness of the obligations of self-development and public leadership, and on faith in the natural instinct of the masses of mankind to follow a true guide; he would give to education the place in society which Burke gave to prerogative. But I do not raise these perplexing questions for the sake of criticising Liberalism or for the purpose of considering plausible remedies. My aim is entirely the more modest one of pointing to a certain thoughtlessness, a certain unheeding straightforwardness, in the mind of a man like Morley who, while enjoying and frankly eulogizing the distinctions of a society based on the higher individualism, yet never hesitated in carrying through measures which, as he himself knew, were laying the axe at the roots of such a society. Though he knew this, you will find, at least within the compass of the *Recollections,* no regret for the ambiguity of his position, no anxious self-questioning such as troubled Mill.

This difference between Mill and Morley is significant of much, but we are brought even closer, I think, to the heart of Morley's Liberalism by considering his relation to two earlier writers—Burke and Rousseau. Now if there be two names in the history of sociology more antipodal to each other than these, I do not know them; and it is extraordinary, to say the least, that throughout his life Morley has professed himself an admirer and, to a certain extent, a follower of both of these men. This is verily a compromise worthy of a new chapter in his treatise on that subject, a compromise indicative of some dulness of the mind to the law of mutual exclusions, possible only to one who has never really assimilated what is essential to one or both of the terms included. As for Burke, Morley's attitude towards that enemy of destructive innovation is more than extraordinary. One of his earliest ventures in literature was an essay, in large measure eulogistic, on the author of the *Reflections on the French Revolution,* and in 1907 Burke is still, he assures a correspondent, "a high idol of mine." That is consistent enough, but the remarkable thing is the ground of this continued admiration. More than once in the *Recollections* he avows that what he learnt from Burke was the "practical principles in the strategy and tactics of public life," and for this lesson he accepts Macaulay's estimation of Burke as "the greatest man since Milton." Such praise for such a benefit is rather startling, but surprise turns to amazement when we find that this teacher of practical politics was, according to the statement of Lord Lansdowne quoted with approval in Morley's life of Burke, "so violent, so overbearing, so arrogant, so intractable, that to have got on with him in a cabinet would have been utterly and absolutely impossible." And if Morley acquired from Burke a virtue—for of practical politics of the more honourable sort Morley was a past master—of which Burke himself was the doubtful possessor, he quite failed, on the other hand, to take from him the one quality of imaginative perception which gives meaning to the whole of Burke's career. Of this quality, to be sure, Morley's critical intelligence was fully aware when he wrote his monograph. He saw its positive aspect: Burke, he says, "was using no idle epithet, when he described the disposition of a stupendous wisdom, 'moulding together the great mysterious incorporation of the human race.'" And he saw also its negative aspect, the inhibition exercised by the higher centripetal imagination upon the egotistic expansiveness of the individual. This, he avers, was with Burke "the cardinal truth for men, namely, that if you encourage every individual to let the imagination loose upon all subjects, without any restraint from a sense of his own weakness, and his subordinate rank in the long scheme of things, then there is nothing of all that the opinion of ages has agreed to regard as excellent and venerable, which would not be exposed to destruction at the hands of rationalistic criticism." The strange thing is that one who could analyse Burke's political creed so fairly and express it so sympathetically should persistently profess himself a follower of Burke for qualities which Burke possessed superficially, if he possessed them at all. The simple fact is, I suspect, that Morley appreciates Burke by the contact of what may be called a purely literary imagination, and by a certain sympathy of character, whereas in the higher imagination as an actual controlling element of statesmanship, or in that deeper wisdom of the human heart which goes with it, he is profoundly deficient. So it is I explain to myself his almost callous indifference, so far as the records show, to the destructive hazard in a rationalistic programme, which even a Mill could perceive.

In the case of the other great leader to whom Morley remains addicted throughout life, the procedure is of a reverse order. With Burke our statesman feels himself in sympathy, whatever he may say of Parliamentary strategy, chiefly by reason of the British tradition of sturdy character, while he rejects the principle upon which that character is really based. To Rousseau he is drawn in a contrary manner. Here it is the central impulse of the heart, the generating principle of conduct, that holds his loyalty. Early in the *Recollections* he quotes, as justifying his own addiction to Rousseau, a passage from a letter of George Eliot, that throws a flood of light on the nature of his Liberalism. "I wish you to understand," the novelist had written, "that the writers who have most profoundly interested me—who have rolled away the waters from their bed, raised new mountains and spread delicious valleys for me—are not in the least oracles to me. It is just possible that I may not embrace one of their opinions—that I may wish my life to be shaped quite differently from theirs. For instance it would signify nothing to me if a very wise person were to stun me with proofs that Rousseau's views of life, religion, and government are miserably erroneous. . . I might admit all this, and it would be not the less true that Rousseau's genius has sent that electric thrill through my intellectual and moral frame which has awakened me to new perceptions—which has made man and nature a world of freer thought and feeling to me; and this not by teaching me any new belief."

Now a plain man might be inclined to ask by what right a practical statesman, however it may be with a maker of fiction, dare avow his adherence to a philosopher who kindles a relentless flame of passion, yet whose "views of life, religion, and government are miserably erroneous." It might be in order to observe that this reckless surrender to emotion, without conscientious scruples for the direction the emotion was taking, has been one of the causes which have brought the world to its present dolorous pass. But at bottom Morley has taken from Rousseau something more than the mere shock of feeling. As one may learn from many passages of the *Recollections,* there are involved with this emotionalism two leading ideas, or views of life, distinct in expression, though springing from the same head. One of these is what he calls "Rousseau's resplendent commonplace," and is directly political: " 'T is the people that compose the human race; what is not people is so small a concern that it is not worth the trouble of counting." The other idea is rather the philosophical, or psychological, basis of Rousseauism. It is what Morley in various places upholds as the law of "bold free expansion," "the gospel of free intellectual and social expansion"; it is the "belief in Progress" as the mechanical result of this expansive instinct, which he insistently preaches as a substitute for the belief in God and providence. It might be remarked in passing that these two Rousseauistic ideas are in violent opposition to the doctrine of Morley's other acknowledged master. To conceive society as composed of the people alone (the masses, that is, as contrasted with the privileged classes) is certainly, whatever else may be said of it, to deny any meaning to Burke's notion of the hierarchy of orders forming together "the great mysterious incorporation of the human race"; it is even to forget the reservations of leadership demanded by so complete a Liberal as Mill. And, again, to trust for progress to an instinctive desire of expansion in human nature is certainly to encourage that letting loose of the individual imagination, without any restraint from the sense of a man's own weakness, about which Burke would throw the bulwark of the restrictive social imagination.

But that is by the way. The striking fact is that no one could be more sensitive than Morley to the actual outcome of these principles in character, yet that he should so entirely overlook the nexus of cause and effect. Of Rousseau's personal weaknesses he was an unsparing critic; he has written of them in the spirit of Burke and of an English gentleman. Theoretically, too, he knows that such fine emotional words as "truth, right, and general good," if allowed to usurp the place of plain thinking, may be nothing more than a cloak for factious malignity; he can praise Bishop Butler for "the solid distinction of never shutting his eyes to dark facts in human life and history." Yet one might suppose, for anything said in the *Recollections,* that there is no connection between Rousseau's theory of natural goodness and that lack of personal reticence in speech and conduct which make his character so repulsive. And in his political course, again as reflected in the *Recollections,* Morley is content to reiterate his confidence in the British workman as a being whose desires will instinctively limit themselves without any outer control, as if here the "dark facts" of selfishness did not exist. "My faith," he writes in a letter after the Kaiser's visit to London, "in the political prudence of our democracy is unshaken, and I don't wonder that the German Emperor should have wished that his men of that kidney were half as sensible." It is probable that Lord Morley, in his present retirement, has changed his opinion somewhat in respect to William, and does not now, as he did in 1907, when cajoled by that Monarch's table talk, regard the Imperial Government as solely intent on preserving "a little decent calm all over Europe." One wonders whether he has seen a light also in respect to the possible greed of a class of men who find the way open to grasp at unlimited political power. Will it occur to him that in the one case as in the other, in the Pan-Germanism of Berlin as in the programme of British Radicalism, there is at work the same law of untrammelled expansiveness, and that there may be some peril in following the electric thrill of freer feeling as a force beautiful and ennobling in itself, whatever may be the accompanying views of life, religion, and government? Long ago the first Marquess of Halifax, who had learnt much in the hard school of revolution, discovered that "the greatest part of the business of the world is the effect of not thinking." How far is the business of the world to-day the result of feeling without thinking?

I must say again, and emphatically, that I am not writing a political treatise, nor am I attempting to weigh the good and evil of Radicalism in general. My task is the humbler one of trying to analyse the character of a particular Radical. Here before us lies his autobiography: it is a life replete with charm, most of what was best in the literature of the day is reflected in it, and much of the culture of antiquity; the traditional graces of society give it lustre, and it is actuated by a steady and unselfish purpose; yet what

is the conclusion? At the end of the record, as a
kind of epilogue, the statesman who had played a part
in the social changes of an epoch, describes a walk
in a Surrey upland with little Eileen, a four-footed
favourite, and these are the closing words:

A painful interrogatory, I must confess, emerges. Has not
your school—the Darwins, Spencers, Renans, and the rest—
held the civilized world, both old and new alike, European
and transatlantic, in the hollow of their hand for two long
generations past? Is it quite clear that their influence has
been so much more potent than the gospel of the various
churches? *Circumspice.* Is not diplomacy, unkindly called
by Voltaire the field of lies, as able as it ever was to dupe
governments and governed by grand abstract catchwords veil-
ing obscure and inexplicable purposes, and turning the whole
world over with blood and tears to a strange Witches' Sabbath? These were queries of pith and moment indeed, but
for something better weighed and more deliberative than an
autumn reverie.

Now and then I paused as I sauntered slow over the fading
heather. My little humble friend squat on her haunches,
looking wistfully up, eager to resume her endless hunt after
she knows not what, just like the chartered metaphysicians.
So to my home in the falling daylight.

I am not wrong, I think, in being disconcerted by
such a conclusion to such a record. Is all our intelligence and all our aspiration after the truth no
more than the wistful and aimless searching of a dog?
I believe that no man is justified in laying his hand
on the complicated fabric of society until he has a
surer sense of direction than this; and I am tempted
to ask whether the Witches' Sabbath into which we
had reeled (this was the time of the war) may not
have been the natural goal of a world divided between
those who follow the instinct of expansion without
feeling, and those who follow the same instinct with-

out thinking. If British statesmen like Lord Morley and Sir Edward Grey and British scholars like Gilbert Murray had not been so steeped in the illusion of human righteousness as to discredit the possibility of war, would the war have occurred? It may be unfair to drag in these stupendous issues when criticising the work of one who was, after all, a minor figure in the politics of the day; but Lord Morley is a type. And waiving these considerations, there is still the uncomfortable fact that Lord Morley seems never to have reflected seriously—never, at least, until too late—on the ambiguous position of a statesman who accepted the ungrudged gifts of a culture and a society which all the while he was deliberately undermining. Such action bears at least the semblance of ingratitude. And if it is the ingratitude born of magnanimous sympathy for the less fortunate, one must still ask whether sympathy, unbalanced by clear understanding of human nature and uncontrolled by the larger imagination, may not be found in the end on the side of the destructive rather than the constructive forces of civilization. These disturbing doubts, despite our admiration for Lord Morley, will arise in regard to the special form of utilitarian Liberalism which he took from Mill, without Mill's anxiety; they bring to mind the strong words of Leopardi:

> Stolta, che l'util chiede,
> E inutile la vita
> Quindi più sempre divenir non vede.[1]

---

[1] *Il Pensiero Dominante:* "Blind! that demands the useful, and sees not that ever thence life becomes more useless."

OXFORD, WOMEN, AND GOD

M RS. HUMPHRY WARD has the unenviable portion of a reformer who wrought manfully —should we say womanfully?—to lead England out of the Cimmerian bogs of Victorianism, yet somehow is heartily despised by the younger generation which walks the sunlit ways of our peaceful, spacious Georgian world. It would be an instructive pastime, with her autobiography in hand, to study the causes of this cruel injustice; but that is another story. My present interest in her autobiography [1] has been centred not so much on her own career as on her account of life in Oxford during the sixties and seventies. The four chapters in which she collects her reminiscences of these years are quite the most entertaining of the record—are, in fact, the only part that offers much entertainment of any sort; and if this were my theme, I might suggest that it was the spell of Oxford, however reformed an Oxford, still haunting her mind that makes her so unacceptable to the very much otherwise reformed young wits now gasping their discontent in London. Her first novel, *Miss Bretherton,* was a tale of the university, and *Lady Connie,* her latest novel written before her autobiography, returns to the same scenes; and these, with the chapters of her *Recollections,* might give the lie to Andrew Lang's pleasant witticism that there are no good books about Oxford because they are all composed by women who have spent one day in—Cambridge.

Jowett and Mark Pattison are her heroes, the Master of Balliol in his triumphant days of educational

---

[1] *A Writer's Recollections.* By Mrs. Humphry Ward. New York: Harper & Brothers. 1918.—This essay, it need scarcely be noted, was written while Mrs. Ward was living.

supremacy, and the Rector of Lincoln socially tamed by the restless, keen, very æsthetical "Mrs. Pat.," yet otherwise savage enough with his gibes at the unteutonized scholarship of Balliol and the persistent priestcraft of Christ Church. But other figures, denizens and visitors, flit through her pages—Swinburne, Renan, George Eliot, Mandell Creighton, Taine, Green—each the subject of an anecdote or the occasion for moralizing. Perhaps the most memorable of these stories is that which reports a conversation with Walter Pater in the days when the critic had yielded something of his earlier paganism and was lapsing into a kind of artistic dalliance with the charms of Christianity. Mrs. Ward had been proclaiming the near downfall of orthodoxy and the impossibility of its maintaining itself long against the attacks from the historical and literary camps. To her surprise, Pater shook his head and looked rather troubled. " 'I don't think so,' he said. Then with hesitation: 'And we don't altogether agree. You think it's all plain. But I can't. There are such mysterious things. Take that saying, "Come unto me, all ye that are weary and heavy-laden." How can you explain that? There is a mystery in it—a something supernatural.' "

It was the spirit of the place that would not be exorcised from Pater's thought, and it is curious to observe how this same shadow from the past lay over Mrs. Ward's mind, despite her absorption in modern tendencies and her expressed surprise. She was thinking more of her own young life than of her heroine's when she wrote, in *Lady Connie,* that "in those days Oxford was still praising 'famous men and the fathers who begat' her; their shades still walked her streets." Only Mrs. Ward was rebellious under the spell, while Pater was gently acquiescent. Again she is speaking for herself through the mouth of her heroine: "We who are alive must always fight the past, though we owe it all we have. Oxford has been to me often a witch—a dangerous—almost an evil witch. I seemed to see her—benumbing the young forces of the present. And the scientific and practical men, who would like to scrap her, have sometimes seemed to me right." It is, in fact, just this mingling of the past and the present in her mood that piques our interest; and involuntarily, as we see her picture of Oxford under Jowett and Pattison, another picture arises of the city as it was a generation earlier under Newman and Pusey, and her anecdotes of contemporaries recall a host of stories of the men who preceded or were lingering on as ghosts of themselves. It is all so much the same, yet so different. What change has come over the place so reluctant to change?

If it were my vein to attempt the smart style now in fashion, I should think it enough to describe the change as consisting in the banishment of God and the admission of woman. At any rate, whatever else was happening in Mrs. Ward's time, the gods were going and women were coming; and of one, at least, of these events she is fully aware, and might even boast that she was *pars magna*. In her maiden days, she says, Oxford was a city of young men, "it was not also a city of young women, as it is to-day." But they were already creeping in, and before she left had conquered the right of domicile, much after the manner of the fabled camel; in fact the encroachment of the feminine into a society so archaically masculine is the real theme of her university novels, and her *Recollections* show how much her own activities as writer and talker helped on the invasion. But it was not only the presence of the undergraduate in petticoats that marked the revolution; wives, too, were multiplying, and with them came a great alteration in the habits of the faculty. In the generation preceding none of the tutors were married and very few of the professors; Oxford was still under the old conventual rule, though, with the disappearance of the religious ideal and purpose of celibacy, the peculiarly monkish traits of character had vanished and left behind only the bare "character," as that word used to be understood. This indeed is the chief impression one gets from the memoirs of the age. There was purpose enough in the lives of Newman and his group, but all about them was a society of happy egotists whom isolation from the shaping contacts with the world had allowed to develop each as whim or passion guided him. Even the throngs of boys, who were so conspicuous to Mrs. Ward at her first coming, seem somehow to have been pushed into the background of the picture by these crusty bachelors. Of a certain "Mo." Griffith, Senior Fellow of Merton, who used to fly from Oxford in term-time to avoid the Philistines, as he called the undergraduates, the story is told that once in vacation, when dining alone in Hall, he was confronted with the sight of a single scholar who had not gone down. "Fetch a screen, Manciple!" he cried. It is the Fellows' side of the screen we see in the annals of that age.

And one can imagine what went on there on this occasion, if our Don was faithful to his creed. It is related that a physician, having dined with him and eaten too sparingly, excused his abstinence by pleading the maxim, "Eat and leave off hungry." Mo. threw up his hands: "Eat and leave off hungry! Why not wash and leave off dirty?" No doubt, too, he would have been ready, with most of his contemporaries, to exclaim in the same manner over the command to drink and leave off thirsty—sober their forefathers would have said. For, if the *Logic* of Dean Aldrich

of Christ Church was still after a century and a half
the textbook of Oxford, it is to be feared that some
of the logicians of the day had not forgotten the
Dean's practical example of the art of ratiocination:

> Si bene quid memini, sunt causæ quinque bibendi:
> Hospitis adventus, præsens sitis atque futura,
> Aut vini bonitas, aut quælibet altera causa—

which may be translated for a less genial and less
erudite generation:

> If I remember well, these be the sum
> Fivefold of drink's occasions and its laws:
> A guest arrived, thirst present or to come,
> Virtue of wine, or any other cause.[1]

The same Moses (or Edward as he chose to call
himself) Griffith was one day walking round Christ
Church Meadow with a brother Fellow named Frowd,
who began, as *laudator temporis acti,* to lament the
disappearance from Oxford of the strange originals
of their young days. "Does it not occur to you, Dr.
Frowd," was the reply, "that you and I are the 'characters' of to-day?" I ask my reader: Does our world,
of which we sometimes boast, possess such naïve sub-
limity of assurance? But Mo. and his friend flattered
themselves, if they thought their originality outlawed
and peculiar at that date. As I stand in the corner
of my library in which the Oxford memoirs of the day

---

[1] The old, freer translation is well known:

> If on my theme I rightly think,
> There are five reasons why men drink:
> Good wine, a friend, because I'm dry.
> Or lest I should be by and by,
> Or any other reason why.

are gathered, and as I turn over the pages of book after book looking for examples, I am embarrassed by the need of selection among so many doughty heroes and so many combats of wit. Like Æneas, I see

> Battles through all the world made known to fame.

The easiest way out of the difficulty, were it permissible, would be to copy off a chapter of the Reverend W. Tuckwell's *Reminiscences,* and perhaps the best of permissible ways is to direct any reader not already acquainted therewith to that storehouse of entertainment. If there is any more exhilarating book of the sort in English, I do not know it; and if there is a more captivating group of oddities than the scholars who congregated by the Isis before the advent of Mrs. Ward's petticoats, and who live again in Mr. Tuckwell's memory, I have not met them in my literary pilgrimage. Whatever Oxford may not have been, it was vastly amusing. If our friend Mo. left the impression of a rather gluttonous and bibulous curmudgeon, it is not to be inferred that the story of that society is a mere "gastrology," like the work of the ancient Epicurean who, as Athenæus says, "made a voyage round the inhabited earth for his belly's sake" (I omit the rest of the quotation), and wrote up his adventures in epic form. No, these Dons were true *deipnosophists,* dinner-philosophers, whose talk was as much wittier than their successors' as their appetites were more capacious. Mr. Tuckwell draws the comparison neatly:

> The Commons Rooms to-day, as I am informed, are swamped by shop; while general society, infinitely extended by the abolition of College celibacy, is correspondingly diluted. Tutors and Professors are choked with distinctions and redundant with educational activity; they lecture, they write, they edit,

they investigate, they athleticise, they are scientific or theological or historical or linguistic; they fulfil presumably some wise end or ends. But one accomplishment of their forefathers has perished from among them—they no longer *talk*: the Ciceronian ideal of conversation, σπουδαῖον οὐδέν, φιλόλογα multa, "Not a word on shop, much on literature," has perished from among them. In the Thirties, conversation was a fine art, a claim to social distinction: choice sprouts of the brain, epigram, anecdote, metaphor, now nursed carefully for the printer, were joyously lavished on one another by the men and women of those bibulous, pleasant days, who equipped themselves at leisure for the wit combats each late supper-party provoked.

That is well put, and is in the main true; but I should like to discourse on one of Mr. Tuckwell's points—his unreserved condemnation of "shop," which he connects with rather an unfair translation of Cicero's Greek. The comparative dulness of conversation in the modern Hall, or in the American equivalent, is not to be laid to the intrusion of shop, but to the wrong kind of shop. The minute specializing of studies has brought about such a division of interests among scholars that you will scarcely find any body of men, nominally united, who have less in common intellectually than the faculty of a university. Only the other day I heard a biologist girding at a teacher of Greek for his concern with a remote and outworn civilization. It was easy for the Grecian to retort that after all the polity of the coral insect represented a stage of evolution immensely more antique than the constitution of Athens two thousand years ago, and that the art of Sophocles and the philosophy of Aristotle were closer to the business and bosoms of mankind than the skeleton deposits of the Anthozoan polyp. (Which last heavy-loaded phrase, however, I got from the encyclopædia, not from the professor's

lips.) The retort was effective, but it did not bring
the two gentlemen closer together. And so, in the
absence of any intellectual meeting-ground, except that
of mere transient curiosity, college men are driven to
the interchange of personalities and the discussion of
departmental wire-pulling, from which their only
escape is the political news of the morning paper.
Their shop is no better, for conversational purposes,
than a department store. But it was not so when
scholars were interested in the same group of subjects, with, of course, a human variety of views. Even
the personal gossip of such a society took colour from
their more serious pursuits; even malice and back-
biting spoke the dialect of the Muses, as any one may
discover for himself if he will read the memoirs of
the day. Mr. Tuckwell, for instance, has a good deal
to say of a certain "Horse" Kett, of Trinity, as he was
called by reason of a long face dominated by a straight
bony nose—an estimable gentleman withal, and not
without critical acumen of a sort that won the respect
of De Quincey. But his academic renown was owing
to that equine countenance and to its power of "in-
spiring from the seniors jokes in every learned language, and practical impertinences from the less erudite youngsters." This Kett put out a rival to Aldrich's book, which he entitled *Logic Made Easy*. It
was a feeble and blundering thing, but provocative of
high mirth, when Copleston of Oriel reviewed it in a
scathing pamphlet, with the motto—

Aliquis latet error; Equo ne credite, Teucri!

Mr. Tuckwell would have come closer to the mark
if, instead of contrasting shop and literature, he had
said that the two were then one thing. We sometimes speak slightingly of the erudition of those clois-

tered Dons, and use their idleness to point a moral or adorn ourselves; yet as a matter of fact many of them were prodigiously learned—only with a difference. What they knew, they knew. Perhaps the long-forgotten name of James Endell Tyler may be recalled as a type. "He was not a reformer of Churches and creeds," we read of him in Mozley's *Reminiscences,* "but he was an able and effective lecturer. He was no genius, it used to be said of him, but he could construe Thucydides 'through a deal board.'" No doubt their reading was circumscribed, but that very circumscription had its advantages, in so far as it made learning a bond of sympathy rather than a dyke of separation.[1] The great masters of human experience were in their blood; they knew them by heart; thought as they thought; spoke their language, with perfect assurance that the most recondite play of wit or wisdom would be caught up immediately and an-

[1] One may find an amusing illustration in Mark Pattison's *Memoirs* of the common confusion of mind on this matter of scholarship. On page 237 he says: "Probably there was no period of our history during which, I do not say science and learning, but the ordinary study of the classics was so profitless or at so low an ebb as during the period of the Tractarian controversy. By the secession of 1845 this was extinguished in a moment, and from that moment dates the regeneration of the University." This is the voice of the anti-theologian. Hear now the words of the educator on what is really one aspect of the extinction of the hated movement (p. 240): "The sudden withdrawal of all reverence for the past has generated a type of intellect which is not only offensive to taste but is unsound as training. The young Oxford, which our present system tends to turn out, is a mental form which cannot be regarded with complacency by any one who judges an education, not by its programme, but by its *élèves.* Our young men are not trained; they are only filled with propositions, of which they have never learned the inductive basis."—Might not this second passage have come straight from Newman's *Idea of a University?*

swered in kind. Some of them may have quoted with the awful profusion of a Porson, who, as Byron declared, "used to recite, or rather vomit, pages of all languages, and could hiccup Greek like a Helot"; but Porson was a Cantabrigian, and a beast; and all good things may be abused—even temperance. And to the drunkenness of Porson we owe, it must be granted, the profoundest utterance of pessimism that has ever fallen from mortal lips. He was in his customary state one night. Wishing to blow out his candle, and seeing, as is said to be the way of the inebriated, two flames side by side where there was only one, he three times directed his swaying steps to the wrong image, and three times blew, with no effect, for the non-existent cannot be extinguished. Whereupon he drew back, balanced himself, and gave verdict: "Damn the nature of things!" [1]

It may be objected that all this erudition was sterile; it produced few books, and some of these were bad. The charge is fair, but there are alleviations. The barrenness is attributable in part to the kind of scholarship in vogue; it was not the business of these men to decipher manuscripts and investigate sources, and when they did turn to such work they were capable of making a mess of it. But if they had been better editors, does it follow necessarily that they would have been more interesting men? And there was another cause, a tradition that still lingers at Oxford through all the changes of the past fifty years. I remember not long ago talking with an Oxonian, of all

---

[1] So the story was once told me on a memorable occasion by a friend, now one of the editors of the *Weekly Review*, and so I repeat it. But my genial authority is only a mathematician after all; for another and I fear truer version the reader must be referred to the Porsonia at the end of the *Table-Talk of Samuel Rogers*.

places in a New York elevated train, about these matters. Somehow we had got to the question of the best model for the writing of Greek prose, and he appealed to the opinion of one of his teachers in favour of the simpler narrative style of Thucydides. I had never heard the scholar's name—nor do I now recall it—and inquired about him. "Why," said my friend, "he is probably the most learned man in Oxford, so nearly omniscient that his colleagues live in constant terror of his criticism." I still expressed my surprise that a pundit of such renown should be unknown to me. "That is not strange," was the reply, "for he has never published anything." My surprise was increased, and I asked the reasons. "Well, you know," said my friend, who to his other charms adds a slight impediment of speech, "it isn't quite g-good form in Oxford to p-print."—A foolish tradition, I dare say; yet I challenge any one familiar with the growing custom among us to appraise a man's academic standing by the quantity of his output—often enough in the form of petty source-hunting—I challenge him to deny that such a tradition has its good side.

It is not to be supposed that the scholarship of Oxford passed without comment at the time. Critics were ready then as now, though with less immediate effect, to denounce the narrow exclusive spirit of the place; and one series of criticisms in particular, appearing in the *Edinburgh Review,* drew out apologies from Copleston, published in 1810 and 11, which contain paragraphs still readable to-day with profit and interest. To the reviewer's charge that classical studies are frivolous because they do not tend directly to what is called practical good, Copleston replies finely with a plea for "cultivation of mind which is itself a good, a good of the highest order, without any immediate reference to bodily appetites or wants of any kind," and then appeals to what the Oxford tradition had done for the formation of character, and specially for character under the testing strain of war. "If classical education be regarded in this light," he says, "there is none in which it will be found more faultless. A high sense of honour, a disdain of death in a good cause, a passionate devotion to the welfare of one's country, a love of enterprise, and a love of glory, are among the first sentiments which those studies communicate to the mind. And as their efficacy is undoubted in correcting the narrow habits and prejudices to which the separation of the professions gives birth, so in the rough school of war is it more especially exemplified in mitigating the tone of that severe instructor and in softening some of his harshest features."—Can any one read the letters of Arthur Heath and of other Oxonians who went out the other day into the battle line and did not return, without feeling that even the remnant of the old tradition has not lost the power claimed for it by the Provost of Oriel?

> God rest you, happy gentlemen,
>   Who laid your good lives down,
> Who took the khaki and the gun
>   Instead of cap and gown.
> God bring you to a fairer place
>   Than even Oxford town.

I wish there were space to quote the striking words of Copleston on the mischief, even then threatening, of the undue predominance of Political Economy in education and among "the clamorous sciolists of the day"; what was once prophecy is now fact; but this is not my present theme. It is more to the point to show how the old tradition, with all its exclusions, perhaps on account of them, caught the abler youths

of the day—and they are the only ones who count—
in its spell and stimulated their ambition. Pusey's
mother, who as an old woman loved to talk of her
famous son, used to tell how he had asked his father
for a complete set of the Fathers as his reward for
gaining a First Class; "and how in the Long Vacation
he used to carry his folios to a shady corner in the
garden which she pointed out, and sit there reading
with a tub of cold water close at hand, into which he
plunged his curly head whenever study made it ache."
Quite as significant is the account of the excitement
roused by the success of Jowett, Pusey's lifelong rival,
when he won a Balliol Fellowship in 1839. In the
candidate's home there is an outburst of joy as great
as if he had been appointed Lord Chancellor, and in
the university, as one of his friends writes, "nothing
has been talked about here so much for a long time. . .
'Little Jowett' was nearly pulled to pieces." Frankly,
do we think so highly of getting a fellowship to-day?
Is the business of education quite so serious an affair
or so enthralling?

Part of that ancient enthusiasm may be explained
by the fact that success in the schools was an open
door to the great prizes of State and Church; it was
still true that knowledge of Greek seemed a proper
claim to a bishopric. (I heard one of our bishops the
other day derive "disciple" from the Greek *didasko,*
"to teach"!) And this truth a Winchester lad of the
day expressed with delightful naïveté in the closing
lines of an *Address to Learning:*

> Make me, O Sphere-descended Queen,
> A Bishop, or at least a Dean.

What prize, if any, his school bestowed on the poet I
do not know, but he ended his well-planned career as

Warden of New College and Bishop of Chichester. Nor was it the young visionary alone who beheld Learning as the patron of success. In one of his Christmas sermons the redoubtable Gaisford (to whom as an undergraduate his Dean had observed, "You will never be a gentleman, but you may succeed with certainty as a scholar"—and become yourself a Dean, he might have added) stated the same truth with prosaic candour: "Nor can I do better, in conclusion, than impress upon you the study of Greek literature, which not only elevates above the vulgar herd, but leads not infrequently to positions of considerable emolument."

It sounds a little queer and mercenary, put that way, though we can wish that the emoluments of scholarship were rather more considerable to-day; but there is another version of Gaisford's words—I do not know which of the two is *verbatim* correct—which sets the matter in a different light. According to this report his exhortation to the study of Greek was on the ground that it would enable a man "not only to read the oracles of God in the original, but also to look down with contempt upon the vulgar herd." And on the whole this second version is the fairer representation of the spirit of the age. Lawn sleeves may have been a pleasant, and quite legitimate, incentive to the young student poring on his Aristotle and Origen, but I think he went to those great philosophers and theologians seeking first the oracles of God. I have said much of the more eccentric, even the coarser, habits of these cloistered scholars. We must take the good with the bad, and I fear that the old charge made in the time of Charles II might still be repeated of a certain Oxford set: "At a dingy, horrid, scandalous ale-house over against the college, Balliol men by perpetual 'bubbeing' added art to their natural stupidity to make themselves perfect sots." Yet there was another side even to the indulgence in Port.

> "Narratur et prisci Catonis
> Sæpe mero caluisse virtus,—

with all its faults there is something generous about it, and if the Latin proverb says right, it is at least no enemy to truth," was the reply of Copleston to the *Edinburgh* reviewer who had scourged the university for its guzzling. Though a sprinkling of "bubbeing" sots was to be reckoned with, nevertheless the real mark of this society was its conviction that it held a place set apart amid a world of indifference, as guardian of the truth; it still believed that scholarship was primarily concerned with the oracles of God. If we look below the surface, we shall find the very zest of those quaint characters that move through the memoirs of the day in their extraordinary mingling of personal eccentricity with religious regularity. Nor must we forget that the Oxford of Mo. Griffith and his brother oddity was also the home of Newman and Keble and Pusey, in whom, however we may be disposed towards their particular dogmas, we must acknowledge that the zeal of God burned with a steady, almost a devouring, flame.

But perhaps the best type of the Oxford I have in mind is not one of those eagles of the faith, but their servant and drudge in the intellectual battle, if I may so designate Charles Marriott without injustice to his noble simplicity. Eccentric he was, almost beyond credence. In the street his strange figure could be recognized afar by its involved mufflings of cloak and wrapper and veil. Indoors he wore a black silk skull-cap, which, from his habit of slumbering in public places, might often be seen nodding, with the drollest effect—yet somehow he contrived to hear more in his sleep, and remember better, than other men who listened with head erect. His somnolence, apparently, was only a deeper lapse in his normal state of absent-mindedness. If accosted suddenly in the street he would start and stare at you for a moment in utter silence, as though he had been walking awake in some other world, as no doubt he had been. And like the man were his rooms. In a biographical sketch, aptly entitled *The Man of Saintly Life,* Dean Burgon gives a vivid account of one of Marriott's breakfasts, to which, as usual, the careless host had invited guest after guest at random with no thought of their number. What happened may be told in Burgon's own words:

On entering the dear man's rooms next morning, whereas breakfast had been laid for ten, [we found] fifteen guests had already assembled. While we were secretly counting the teacups, another rap was heard, and in came two University Professors. All laughed: but it was no laughing matter, for still another and another person presented himself. The bell was again and again rung: more and more tea and coffee,— muffins and dry toast,—butter and bread,—cream and eggs,— chops and steaks,—were ordered; and "Richard" was begged to "spread my other table-cloth on my other table." The consequence was that our Host's violoncello,—fiddle-strings and music-books,—printers' proofs and postage stamps,—medicine-bottles and pill-boxes,—respirator and veil,—gray wrapper for his throat and green shade for his eyes,—pamphlets and letters innumerable,—*all* were discharged in a volley on to the huge sofa. At last, by half-past nine (thanks to Richard's super-human exertions) twenty of us (more or less) sat down to breakfast. . . . I am bound to say that the meal was an entire success,—as far as the strangers were concerned. They were greatly entertained,—in more senses than one.

Yet this same absentee from the world was a scholar of indefatigable industry, to whom Newman and Pusey could always turn for any onerous task of editing or translating in their paper warfare with rationalism. Nor would it be easy to say where, with such a man, scholarship ended and saintship began, so thoroughly were heart and brain in accord. He was one in whom the thought of self was lost in uninterrupted contemplation of God, one in whom the consummation of Aristotle's *theoria* might seem to have been realized in Christian worship. "There was," says one who knew him well, "something unspeakably sweet and pure and simple, in the outcome of his habitual inner life. . . To me he seemed habitually to walk with God . . . He was of a kindred nature to the Saint who said, 'When I am in heaviness I will think upon God'; and who habitually spoke of God as 'his stronghold whereunto he might always resort, his house of defence and his castle.'"

Now what strikes one in the Oxford of Mrs. Ward, as it would strike one still more in the Oxford of to-day, is the impossibility of meeting with such a character as that of Marriott: the eccentricity is gone, vanished with the last relics of medieval isolation; gone, too, the spiritual sense of an actual presence of the Deity. As for the eccentricity, its disappearance, Mrs. Ward herself would probably admit, was caused in no small measure by the influx of women into a society of bachelors. With petticoats came the world and the conventions of the world; manners were softened, the tongue was filed, angles of originality were ironed out; the drawing-room conquered the cloister. As for the second change, whether the intrusion of women had anything to do with the synchronous extrusion of God, you will not hear from me; even if I believed in such a causal relation, I have too many misoneistic quarrels already in hand to risk the charge of misogyny. But I can tell you what Mrs. Ward would say: she would simply deny the fact of ex-

trusion. That the religiosity of Newman and Pusey
had been expelled, she would grant, and would boast,
with reason, that her own pen had been one of the
effective instruments of the expulsion; but she would
uphold her sincere conviction that the idea of God
had been merely purified by the process. For such
a tenet she does actually argue vehemently in a dialogue on *The New Reformation* contributed to the
Nineteenth Century for March, 1889, as a part of the
acrid debate then waging between Huxley and the
enemies of agnosticism. "The point is," she declares,
in reply to the fears of orthodoxy—"the point is, What
religion is possible to men, for whom God is the only
reality, and Jesus that friend of God and man, in
whom, through all human and necessary imperfection,
they see the natural leader of their inmost life?"
And, more succinctly, she adds: "God—though I can
find no names for Him—is more real, more present
to me than ever before." In like manner, with tacit
reference to the criticisms that still emanated from
the unreformed stronghold of Christ Church, she
dwells in her *Recollections* on the deep religious spirit
of her beloved heretic, Jowett:

If ever a man was *Gottbetrunken*, it was the Master, many
of whose meditations and passing thoughts, withdrawn, while
he lived, from all human ken, yet written down—in thirty or
forty volumes!—for his own discipline and remembrance, can
now be read, thanks to his biographers, in the pages of his
Life. They are extraordinarily frank and simple; startling,
often, in their bareness and truth. But they are, above all,
the thoughts of a mystic, moving in a Divine presence. An
old and intimate friend of the Master's once said to me that he
believed "Jowett's inner mind, especially towards the end of
his life, was always in an attitude of Prayer. One would go
and talk to him on University or College business in his study,
and suddenly see his lips moving, slightly and silently, and
know what it meant."

Now that there is an element of truth in what Mrs. Ward maintains, I would not deny; yet as I read the life of Jowett I cannot divest myself of the feeling that his religion is a kind of reverberation from forces which have ceased to operate—like the prolonged intonation of a bell after the last stroke of the hammer. It was Jowett who avowed that "Voltaire has done more good than all the Fathers of the Church put together"; and as he grew older his faith took on more and more the form of a belief with nothing to believe. "Litanies should have no creeds"; all dogmas, including belief in a personal God and in immortality, should be surrendered, and in their place religion should be steadied on what he understood—erroneously, it must be added—as Buddhistic nihilism. The "Divine presence" with him was "mystic"; what, one asks, was actually present? No doubt Jowett continued in the habit of inner worship, but the shrine before which his lips moved in meditation was empty, and what vitality his faith possessed was drawn, vampire-like, from the heart of men whose creed he had shattered. No doubt the idea of Deity, as Mark Pattison declared, misapplying a phrase of Coleridge's, had been "defæcated to a pure transparency"; would it be unfair to reply that a pure transparency, so far as our corporeal or spiritual vision is concerned, means only a vacuum? The Oxford of Newman may have been superstitious; the Oxford of Jowett, despite Mrs. Ward's protests, was rapidly becoming Godless. The new scholarship is busied with investigation of sources and scientific phenomena, and has no need of the hypothesis of a divine presence. So far as religion prevails, it is the religion of humanity, such as that for which Mrs. Ward pleaded in *Robert Elsmere,* not Newman's religion of God and the individual human soul. Worship has been transferred from the pulpit of Saint Mary's to the recreation room of the Passmore Edwards Settlement.

What this change means to education I have found curiously intimated in one of the smart sayings of Stephen McKenna's *Sonia*. He has been describing his experience in an East End university mission, where, as he says, thirty per cent of his Oxford generation worked for longer or shorter periods, and he concludes: "I doubted, and still doubt, the possibility of friendship between a Shadwell stevedore and the angular, repellent product of an English public school and university; this is not to put one above the other, but merely to disbelieve the existence of a common intellectual currency."—*Not to put one above the other:* can you imagine a scholar of Gaisford's generation doubting in his mind whether the product of Winchester and Oxford, *ceteris paribus,* is higher than the product of the Shadwell docks? Yet just such a query, in less paradoxical terms, you may find in almost every recent book that reveals what is going on inside the minds of serious university men. Even Jowett could exclaim over his college as "a bad school for character," where a "sort of weak cleverness" is fostered and "manliness" is impaired. If the modern report of university life is true, I wonder why we go on spending millions of dollars and pounds to maintain institutions which make men no better than stevedores, and why, on the other hand, we waste so much sympathy on life at the docks which makes men no worse than professors. Our ears have grown too squeamish to endure Gaisford's blunt association of the oracles of God with contempt for the vulgar herd, nor do I think his a happy or a true definition of the aims of education; but one thing is certain: if the college as an institution is to retain any value above the shop and the market-place, if the pursuit

of scholarship as an end in itself is to offer any satisfaction for the finer spirits of men, then, in some way,
those studies must be restored to authority which give
zest and significance to the inner life of the soul; and
at the centre of that life, binding all its interests into
one, lifting them above the grosser forms of utility,
irradiating them with joy, must be the idea of God.

I did not intend, when I began this account of Oxford before and after the reforms of the mid-nineteenth
century, to end on so solemn an argument. What
impressed me most while going through Mrs. Ward's
Recollections and recalling the reminiscences of the
preceding generation, was the simple fact that college
society as portrayed in these books had grown in a few
years comparatively less amusing to read about and
distinctly less interesting to itself. I do not mean that
Mrs. Ward's chapters are without entertainment—I
have said they were the most entertaining part of her
memoir—but the college life she depicts has lost much
of its peculiar tang and proud independence; already
its main significance is in the comparison it evokes.
The change, I think, will scarcely be disputed by any
one conversant with the literature, though some may
contend that the loss of interest is more than com-
pensated by the suppression of quaint or ludicrous ec-
centricities. For my part I would not hold a brief
for mere eccentricity, however fond I may be of the
well-crusted "character." But that is only half the
story. The waning of interest, in its deeper aspect, is
typical of an intellectual revolution which has grown
more and more evident with the passing of the years,
until now the ancient pride of the scholar and the self-
content of the scholars' career seem to have been swallowed up in the one prevailing note of distaste and
dissatisfaction and apology. Professor Gilbert Murray,
who is qualified to speak for the Oxford of to-day,

complains of the satiety that pervades college life, and attributes it to the very liberation of mind and the enriching of the means of personal satisfaction. "Whatever gifts Oxford may bring her children," he says, "she is apt to bring steeped in the one poison that is fatal to poetry, the poison of satiety. A spirit of satiety broods over the rich meadows and the slow streams, over streets and towers and quadrangles and playing-grounds. Do you wish for games? There they are waiting for you, laid on like water or electric light, all the games that exist. If you can think of another it shall be brought; there shall be no trouble to you in the preparing of it, and no time for your hunger to grow. Do you wish for books? There they are, old and new, in convenient libraries and magnificent bookshops, more than you can ever read or look at; so many that the sight wearies you, and suggests, not a desire to be richly gratified, but an ever-mounting and fastidious duty." This is no doubt a true account of the matter, true in a way; but going back to an earlier day, and studying the transition from the Oxford of Newman to the Oxford of Mrs. Ward, I seem to see other causes at work than that heaping up of material resources which has turned the delight of scholarship into a fastidious duty. At least one can safely say that a unique interest was lost to learning with the admission of women into Oxford's cloistered society and with the banishment of God.

THE END

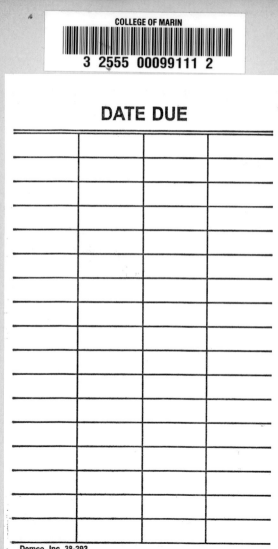

DATE DUE